Smithsonian

Q&A

THE ULTIMATE QUESTION
AND ANSWER BOOK

THE AMERICAN
REVOLUTION

Stuart A. P. Murray

Collins

An Imprint of HarperCollinsPublishers

THE AMERICAN REVOLUTION

Contents

Sculptor Daniel Chester French honored the Massachusetts Minutemen of 1775 with this bronze sculpture.

Smithsonian

Q&A

THE ULTIMATE QUESTION
AND ANSWER BOOK

THE AMERICAN
REVOLUTION

Produced for HarperCollins by:

HYDRA PUBLISHING
129 MAIN STREET
IRVINGTON, NY 10533
WWW.HYLASPUBLISHING.COM

FIRST EDITION

Library of Congress Cataloging-in-Publication Data has been applied for.

ISBN-10: 0-06-089113-0
ISBN-13: 978-0-06-089113-8

06 07 08 09 10   QW   10 9 8 7 6 5 4 3 2 1

American-made cavalry saber with typical curved blade.

Long and short beats on this American regimental drum sent orders to troops.

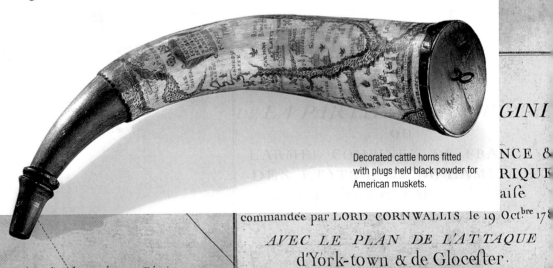

Decorated cattle horns fitted with plugs held black powder for American muskets.

commandée par LORD CORNWALLIS le 19 Oct.^bre 178

AVEC LE PLAN DE L'ATTAQUE
d'York-town & de Glocefter.

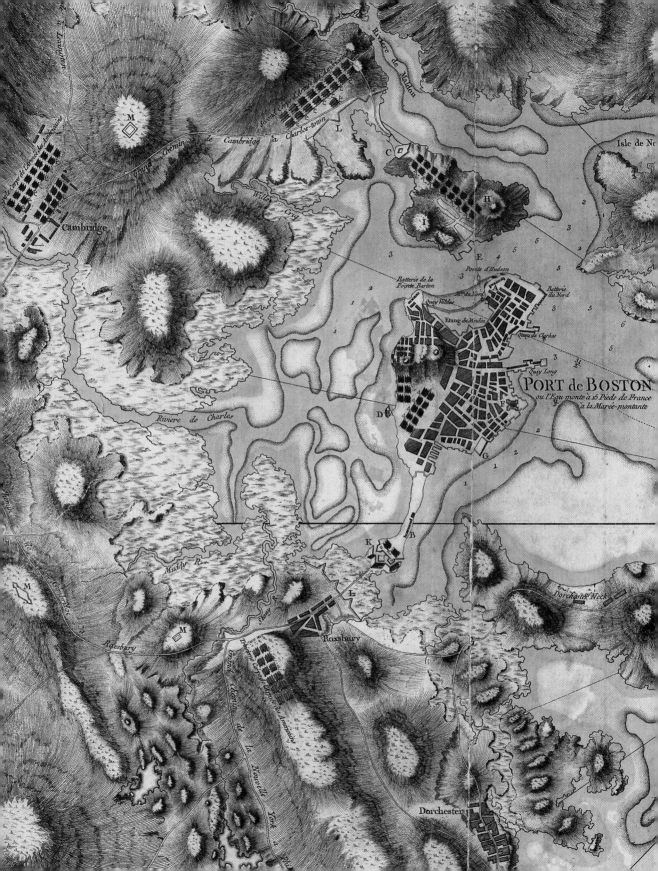

Lexington

Second Corps de l'Armée Americaine

Rivière de Maldon

Grand Chemin de Cambridge à Charles-town

Charles-town

L

C

Isle de No...

Willis Cry

H

I

M

Cambridge

E

Pointe d'Hudson

Batterie de la Pointe Barton

M.r du Nord

A

Batterie du Nord

Quay Valetas

Etang du Moulin

Quay de Clarkes

Riviere de Charles

Quay Long

PORT de BOSTON
ou l'Eau monte à 16 Pieds de France
à la Marée-montante

D

F

G

Muddy R.

B

K

L

Dorchester Neck

M

Roxbury

M

M

Roxbury

Troisième Corps de l'Armée des Americains

Quatrième Corps de l'Armée des Americains

Dorchester

THE AMERICAN WAR FOR INDEPENDENCE

To the Patriots the war was for a "Glorious Cause," a struggle for liberty and against tyranny. But to the Loyalists and neutrals it was a curse upon their prosperous, once-peaceful homeland. And to King George III and his government the revolt in the American colonies was a rebellion that had to be crushed: The rebels had to be compelled to submit.

The American Revolution was a social and political movement that lasted from 1763 until the founding of the United States of America in 1789. Open warfare, the War of American Independence, raged from 1775 to 1783, a conflict that tore America apart. When the war was over, the victorious Patriots had to begin again and rebuild their country, while the defeated Loyalists found themselves banished from their homeland. As for the king, he had lost the most valuable part of Britain's overseas empire.

This hand-colored 1776 French map of Boston and its harbor shows the position of American forces in red and the British in a dark tone. The king's troops occupy the Charles Town peninsula, scene of the bloody battle of Breed's Hill the previous summer.

Thomas Paine's 1776 pamphlet *Common Sense* called on "Inhabitants of America" to stand up and fight for their natural rights. In three months more than 120,000 copies were sold, inspiring Americans to revolt.

> " I am well aware of the toil and blood and treasure it will cost us to maintain this declaration and support and defend these States. Yet through all the gloom I can see rays of ravishing light and glory. I can see that the end is more than worth all the means. . . . "
>
> —JOHN ADAMS

After the War of American Independence—better known as the Revolutionary War—a union of thirteen states stood where thirteen separate colonies had been. Americans faced the world as a free people who had wrenched independence from the most powerful empire on earth. Their cause was indeed glorious, but its success had required battles with muskets and bayonets, with fire and sword, and too often with the hangman's noose so common to revolutions. The Revolutionary War was not a grand panorama of mighty contests between enormous armies. In comparison with the great European wars of the age it was little more than a series of skirmishes with minor losses on each side. Yet every engagement was meaningful. Every clash won or lost some part of a land that was too large to be held by a royal army from across the sea. And in the end it was the Patriots who won it all, taking control bit by bit, town by town, region by region. Where they were outnumbered, they withdrew. When the enemy departed, they returned.

The king's troops could not move without Patriots harrying their flanks, attacking foragers, making it dangerous for a man to wander from the main column. By 1778, just three years into the war, the Continentals marched confidently out of Valley Forge looking for a fight they believed they could win. Final victory would yet cost more blood and treasure, but it was possible as long as the Patriot leaders stayed true to the Glorious Cause.

Those leaders were captains of militia companies, colonels of Continental regiments, masters of fast warships, and scouts on frontier patrols. They were women tending the wounded and tending the family, financiers finding a way to supply the Continental army, members of Congress signing the Declaration of Independence under the shadow of the gallows and then rising above their states' petty jealousies to vote for the Articles of Confederation that laid the cornerstone of the United States of America.

And, in battle, the first leaders were the generals, most learning from their mistakes and making up for them with courage and unshakable honor. First among these was Washington, conspired against by

George Washington: A marble bust attributed to French sculptor Jean-Antoine Houdon, who came to America to study Washington in person. Houdon arrived at Mount Vernon for a two-week stay in October 1785.

American artist and former soldier John Trumbull portrayed the drafting committee of the Second Continental Congress presenting their first version of the Declaration of Independence to president of Congress John Hancock, seated, on July 1, 1776. Committee members, standing, from the left: John Adams, Roger Sherman, Robert Livingston, Thomas Jefferson, and Benjamin Franklin. After much debate by the delegates, also depicted by Trumbull, a revised document was adopted by Congress three days later, on July 4.

lesser men who could not remove him, admired by enemy commanders who could not conquer him, and adored by his soldiers and the American people. When all else failed, love for the man who was "Father of the Country" kept the revolutionary spirit alive. In the end, this struggle, this American War of Independence, won the American Revolution and gave birth to a new nation. The story of Americans fighting for their Glorious Cause is mythical, but it is not a myth. It is a story of men and women who once lived and whose deeds are an inspiration to everyone, everywhere in the world, who believes in the Glorious Cause: the right to "Life, Liberty, and the Pursuit of Happiness."

"It is not a field of a few acres of ground, but a cause that we are defending.

—*THOMAS PAINE, 1778*

CHAPTER 1

THE COLONIAL ERA

The race to possess North America began in the late sixteenth century as the French and Spanish established their first footholds. By the early 1600s, the Dutch, Swedes, and British were planting colonies along the East Coast from New England to Virginia. The British became dominant on the coast, mainly as a result of international treaties, and no major conflict developed in America until late in the century. In the next decades, competition between French and British America sparked several clashes that finally erupted in 1754 and became part of the Seven Years' War, a world-wide conflagration. Known in North America as the French and Indian War, this struggle ended in 1763 with the defeat of the French. British America now developed rapidly, and cities such as Philadelphia, Savannah, Boston, and New York prospered and grew. A dynamic new generation of colonial leaders arose from the war, aware of America's importance to the empire and determined to take hold of their own destiny.

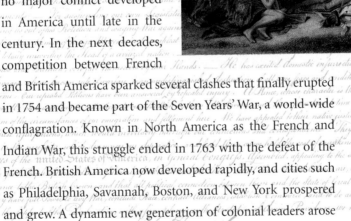

Above: English general James Wolfe dies moments after hearing of victory as Quebec falls in 1759, dooming French colonies in America.

Left: After the French and Indian War ended in 1763, the colonies of British America extended over the eastern seaboard from Canada to Florida.

The Rise of British America

Q: Why did Britain's American colonies develop and grow faster in population than their main rivals on the eastern half of the continent during the 1600s—the colonies of France and the Netherlands?

A: The British colonies in North America were for the most part settled—or "planted"—by colonists who intended to stay and raise families. New France and New Netherland, on the other hand, were primarily intended as commercial ventures for the benefit of the nobility and the mercantile class. Most French and Dutch colonists were there for the fur trade—as buyers journeying to native villages, as shopkeepers, artisans, farmers in the settlements, or as soldiers in the posts. These governments did not want to go to the great expense of sending over colonists who would then have to be ruled and protected.

French colonists, moreover, were answerable to the Roman Catholic Church, which had to approve every emigrant who wished to depart for New France. Protestant Huguenots, in particular, were not allowed in the colonies, so thousands of them sailed instead to British America, where they became stalwart pioneers on the frontiers.

Dutch New Amsterdam was a small seafaring port of a few thousand inhabitants in mid-century, where at least sixteen different languages were spoken in a polyglot society devoted to the fur trade and shipping. The entire colony—from Long Island to the Delaware River, and north up the Hudson River to the Mohawk—had only twelve thousand white inhabitants. They all were required to be in the service of the Dutch West India Company, which ruled the colony by royal decree. Neighboring New England, on the other hand, was not ruled by a mercantile company and as a result became the permanent home to generation after generation of deeply rooted colonists.

New England had a burgeoning population of forty thousand at mid-century, when war broke out between England and the Netherlands. A small English fleet and an army of New Englanders took over weakly defended New Amsterdam without a fight in 1644, and New Netherland was soon no more. New Amsterdam was renamed New York, and the city fast became a major port for the thousands of British merchant ships trading with the Caribbean.

There was little other armed conflict between the colonies in North America until 1690, when war between Britain

This French halberd, was once an effective "pole arm." Made obsolete by firearms, it was carried by junior officers as a symbol of authority.

Branded with "Newtowne" for its place of origin, this matchlock musket was likely used by seventeenth-century Massachusetts militia.

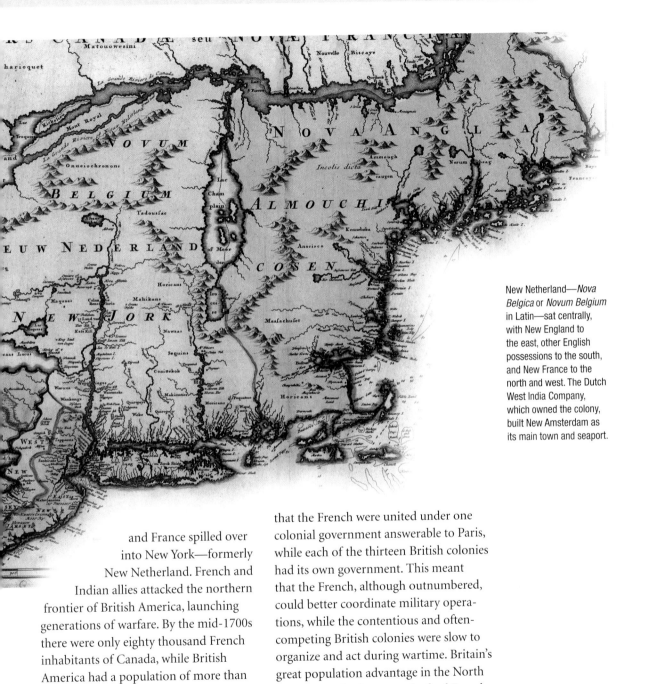

New Netherland—*Nova Belgica* or *Novum Belgium* in Latin—sat centrally, with New England to the east, other English possessions to the south, and New France to the north and west. The Dutch West India Company, which owned the colony, built New Amsterdam as its main town and seaport.

and France spilled over into New York—formerly New Netherland. French and Indian allies attacked the northern frontier of British America, launching generations of warfare. By the mid-1700s there were only eighty thousand French inhabitants of Canada, while British America had a population of more than one million. One key difference between New France and British America was that the French were united under one colonial government answerable to Paris, while each of the thirteen British colonies had its own government. This meant that the French, although outnumbered, could better coordinate military operations, while the contentious and often-competing British colonies were slow to organize and act during wartime. Britain's great population advantage in the North American colonies assured a final French defeat in 1763.

> **Every man in England seems to consider himself as a piece of a sovereign over America . . . and talks of our subjects in the colonies.**
>
> —BENJAMIN FRANKLIN, *1767*

New men will come in . . . with new ideas; at this very instant the causes productive of such a change are strongly at work.

—*EDMUND BURKE, BRITISH STATESMAN, 1765*

Q: Why did Parliament refuse the colonial request for mounting a military campaign against Fortress Louisbourg, Cape Breton, in 1745?

A: War between New France and the northern British colonies of New England and New York had broken out several times in the 1700s, with many frontier raids and counterraids and occasional major expeditions. These wars were named after the current British sovereign: King William's War (1689–97), Queen Anne's War (1702–13), and King George's War (1744–48). They were part of a larger European conflict, the settlement terms of which usually involved trading colonies captured or lost during the struggles. Always, these wars drained the royal treasuries and interrupted economic intercourse. So when the American colonies demanded that King George and Parliament destroy a huge fortress the French were building on the coast of Cape Breton, the British government saw only the prospect of great expense and little advantage to the mother country.

For the Americans, however, the fortress would be a safe haven for French warships as well as fishermen, and that meant the rich fishing banks of the North Atlantic could be brought under French

New France's Fortress Louisbourg on Cape Breton fell twice during the colonial wars of the eighteenth century: first in 1745, captured by American colonial militia, and again in 1758, by British regulars, who landed from Royal Navy ships.

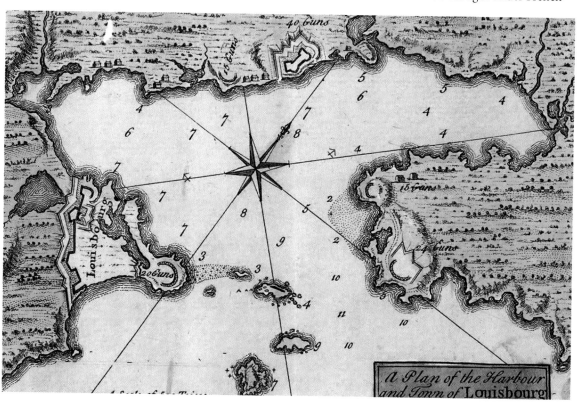

A Plan of the Harbour and Town of Louisbourg

control. Fishing was a mainstay of colonial economies, and these British-Americans were furious when the government declined to act militarily against Louisbourg.

When the colonies determined to mount their own expedition, the British government and military just laughed. The fortress was reputed to be the most powerful in the world. No motley colonial expedition could ever hope to take it.

But take it they did. Fortress Louisbourg was captured in June 1745 after a brief siege by mostly New Englanders and New Yorkers operating with a small Royal Navy squadron that happened to be patrolling at the time. Fewer than a hundred British lives were lost. When the proud colonials prepared to set out for home to work the harvest, the government demanded that they leave thousands of men behind to hold the place until British soldiers were sent to be the garrison. The colonials stayed, but no soldiers arrived. Through a brutal winter, the militiamen sickened and died at Louisbourg, losing at least a thousand men.

Colonial resentment at the British government began to simmer, and when the 1748 peace terms gave Louisbourg back to the French in exchange for other possessions, that resentment became an abiding anger. This bitterness was a

British naval power closes in on Louisbourg during the siege of 1758. This contemporary engraving shows a view over the lighthouse toward French vessels in the harbor and a Royal Navy fleet beyond.

cornerstone of colonial hostility to the British government—hostility that less than thirty years later erupted into the Revolutionary War.

Q: What was New York City's importance to the British military establishment in America?

A: For the first century of colonization few professional soldiers were stationed in British America. The colonies raised their own forces as needed. Other than the formidable presence of the British navy along the coast, British troops were seldom seen. By the mid-1700s there was a small military establishment, known as the "Four Independent Companies," a couple of hundred men sprinkled through the colonies. With the French and Indian War in the 1750s, thousands of British troops arrived. The army made its headquarters in New York City, where the magnificent harbor was becoming one of the most important in the world.

The English naval cutlass, a short, single-edged sword, was designed for hand-to-hand fighting. Its heavy guard was effective when delivering close-combat blows.

British Conquest of New France

Q: Why is the Seven Years' War, lasting from 1756 to 1763, considered the first worldwide conflict?

A: The Seven Years' War was ignited as the French and Indian War began in North America, where the British and French battled for control of the waterways and frontiers of the Ohio country. At first, the French colonials and their Native American allies were triumphant, expelling a small expedition led by Virginia colonel George Washington in 1754, and then in 1755

Braddock gave this pistol as a gift to Washington, an officer on the doomed campaign against Fort Duquesne.

slaughtering a British force of regulars under General Edward Braddock along the Monongahela River. Within a year, France and Britain were in conflict around the world as never before, attacking each other's colonies and fighting naval battles. They made alliances with other European powers —Britain with Prussia and Portugal, and France with Austria, Spain, Sweden, Holland, Poland, and Russia. This war was part of a broader struggle for supremacy in Europe, and its greatest land engagements were fought on

General Braddock meets his death as his expeditionary force is ambushed and almost wiped out by French and Indian forces defending Fort Duquesne in the Ohio region in 1755.

the continent. France and Britain's most decisive battles, however, were for their colonies, from India to North America. By 1760, the British had defeated the French in Canada, and Britain acquired the colony by the terms of the 1763 peace treaty. British America at last felt secure now that French military power had been removed from its borders. Before long, many colonies would be ambitious to expand westward into the wilderness.

An English official meets with chiefs of the "North-west"—the lands beyond colonial boundaries; this large native lodge may have been specially built for a major gathering of Indian and colonial leaders. This illustration depicts the English official incorrectly, in seventeenth-century clothing.

Q: What was the "Year of Miracles"?

A: Great Britain's triumphs were so numerous in 1759 that this became known as the "Year of Miracles." In North America the British captured one key fortress after another, including Ticonderoga and Crown Point, then took Quebec and laid siege to Montreal, which fell in 1760. British Secretary of State William Pitt led the nation through the war and was credited with military successes that shattered French power in India, Africa, the West Indies, and North America. Britain now was ruler of the seas and more powerful than her longtime adversary, France.

Q: What was Pontiac's Rebellion?

A: After the French and Indian War, Native Americans who had been allied with the defeated French remained hostile to the British. These included the Shawnee, Ottawa, Mingo, and Miamis—all objecting to the British occupation of former French forts in their country. In June 1763, the Ottawa war chief, Pontiac, organized an uprising from the Ohio Valley to Detroit, capturing nine military posts. Fort Detroit and Fort Pitt held on under siege as the frontier was swept with fire and destruction, with more than two thousand settlers killed. In August, the British defeated a major Indian force at Bushy Run, near Pitt, turning the tide against the uprising, which ended a year later. For now, the border between the colonies and Indian territory would be respected, but the colonials were hungry for new lands. Native peoples west of the Ohio recognized this threat, and they were determined to fight to the last for their homelands.

The pipe tomahawk was hollow and could be used for smoking or battle.

The 1760 enlistment papers of John Edwards, signed in Boston, inducted him into His Majesty's Provincial Service as a soldier for the final campaign against the French in Canada. His bounty money for enlisting was paid by Massachusetts Bay Colony. Provincial soldiers were short-termers compared with the king's regular soldiers, who often served for life.

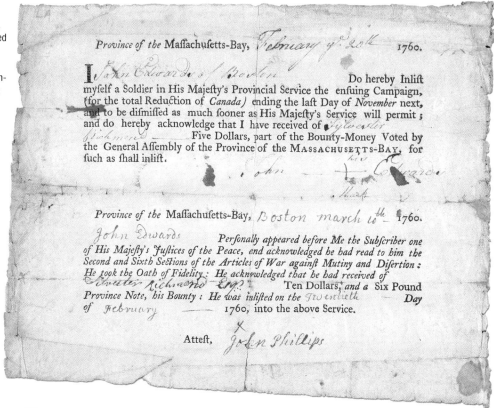

This idealized nineteenth-century depiction of colonial commander Robert Rogers conferring with Pontiac expresses the longstanding fascination of later Americans with the colonial period's Indian conflicts.

Q: How effective were American colonials in the French and Indian War?

A: Colonials were essential to the British military, with militiamen called up by the thousands to join expeditions or defend the frontiers. Colonial patrols countered French and Indian raiding parties that otherwise would have wiped out frontier communities.

Militia troops did not have the battlefield discipline or training of the British regulars, and for that reason many British officers despised them. Yet colonials showed notable courage and stalwartness, even in pitched battles, when well led. They especially shone as scouts cooperating with the regulars. Among the most famous were Rogers' Rangers, whose exploits on the New York–Quebec frontier are legendary.

In one crucial role Americans were the match of anyone in the world: as seamen and shipbuilders. New England sailors, in particular, were highly regarded, and many fast Yankee-built ships served as privateers hunting French vessels. Furthermore, if not for the great pine trees of New England, the British navy would not have had a secure source of tall masts for its warships or pitch to caulk their hulls watertight.

Q: What was the relationship between the colonies and the Indian nations in the first part of the eighteenth century?

A: During the first century of colonization, each colony had a different history with the native peoples—and that history was mainly peaceful. Trade between the fledgling colonies and the nations was essential to both sides: to colonials for furs and foodstuffs, and to the natives for firearms. As the colonies grew stronger and expanded, clashes increased, invariably to the detriment of the nations.

By the mid-1700s, when the British and French warred on the frontiers, most eastern Indians took one side or the other. The French depended on the Huron, Shawnee, Ottawa, and Wyandot tribes, and the British had enlisted most of the Iroquois as allies.

In the French and Indian War, however, the Iroquois generally kept out of the fighting. After the final French defeat, their former allies were left to face a fast-growing British America that was now hungry for Indian land rather than furs.

British officers wore metal "gorgets" hanging from their necks and engraved with the royal arms.

The ball-headed wooden war club was a lethal weapon in the hands of the Iroquois fighting man who wielded it.

Q: How did the Iroquois Confederation inspire Benjamin Franklin to conceptualize an American colonial alliance?

A: The Six Nations of the Iroquois League, occupying what became western New York State, were officially recognized by colonials as a political confederation. Well-organized into clans, tribes, and nations, with clearly understood rules and regulations, the Iroquois impressed Franklin with their governance through traditional ceremonies, skillful negotiating, frequent meetings, and deliberation in councils of respected leaders. Franklin adapted Iroquois diplomacy for his 1754 Plan of Union, conceived in Albany, New York, during treaty negotiations with the Iroquois. Franklin's Plan of Union was a precedent for the convening of the Continental Congress in 1774.

Q: Which colonial city was the second-largest city in the British Empire in the mid-eighteenth century?

A: Philadelphia, a hundred miles from the sea on the Delaware River and seat of the prosperous colony of Pennsylvania, was second only to London. With a population of around 35,000, Philadelphia was dwarfed by London's 750,000, but this colonial city was home to many of the wealthiest, most cultivated, and most influential American families. A major market for the southern colonies, Philadelphia was also within reach of New York and New England and was the gateway to the western frontier lands that so many colonists coveted.

Benjamin Franklin, a Boston native and citizen of Philadelphia, was one of the world's most renowned diplomats and intellectuals. He represented colonies in negotiations with native peoples, then to the government and king in London, and later went to Paris on behalf of the revolutionary Continental Congress.

Q: How did the British victory in the Seven Years' War (and French and Indian War) lay the foundations for the American Revolution?

A: The breaking of French power left the British unchallenged and supreme in North America, with only the native peoples standing in the way of westward expansion. The British government was determined to control development of this Northwest Territory, although colonies were staking claims there.

During the war, American colonials had prospered from military expenditures. Artisans and merchants were strengthened by supplying the thousands of troops. The British Empire was also prospering, bringing increased trade through American seaports, and there were a greater number of markets for colonial foodstuffs and raw materials. At the same time, the British government had gone deeply into debt for the war, and the controversial issue of taxing the colonies to repay that debt became a subject both in Parliament and colonial assemblies.

Further, American manufactures were developing in competition with British-made goods, such as ironwork. The enormous colonial market was becoming self-sufficient, troubling those British whose interests lay in selling to Americans. Victory in the French and Indian War set the stage for an irreconcilable collision between the mother country and thirteen of those upstart American colonies.

The classic design of the mid-seventeenth-century fortress is seen in this diagram of Crown Point, a strategic post on Lake Champlain built by the French as Fort St. Frederic.

The world was changing fast when George III came to the throne in 1760 at the age of twenty-eight. His most difficult challenge of all was how to rule the independent-minded American colonials.

Q: What were the British colonies in North America in 1768?

A: British America was roughly viewed as comprising five or perhaps six regions. The New England colonies were Massachusetts, Connecticut, Rhode Island, and New Hampshire, with Boston and Newport the major cities. The middle colonies were New York, Pennsylvania, New Jersey, and Delaware, with the cities Philadelphia and New York. The southern colonies were Maryland, Virginia, North Carolina, South Carolina, and

The Colonies are not to be emancipated from their dependence on the supremacy of England.

—*King George III*

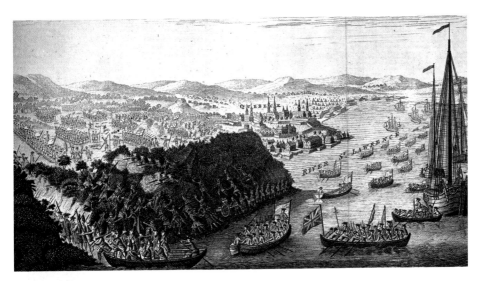

The most famous battle of the French and Indian War, the September 1759 British assault on powerful Quebec began by transporting soldiers across the St. Lawrence River. They then climbed a little-known path that ascended the cliffs and brought the troops to the plains before the city. The defenders sallied out to counterattack and were defeated.

Georgia, with Charleston and Baltimore the major towns. In the north were Quebec and Nova Scotia, with the cities of Montreal and Quebec. Upper Canada was west of Quebec, and Indian Territory, with several military posts, stretched beyond the Ohio River. In the far south were East and West Florida, with a minor military presence.

George Washington was in his Virginia militia colonel's uniform when he sat for painter Charles Willson Peale in 1772.

Q: Which key colonial military leaders came to prominence during the French and Indian War?

A: Most veterans of the French and Indian War were aging by the time the Revolutionary War appeared on the horizon, almost fifteen years later. Among the important American colonials were Virginia colonel George Washington; Philadelphia statesman Benjamin Franklin; Louisbourg veteran David Wooster; John Stark, Robert Rogers, and John Butler of Rogers' Rangers; Mohawk chief Thayendanegea, also known as Joseph Brant; and military wagoneer Daniel Morgan. British officers who after the war lived in America included Thomas Gage, Frederick Haldimand, Simon Fraser, Horatio Gates, and Guy Carleton. All these men returned to the field when the Revolutionary War began. Colonials Washington, Franklin, Wooster, Stark, and Morgan served as Patriots, joined by Gates. The others were Loyalist or—like Carleton, who was governor of Canada, and Fraser, who was a high-ranking officer—remained in the king's service.

A historical map of New England showing Massachusetts Bay, New Hampshire, Maine, Connecticut, Rhode Island, and the surrounding coastline.

HAMPSHIRE

MASSACHUSSETS BAY

MAIN

CONNECTICUT

RHODE ISLAN

Connecticut River · White Mountains · Cohasset · so called

Cape Anne · Cape Codd · Boston Harbr · Jeffreys Ledge

Nantucket I. · Martha's Vineyard I. · Block I. · Elizabeth Is. · Buzards B.

Rhode I. · Newport · Providence · Glocester · Warwick · French T. · Greenwich · Derby · Kingstown · Charlestown

Hartford · Weathersfield · Middleton · Seabrook · Killingworth · Guilford · Saybrook · Windsor · Simsbury · Suffield · Enfield · Springfield · Westfield · Northampton · Hadley · Deerfield · Halfield · Sunderland · Northfield · Fort Dummer · Winchester · Ashuelot

Boston · Cambridge · Concord · Dorchester · Milton · Braintree · Weymouth · Hingham · Scituate · Marshfield · Duxbury · Plymouth · Barnstable · Sandwich · Falmouth · Rochester · Dartmouth · Taunton · Bridgewater · Attlebrough · Wrentham · Mendon · Hopkinton · Rutland · Leicester · Worcester · Grotton · Tewksbury · Newbury · Ipswich · Beverley · Salem · Lynn · Marblehead · Manchester · Gloucester

Portsmouth · Piscataqua Hr · I. of Shoals · Kittery · Berwick · York · C. Nedock · Boon I. · Wells · Wells B. · C. Porpoise · Winter Harb · C. Elizabeth · Casco Bay · Falmouth · Saco · Scarborough Fort · Biddeford · Brunswick · Topsam · Richmond Ft

Cape Anne · Salisbury · Plumb I. · Newbury · Bradford · Haveril · Kingston · Exeter · Durham · Chester · Litchfield · Nottingham · Peterborough · Sowhegan · Tings T. · Suncook · Rumford · Bow · Canterbury · Contocook · Gerrish T. · Gilman T.

Old Rose and Crown · New Rose & Crown · South Channel · Sandy Pt · Chatham · Harwich · Eastham · Truro · Barnstable Bay

CHAPTER 2

CAUSES OF THE REVOLUTION

British America's population burgeoned from almost 1.6 million in 1760 to 2.14 million in 1770. African Americans were approximately a fifth of the colonial population, and the slave trade steadily increased to meet the demands of southern plantations. Cities grew, but most colonials lived and worked on family farms. Manufacturing was restrained by repressive British policies that inhibited the growth of American industry in order to promote the sale of British-made goods to colonials. The heavy-handed attempts by King George III and Parliament to rule and regulate the flourishing colonies were doomed to failure. Americans grew resentful of being taxed without their consent and of being governed by rulers who did not understand their way of life. As red-coated British soldiers arrived to police them, resentment deepened. When royal proclamations prevented settlement of western lands, the colonies felt barred from their natural expansion. The combination of long-standing animosities with new notions of the "rights of man" made it apparent by the early 1770s that a great and decisive struggle with the mother country was fast approaching.

This map of the colony of Massachusetts in 1774 shows how the waters of Boston harbor once dominated where land and city now exist. The harbor was busy with British navy vessels and cargo ships supplying the garrison that occupied the city as punishment for defiance of royal taxation and navigation regulations.

"Triangular Trade" and Smugglers

Q: How important were the North American colonies to the British Empire before the Revolution?

A: These colonies differed from others in the British Empire in that the majority of the population were white and considered themselves British citizens—except for the French of Canada. Most Indians lived in what was then the Northwest Territory, not officially considered a colony. Important colonies in India, Asia, Africa, and the Caribbean had a tiny ruling white minority with an overwhelmingly large, but subjugated, native population. America had valuable raw materials and commodities, from timber to molasses, but more important, the colonials were an extremely lucrative market for British manufactured goods—wares that the home government forbade Americans from producing on a large scale.

One important export from America was "naval stores," the production of which was encouraged by the British government. As a maritime power, Britain needed the tar, pitch, turpentine, resin, hemp, and lumber for building and maintaining ships. Even more critical to the empire was the colonial shipbuilding industry, which accounted for more than one-third of all British tonnage. More than twenty-five thousand tons of shipping were turned out each year in the American colonies, where manufacturing costs could be half that in Britain.

Some very tiny colonies were considered more valuable to British business than most North American colonies, however. West Indies islands were extremely profitable, producing molasses and sugar for rum and taking part in the slave trade.

Q: How did the "Triangular Trade" work, and what were the commodities being shipped?

A: "Triangular Trade" describes commerce that brings goods from one port to another, which processes or sells those goods and ships the end product to a third port, where the transaction results in product or goods that are in turn sold to the first port—a perpetual motion. In the 1700s, one triangle included the West Indies, the North American colonies, and Britain. The West Indies produced molasses and sugar that was sold to New England, where it was used to produce rum. The rum went to Britain, where much of the profit from its sale was used to buy African slaves. Those slaves were then sold in the West Indies or in North America.

In another variation New Englanders shipped rum to Africa to purchase slaves that were then carried to the West Indies or to the South for sale. Another trade

Thousands of fishermen and whalers set out from Marblehead, one of the busiest seaports in New England during colonial and revolutionary days. This Massachusetts port also had its share of smugglers slipping past government patrols.

1763

The west coast of Africa was the leading source of slaves, who were shipped to Caribbean "sugar islands" to work in the cane fields. Thousands were also sold to British colonies on the continent, most to work as field hands in the growing plantations of the South.

route included New England fish and lumber going to Britain in exchange for manufactured goods that were brought back to America. Each commodity, from sugar to human beings, helped finance the purchase of the other, with middlemen profiting from the sales and shipping.

British "Navigation Acts" were laws that prevented foreign vessels from carrying shipments to or from British ports—including those in North America. These laws required that almost all commodities had to first pass through a port in the British Isles before being sent to the colonies. The result was added cost that colonials came to resent. In this way the colonies were prevented from trading with countries outside the empire, making smuggling a profitable enterprise.

Q: Why was smuggling such a point of hostility between the colonies and the British government?

A: As the American colonies prospered, British regulations such as the Navigation Acts slowed their growth. Colonials were unhappy about tariffs, fees, and middleman costs placed on trade goods and merchandise imported into the colonies. Smugglers could sail to the Caribbean and make secret purchases, and then return to North America to sell them—slipping them past coastal patrol vessels. Some of America's leading families, including the Hancocks of Massachusetts, made great fortunes as smugglers. Smugglers cut into British mercantile profits and reduced government revenues.

John Hancock was an influential New Englander whose opposition to the British Parliament sprang in large part from his hatred of port fees and tariffs. Much of Hancock's fortune came from his profitable smuggling enterprises.

A Rich, Productive Land

Q: Which American colonies were the most populous?

A: Of the approximately 2.14 million inhabitants of the original thirteen colonies in 1770, Virginia had by far the largest share, with 447,000. Of the total colonial

Pennsylvania artist Charles Willson Peale captured an incident in Philadelphia's daily life with this "Accident on Lombard Street."

population, 459,000 were African American, and several thousand were Native American. Virginia's population included more than 187,000 blacks. Pennsylvania was second-largest, with 240,000 persons, but only 5,700 blacks. Next were Massachusetts, at 235,000, including 4,700 blacks; Maryland, 202,000, including almost 64,000 blacks; North Carolina, 197,000, with 69,000 blacks; Connecticut, almost 184,000, including 5,700 blacks; and New York, almost 163,000, and 19,000 blacks. South Carolina's 124,000 included 75,000 blacks; New Jersey, at 117,000, had 8,000 blacks; New Hampshire, 62,000, with 650 blacks; Rhode Island, 58,000, and more than 3,700 blacks; Delaware, 35,000, with 1,800 blacks, and Georgia, more than 23,000, with 10,600 blacks.

Another 55,000 colonists lived along the frontiers, from Maine to Kentucky and Tennessee, including about 3,000 blacks.

Q: What profession and way of life was at the heart of American culture and society by 1770?

A: Most Americans worked on the family farm, whether as owners or hired hands. Some were rough-and-tumble frontier farms on the edge of Indian country, but most were well-tended enterprises. Family farms provided food and also some cash crops and produce for sale, such as maple sugar, butter, cheese, and flax prepared for spinning into linen yarn. The average American was a farmer, not a pioneer backwoodsman, though most country folk could handle firearms. About one hundred thousand colonists lived in the major cities, and cottage industries—including weaving and spinning—thrived in all the colonies.

Hand tools such as this sickle and forged-iron hoe blade were the main implements for farming, the primary colonial occupation.

The cozy New England kitchen was a busy place, with cooking, baking, spinning, butter-churning, and repair work carried out to the sounds of children playing.

Large-scale manufacturing other than shipbuilding was discouraged by British laws, however, so local industry was small and catered to the community.

America had some of the world's finest gunsmiths, and iron manufacturing was developing by 1770, but there was little manufacturing done outside of Philadelphia, which made hats, shoes, stockings, pottery, and soap as well as naval stores and some metal foundry products. Fishing, seafaring, and related industries were also major American endeavors.

Q: How important was slavery to the colonial economy?

A: By 1770, African American slaves were becoming increasingly numerous in the southern colonies, where they were essential for working on the plantations growing major cash crops. While most southerners lived on family farms, most black slaves lived on plantations, generation after generation, and labored in fields of tobacco, rice, or indigo that was grown mainly for export. A small number of plantation owners became extremely wealthy from these crops, which could not have been efficiently produced without the manual labor of slaves. Thousands of blacks were free, especially in the middle and northern colonies. Many others, considered servants, lived with the same family all their lives. While many Americans opposed or questioned the institution of slavery, the steady growth of plantations promised that slave labor would be ever more crucial in the future.

"Negro servant" Phyllis Wheatley was an accomplished poet. She took her last name from the Boston family to whom she belonged; she would not have been considered a slave.

> "Will you sheathe your sword in the bowels of your brothers, the Americans?"
>
> —WILLIAM PITT (THE ELDER)
> in 1766, warning Parliament and king not to push the colonists toward open conflict

"Taxation Without Representation!"

Q: Why, in the 1760s and early 1770s, was Parliament so determined to place tariffs and taxes on the already profitable commerce with the colonies?

A: Not only did Parliament want the Americans to pay some of the cost of the Seven Years' War (French and Indian War in America), but tariffs, duties, and taxes were intended to regulate American trade and manufacturing in favor of British business and industry. The 1764 Sugar Act taxed sugar imported into the colonies, and the 1765 Stamp Act placed a tax on legal documents and printed paper.

The Townshend Acts of 1767 were passed in part because the Americans had refused to accept the earlier taxation, and Parliament was resolved to prove that it had the authority and right to rule America as it saw fit. The Townshend Acts placed duties on imports such as glass, paper, paint, and tea. Many members of Parliament objected futilely to squeezing

Bostonians demonstrate against the Stamp Act. The Stamp Act required the purchase of stamps, to be affixed to official documents.

cash from the American colonies, whose estimated sixty thousand pounds sterling in annual revenues would do nothing to pay down the immense British national debt of 130 million pounds. One contemporary cartoon showed members of Parliament about to kill the American golden goose.

Americans united in protest that they were being taxed by a Parliament that they had not elected, a violation of their rights as British subjects.

Q: What was the meaning of "taxation without representation"?

A: The entire phrase, "Taxation without representation is tyranny," had been hurled at British royalty and the government more than a hundred years previous. This phrase

Official colonial documents once needed revenue stamps to prove the owner had paid the tax. Stamps were kept in this leather box.

Benjamin Franklin speaks
for American colonies to
the British Parliament's
House of Lords, with
their ladies in attendance,
at Whitehall Chapel in
London in 1774.

was well understood and respected by
the British, so when American colonists
asserted they were not represented in
Parliament, it touched a nerve.

American colonials elected their own
governing bodies, but they did not vote
for members of Parliament, who were
passing the taxation and trade acts. The
colonists insisted that only their own
elected governments in America had the
right to levy taxes. In response, Parliament declared that its members did not
represent individuals, but "estates"—for
example, landed gentry, doctors, lawyers,
and merchants. According to this logic,
colonials from these various estates were,
like citizens in the British Isles, represented in Parliament.

Colonials were not convinced,
however, and this phrase became the
theme and cry of the buildup to the
Revolutionary War.

Q: Did the colonies have any official
representation before Parliament?

A: Yes, colonial governments had
appointed "agents" in Britain, someone
who looked out for the colony's interests,
lobbied Parliament and the king upon
issues important to the colony, and kept
Americans informed of developments
in London. Benjamin Franklin at one
time served as agent to the governments
of three colonies: Pennsylvania,
Massachusetts, and Georgia. Agents had
no authority in the British government,
but they were heard when they spoke
on behalf of their colonial clients. The
agent's diplomatic skills and intelligence
were keys to their colony's influence in
London's halls of power. In Franklin's
case, the office of agent contributed to
his considerable stature in both America
and Britain.

" Parliament cannot well and wisely make laws suited to the colonies, without being properly and
truly informed. "
—*Benjamin Franklin*

Royal Coercion Meets Resistance

Q: Which British statesman said, "An Englishman is the unfittest person on earth to argue another Englishman into slavery"?

A: Edmund Burke (1729–97), on the eve of the War of American Independence, thus expressed his objection to using force against American resistance to harsh, punitive acts of Parliament. Burke, a native of Dublin, also said, "The people of the colonies are descendants of Englishmen. England, Sir, is a nation which I still hope respects, and formerly adored, her freedom."

Influential Member of Parliament Edmund Burke spoke out in support of the American colonies.

Q: What did King George III think about colonial unrest?

A: He was infuriated. As America defied various acts to tax or dominate the colonies, King George resolved that the colonists must be put in their place. He feared that open resistance, or rebellion, in America might encourage rebellion in Ireland, and the result might even be the breakup of Great Britain. Also ominous to him was the possibility that the Americans might ally themselves with the French against Britain.

When the Stamp Act was repealed as a result of American resistance, the king and his closest advisers resolved to assert Britain's right to tax the colonies. One

Silver teapots such as this one made for a Newport, Rhode Island, lady, were fashionable items in the wealthiest colonial American households.

White colonists, dressed up as Indians in order to mock government officials with their superficial disguises, throw British tea into Boston harbor in 1773 to protest royal trade regulations.

result was the Townshend Acts, levying import duties. The colonies erupted in riots and boycotts, winning some concessions, but the king stubbornly maintained the duty on tea. Colonial turmoil and the Boston Tea Party resulted in the 1774 Coercive Acts, which punished Massachusetts in particular, closing Boston's port. As the colonies united around Massachusetts, King George's own resolve hardened, and he determined to use force to make the Americans obey his rule.

Q: Did the colonists believe they were defying King George III?

A: In the first years of hostility to Britain's colonial administration, the anger of Americans was for the most part directed at colonial governors or at Parliament, not at the king. The colonists appealed to King George for understanding and support in their struggle for the same rights as British subjects in the mother country. The king did not offer that support. By the mid-1770s, George could not find a minister able enough to take the lead in managing the long-running controversy with the colonies. As a result he made many decisions himself, further alienating the colonists, who began to call him a tyrant.

Q: Who were the philosophers whose writings most influenced American aspirations for liberty?

A: The Frenchmen Voltaire and Jean-Jacques Rousseau wrote criticisms of hereditary feudal privilege, social inequality, and the oppression of the lower classes. Their works helped give birth to an "Age of Reason," an "Enlightenment," and their brilliant essays influenced the likes of Benjamin Franklin and Thomas Jefferson. Such profound American thinkers were busy in their minds with the concept of effective government free of aristocratic or religious domination.

Hereditary privilege did not have much standing in the New World, making it easier to establish liberty, equality, and fraternity—although how those ideal "rights of man" would embrace blacks, Indians, and women was to remain a mystery to American social philosophers as they undertook the building of a new nation founded on individual liberty.

A British cartoon made light of the government's frustration with America, showing important officials carrying a coffin holding the short-lived Stamp Act that colonial opposition had killed.

The controversial French essayist and social philosopher Voltaire made many enemies among Europe's rulers by speaking out against the current order—calling for liberty and equality for all.

> ❝ **America must be embraced with the arms of affection.** ❞
> *PRIME MINISTER WILLIAM PITT*
> *(termed the Younger), hoping for reconciliation between Britain and the colonies*

Boston: The Seat of Revolution

A major in the British Forty-fourth Regiment of Foot wore this uniform coat in military scarlet that earned soldiers the name "Lobsterback" long before they were "redcoats," a nineteenth-century term.

Q: What made Boston such a hotbed of unrest and eventually the seat of open rebellion in the colonies?

A: The fact that Boston had a large anti-English Irish population was not the least of the factors involved in Boston's radical temperament. Through the 1760s Boston saw increasing violence against government officers, revenue collectors, and customs officials—even the Massachusetts governor's home was torched by an angry mob. In 1768, hundreds of British troops arrived. This occupying force would be termed the "Boston Garrison." Radicals, led by Samuel Adams, advocated armed resistance, but cooler heads prevailed.

"Lobsterbacks" quartered in and around Boston were a source of bitter resentment to most residents. The authorities refused to provide quarters or provisions for the soldiers, who returned Boston's hatred in kind. Year after year the tension and friction increased, erupting in the "Boston Massacre" of 1770.

Q: What caused the Boston Massacre?

A: Agitation against the British soldiers was led by radicals who wanted to bring on a crisis to embarrass Parliament and compel the withdrawal of the Boston Garrison. There were minor clashes between soldiers and civilians from time to time, but the worst occurred on a wintry March day in 1770, when a surly mob began harassing a sentry standing guard duty, pelting him with snowballs. The soldier

Paul Revere's false depiction of the "Boston Massacre" shows soldiers in ranks firing on the crowd; this widely distributed poster stirred up anger in the colonies.

was joined by ten comrades, and the crowd grew to about sixty, becoming increasingly aggressive. Provoked, the soldiers opened fire, resulting in five civilian deaths. Radicals, including silversmith and artist Paul Revere, seized the opportunity to disseminate propaganda that falsely painted the soldiers as wanton killers. That propaganda, including a rendering by Revere, provoked Americans from other colonies into a fury against the army. There are those who believe that Sam Adams himself instigated the incident in order to agitate Bostonians.

This period engraving memorializes the five civilians who died in the 1774 Boston Massacre.

Q: Who defended the British troops who were tried for the Boston Massacre?

A: Leading colonial lawyers John Adams and Josiah Quincy defended the seven soldiers put on trial. Five were acquitted and two were found guilty of manslaughter. These two were discharged from military service. The incident resulted in the withdrawal of soldiers from within the city to other quarters in the hope of limiting future antagonism. The radical-disseminated myth that the incident was a cold-blooded "massacre" of upstanding citizens has persisted down the centuries, even though in 1887 the Massachusetts Historical Society objected to a memorial being dedicated to the victims. The society criticized the description of the mob as "heroes and martyrs," saying that to do so would be to misinterpret the event and to raise the dead to a historical status they did not deserve.

Outspoken Virginia orator and statesman Patrick Henry urged armed resistance with "Give me liberty, or give me death!"

communicate with each other. The Sons of Liberty were one of the most dynamic of these organizations, leading some of the worst violence against the British and colonial governments, including the tarring and feathering of their opponents. Committees of correspondence were organized in 1772—the first by Sam Adams—to communicate throughout the colonies.

Committees of safety were formed as conditions worsened and became more dangerous in 1775, with the object of calling out the militia to resist the British army. Until revolutionary governments were established, committees of safety often acted, with the approval of the Continental Congress, as state and local governments.

Anti-British committees of safety organized to establish a system of mutual defense that authorized the raising of militia companies to be called out to oppose the government troops.

Q: What were committees of safety?

A: Radicals determined to resist British rule and bring on a colonial revolution formed secret organizations to carry out their plans and to

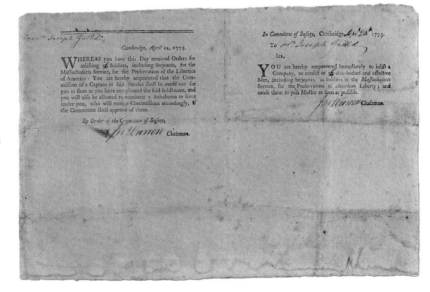

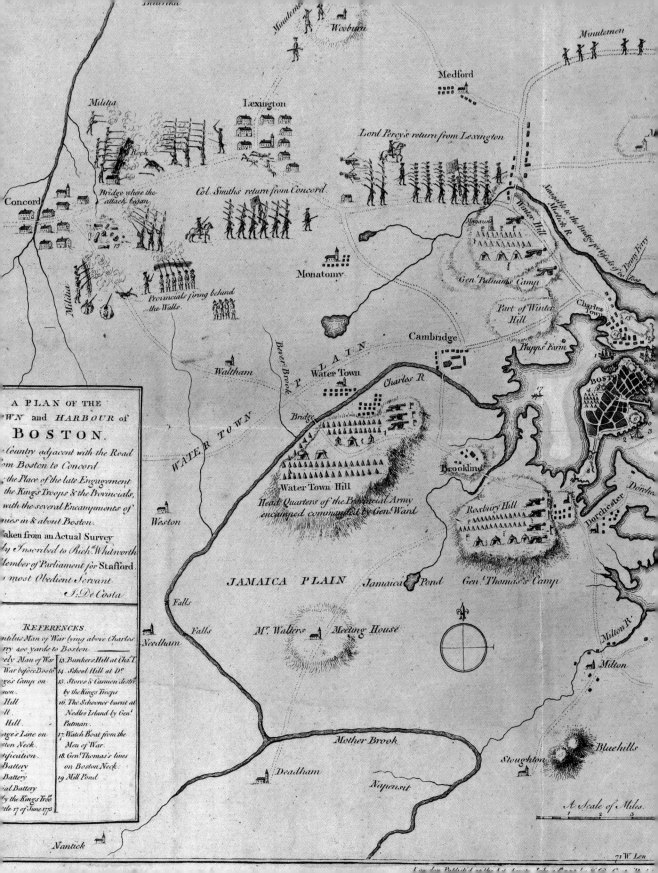

Woobun

Minutemen

Medford

Minutemen

Militia

Lexington

Lord Percy's return from Lexington

Rock

Concord

Bridge where the attack began

Col. Smith's return from Concord

Navigable to the Bridge for Boats of ten Tons

Mistick Hill

Magazin

Gen. Putnam's Camp

Charles Town

Militia

Militia

Provincials firing behind the Walls

Monatomy

Part of Winter Hill

Phipp's Farm

Beaver Brook

P   L   A   I   N

Cambridge

BOSTON

Waltham

Water Town

Charles R.

17

A PLAN OF THE
WN and HARBOUR of
BOSTON.

Country adjacent with the Road
om Boston to Concord
the Place of the late Engagement
the King's Troops & the Provincials,
with the several Encampments of
nies in & about Boston

aken from an Actual Survey
ly Inscribed to Rich.d Whitworth
ember of Parliament for Stafford
most Obedient Servant
J. De Costa

Bridge

Brookline

WATER   TOWN

Water Town Hill

Head Quarters of the Provincial Army
encamped commanded by Gen.l Ward

Roxbury Hill

Weston

Dorchester

Dorchester

JAMAICA   PLAIN

Jamaica Pond

Gen.l Thomas's Camp

Milton R.

Falls

Mr. Walters   Meeting House

Falls

REFERENCES.

antilus Man of War lying above Charles
rry 400 yards to Boston
ely Man of War   13 Bunkers Hill at Cha.T.
War before Boston   14 School Hill at D.o
ge's Camp on   15 Stores & Cannon destro.
non.   by the Kings Troops
Hill   16 The Schooner burnt at
ll.   Nodles Island by Gen.l
Hill.   Putnam.
ge's Line on   17 Watch Boat from the
sten Neck.   Men of War.
tification.   18 Gen.l Thomas's lines
Battery   on Boston Neck.
Battery   19 Mill Pond
al Battery
by the Kings Tro.s
le 17 of June 1775

Needham

Milton

Mother Brook

Stoughton

Bluehills

Deadham

Napensit

A Scale of Miles.
1   2   3

Nantick

71° W. Lon.

CHAPTER 3

WAR BREAKS OUT

Mounting resistance to British rule in 1773 prompted King George to use force to quell the opposition. Policy misjudgments, royal stubbornness, and Tory arrogance infuriated American colonials, who at times resisted violently—British tea was dumped in Boston harbor, and tax collectors were tarred and feathered. In September 1774, delegates to the First Continental Congress met in Philadelphia to declare colonial unity. Then, in April 1775, British troops attempting to destroy military stores at Concord, Massachusetts, were met by militiamen at Lexington Green. Gunfire was exchanged, blood shed, and the Revolutionary War began. The troops then came under fierce attack by thousands of militia, who drove them back to Boston. Now began a yearlong siege of the city, marked by a British assault on Breed's Hill, a costly victory for the king's troops. George Washington took charge of the siege and managed—with often undisciplined and ill-supplied men—to force a British evacuation in March 1776.

Above: Colonial militiamen on Breed's Hill were said to have been ordered to hold their fire "until you see the whites of their eyes!" Up from the Charlestown landings came the regulars, anticipating an easy victory, but they had to charge three bloody times before they captured the American earthworks.

Left: This 1775 English map shows the movements and positions of British regulars and New England militia during the April 19 engagements known as the battles of Lexington and Concord, which began the Revolutionary War.

Symbols, Parties, and Bribes

Q: What was a "liberty pole"?

A: "Liberty trees" and "liberty poles" were trees or raised timbers used as meeting places and for rallies by opponents of British colonial policy. An ancient elm in Boston was considered the first liberty tree when effigies of Stamp Act supporters were hung there by Bostonians in 1765. When British soldiers cut down the elm in 1775, a liberty pole was later raised on the same spot. New York City also raised a liberty pole that became well known in the colonies as the symbol of opposition to British taxation policies.

Right: First cast in London in 1752 and twice recast in Philadelphia in 1753, the bell is inscribed with words from the book of Leviticus: "Proclaim Liberty throughout all the Land unto all the Inhabitants Thereof." In the early nineteenth century anti-slavery groups named it the Liberty Bell.

Q: Why is the famous bell from Philadelphia called the "Liberty Bell"?

A: The bell did not have this name in 1751 when it was ordered by Pennsylvania's provincial council for the State House. The bell cracked the first time it was rung and had to be recast. A symbol of the colony's self-esteem, it was taken down and hidden from British troops who occupied Philadelphia from late 1777 to mid-1778. In 1839 it became known as the Liberty Bell. While ringing for Washington's birthday commemoration in 1846, it cracked again, forever to remain silent.

Q: Who were the Whigs and Tories, and what did they stand for?

A: These terms loosely described the two largest political affiliations in Britain, which themselves were divided into smaller allegiances and parties. The Whigs, founded in the merchant class,

"Raising the Liberty Pole," from a 1776 painting by F. A. Chapman, shows Patriots at work in a crowded village square, as disgruntled Loyalists turn away; in the background, a sign bearing the likeness of King George III is being removed.

had been powerful before George III succeeded in weakening their influence in favor of his own supporters. The Tory party drew power from the conservative aristocracy that favored the king's right to choose and rule his ministers of state. The Whigs asserted that only Parliament had the right to choose ministers and control them. On the eve of the Revolutionary War the "king's friends" were mostly Tories. At the same time, the Whigs favored colonial policies that the American "Patriot Party" favored. As a result Patriot members called themselves Whigs after 1768.

As unrest increased in America, anyone who supported the government against the revolutionaries was termed a Tory, or a Loyalist. Most government officials and revenue collectors were Tories, while proponents of freedom and practitioners of smuggling were Whigs.

Q: What made it so difficult for government officials to stop smuggling?

A: Not only was the American coastline with its innumerable bays and river mouths simply too extensive for the small fleet of government patrol vessels—revenue cutters—to watch, but colonials enjoyed lower prices buying duty-free smuggled tea and other products. Further, there was an efficient and profitable system of moving the contraband from landing place to marketplace.

There were never enough officials or armed vessels to enforce the laws, and many a customs official was bribed, enabling smuggling to thrive. Those officials who tried to enforce the law were often attacked or threatened by smugglers and their allies. By 1773, smugglers were popularly considered heroes who were resisting a tyrannical government.

"The Alternative of Williamsburg," reads this portrayal of a Virginia mob forcing Loyalists to sign a document supporting the Patriots. Those who refuse will be coated with the tar and feathers that hang from the scaffold.

> It is necessary to recur to the law of nature and the British constitution to ascertain our rights . . . and [colonials] have a right to erect what government they please.
>
> —JOHN JAY
> New York delegate to the 1774 Continental Congress

Patience Runs Out

Q: Why was the boycott of British tea such a revolutionary step?

A: In early 1773 Parliament passed the Tea Act to save the corrupt and failing East India Company, which had considerable political and social influence in England. The law cut out middlemen and almost eliminated taxes on the company's tea. This would allow the tea to be sold cheaply in America, undercutting smuggled Dutch tea as well as other legally imported tea. Many colonials considered this act as a blow to their own business interests as well as a devious method of taxing the colonies.

In October 1773 a mass meeting of Philadelphians appointed a committee to prevent East India Company tea from being accepted by a local import business. The same thing happened to tea consigned to New York and Charleston. When a Boston town meeting also called for a rejection of the tea in their city, it proved the colonies could stand unified against Parliament. The Boston merchants importing the tea would not, however, accept the decree of the town meeting, and the result was the Boston Tea Party.

Q: Why did the colonials dress up as Indians and throw tea chests from a merchant ship into Boston harbor?

A: Sons of Liberty leader Samuel Adams was determined not to allow East India Company tea to be landed and sold in Boston. For one thing, he and some allies had a financial stake in their own smuggled tea. Furthermore, he saw the opportunity to spark a popular act of violence against Parliament and its supporters in America. The Indian disguises were intended to prevent easy identifica-

This view of the destruction of British-owned tea by a mob of Patriots in the December 1773 Boston Tea Party was based on a period engraving commemorating the event.

"An attack, made on one of our sister colonies . . . is an attack made on all British America."

—*Thomas Jefferson*
expressing the opinion of Virginia's House of Burgesses, of which he was a member

tion and possible arrest of the sixty insurgents, who on December 16 threw more than 340 chests of tea worth ten thousand pounds sterling into the water. The businesses to whom the tea had been consigned demanded prosecution of the rioters, and Parliament passed what became known as the Intolerable Acts to punish Boston as an example to the rest of the colonies.

Samuel Adams

Q: What were the "Intolerable Acts" and the Quebec Act?

A: After the Boston Tea Party of December 1773, King George was determined to stop American acts of defiance by humiliating Massachusetts. With the king's consent, Parliament passed statutes in May and June 1774 specifically to punish the colony and compel, or coerce, obedience; in Britain these were termed the Coercive Acts. One statute closed the port of Boston to merchant vessels until the destroyed tea was paid for. Another weakened the colony's self-government by giving the king the authority to appoint the governing council, which until then had been elected by the colonial legislature. Another permitted the military to procure housing for soldiers wherever they were needed. This Quartering Act especially angered Bostonians, who wanted the soldiers restricted to military barracks, not scattered around the city, where they could observe militia stockpiling of munitions and weapons. Further, off-duty soldiers quartered in town often brawled with Bostonians, who hated "lobsterbacks." American colonial governments considered these laws to be intolerable, unacceptable, so they were known in America as the Intolerable Acts.

Another hated statute from this time was the Quebec Act, which established a government in Quebec that had no elected assembly or right to trial by jury. The act also recognized Roman Catholicism as Quebec's established religion and extended the province's boundaries along the Ohio and Mississippi rivers, where many other colonies had land claims. Americans feared the same undemocratic government might be forced upon them one day.

Samuel Adams was a Massachusetts legislator and a fiery radical leader of the Sons of Liberty. A second cousin to the more diplomatic John Adams, he won a following during colonial opposition to the 1765 Stamp Act and worked tirelessly for American independence.

In this 1775 cartoon Boston burns as British nobility demand money from a colonial, who declares, "I will not be robbed." A Roman Catholic monk holds up a gibbet and a cross, a Frenchman brandishes his sword, and blindfolded Britannia, symbol of Great Britain, steps toward a pit.

In Congress Assembled

Q: Why did colonial leaders decide to meet in congress in Philadelphia?

A: Anger with the 1774 Intolerable Acts prompted calls for an intercolonial convention, a congress, to decide upon some sort of colonial alliance. Boston suffered most from the Intolerable Acts, and Massachusetts called for the other colonies to rally to her side by holding a congress in Philadelphia. Massachusetts hoped to win a nonimportation agreement calling for a boycott of British-made goods until the Intolerable Acts were repealed.

Early in September, fifty-six delegates from twelve colonies—only Georgia was not represented—met in Carpenter's Hall, Philadelphia, to denounce the Intolerable Acts and the Quebec Act. Going even further, this First Continental Congress criticized taxation and revenue policies, Admiralty Courts (special courts of law established to uphold these policies), the dissolution of colonial assemblies, and the stationing of soldiers in American towns during peacetime. The delegates signed the Continental Association, asserting the rights of colonials as British subjects, and sent a resolution presenting their grievances to the king and the British people.

Q: Which colonial leaders were set on forcing Britain to grant the colonies more liberty, and which wanted to avoid worsening relations with king and Parliament?

A: From the start, colonials who favored unified opposition to British colonial policies were divided into radicals, moderates, and conservatives. The radicals, such as John Hancock and Samuel Adams of Massachusetts and Patrick Henry of Virginia, were quite

Virginia delegate Patrick Henry addresses the First Continental Congress at Carpenters' Hall in Philadelphia in 1774. Congress declared that colonists had the same rights as Englishmen, and it established the Continental Association to boycott British trade goods.

Left: Robert Treat Paine, once a chaplain in the French and Indian War, served as a Massachusetts legislator and a delegate to the Continental Congress. A cautious moderate at first, Paine later became a signatory to the Declaration of Independence.

Right: A conservative delegate to the First Continental Congress, Joseph Galloway of Pennsylvania proposed the "Plan of Union" for a colonial legislature and a written constitution. When his plan was defeated by just one vote, he withdrew from Congress and later fled to England as a Loyalist.

willing to take up arms to assert their colonial rights in the face of British oppression. Moderates such as Robert Treat Paine of Massachusetts wanted the colonies to demand their rights from Parliament, but, as he stated: "Independence? A hundred times no."

A conservative member of the New York delegation to the Continental Congress, John Peters, was beaten by a pro-independence Philadelphia mob for professing his loyalty to the king. Conservative Joseph Galloway of Maryland proposed a Plan of Union to unite the colonies and establish them as a "dominion" in the empire with a royally appointed president-general. Galloway's plan would have given the united colonial government veto power over Parliament's legislation affecting the colonies. The First Continental Congress defeated this Plan of Union by one vote, so infuriating him that he refused to be

a delegate to the Second Continental Congress and eventually became an active Loyalist.

Q: What did the First Continental Congress achieve?

A: The key achievement of the first Congress, which sat for two months, was the approval of its "Declarations and Resolves," a petition to king and Parliament calling for repeal of the Coercive Acts. The Congress condemned the British government for interfering in colonial matters and asserted that the right of self-government and taxation belonged exclusively to the colonies, not to Parliament, which was not elected by colonials. Further, the delegates called for a boycott of British goods and also scheduled a Second Continental Congress to convene in Philadelphia the following May.

> **The distinctions between Virginians, Pennsylvanians, New Yorkers, and New Englanders are no more. I am not a Virginian, but an American.**
> —*Patrick Henry*
> *Virginia delegate to the 1774 Continental Congress*

Seasoned Commanders in America

Q: Who were the key American military commanders in 1775?

A: The Patriot who had achieved the highest rank in the British service was George Washington, a Virginia colonel and commander of a brigade in the 1758 capture of Fort Duquesne. Retired British major Horatio Gates had served in the French and Indian War and was living in Virginia in 1775. Likewise, New York's Richard Montgomery had been a career officer during the French and Indian War and sold his captaincy before settling permanently in America. Some of the most experienced colonial soldiers from the French and Indian War were elderly but still eager for service. These included Israel Putnam of Connecticut, a former wilderness fighter with Rogers' Rangers and a lieutenant colonel in a Connecticut regiment. John Stark of New Hampshire was another former ranger and an officer highly respected by New Englanders. Some top American commanders, such as rangers Robert Rogers and William Butler, opposed independence and joined the Loyalist forces.

Charles Willson Peale painted Horatio Gates from life in 1782. Born in England, Gates soldiered in North America and the Caribbean. In 1772, he purchased an estate in Virginia, and three years later he joined Washington's staff. Gates provided the Continental Army's first disciplinary code, supply procedures, and camp sanitation regulations.

Horatio Gates

Q: Who had more battle-hardened men at the start of hostilities, the British regulars or the American militia?

A: The militia had far more battle-tested soldiers than did the regulars in America. Thousands of colonials had served against the French and Indians, but the British regiments sent to serve in America had seen little action in the previous decade. The regulars were mainly

"General Putnam leaving his plow for the defense of his country" is the title of this fanciful portrayal of Israel Putnam being called from his Connecticut farm to Boston in 1775. "Old Put," a Massachusetts native and a war hero, was the senior commander until Washington took charge.

young men who had enlisted since the Seven Years' War, serving in a time of relative peace.

Most important, however, was the difference in military experience between the colonial militia officers and the British officers. Colonial officers had been seasoned in the French and Indian War, but most of the British officers had acquired their rank by purchase. Many were callow youths, gentlemen out for adventure or fortune, with little or no formal military training. British officers were seldom promoted from the ranks as an award for ability, as colonial officers usually were.

The colonials did not have the rigid discipline or training of the rank-and-file regulars, but their officers were much more experienced than were the British.

New Jersey. As commander of the five-thousand-strong British army in the colonies, and headquartered in New York before the Revolution, Gage was as American as most colonials. He and Margaret had a large family and were active in the best of colonial society. Gage was well liked and considered honorable and competent as a military commander. If not for the Revolution, America surely would have been a permanent home to General Gage and his descendants.

The "tricorne" hat—one folded into three corners—was old-fashioned by 1775, but Whigs wore it proudly as a party symbol. This tricorne belonged to Connecticut militia colonel Jonathan Pettibone, killed in 1776. It next was worn by his son, Jonathan Pettibone Jr.

Q: Did British commanding general Thomas Gage have any special relationship with America?

A: Gage had a very close and longstanding relationship with America. Not only had he been a skilled commander of a regiment of French and Indian War regulars trained and equipped as wilderness fighters, but he married a colonial woman, Margaret Kemble, of

General Thomas Gage

Q: What were Minutemen?

A: In the early 1770s the Massachusetts militia companies were reorganized, with new officers being elected in order to eliminate Loyalists or Tories from their ranks. Certain of these companies were to be ready to muster immediately, in a minute, when alerted of the need to oppose the movement of British regulars.

General Thomas Gage was a career soldier with more than twenty years' service in America when he found himself at war with the rebels in 1775. While commander in chief of British troops in North America, he was also appointed governor of the defiant colony of Massachusetts in 1774.

"Nothing is heard now in our streets but the trumpet and the drum; and the universal cry is, 'Americans, to arms!'"

—AN ANONYMOUS PHILADELPHIA LADY WRITING TO A BRITISH OFFICER

First Blood is Shed

Q: How well did the occupying British troops and Bostonians know each other before open conflict broke out?

A: Most Bostonians had considered themselves under oppressive rule since 1768, when General Gage ordered the Sixty-fourth and Sixty-fifth regiments of foot into the city as the first contingent of the "Boston Garrison." Resentful of being policed by the military, many Bostonians despised the presence of the soldiers. When soldiers also took part-time work in their off-duty hours, they were further resented by local men who wanted those scarce jobs for themselves.

That there often were brawls between soldiers and civilians should have surprised no one, since many Bostonians were Irish and the soldiers came to the city directly from serving in restive Ireland. In turn, the soldiers despised Boston. From the start, city authorities made life difficult for the troops, refusing them housing and provisions.

Regiments were shifted in and out of Boston, until by 1775 Gage had forty-five hundred troops quartered among a restive population of seventeen thousand.

Q: Did the British expect to meet resistance when they marched out to Lexington and Concord?

A: The secrecy surrounding the April 19 expedition to Concord was intended to prevent the colonial militia from being warned

Paul Revere, an ardent Son of Liberty, engraved this portrayal of the 1768 landing of British troops to occupy Boston as punishment for the city's resisting the rule of Parliament. This military occupation was one of the primary American grievances against Britain.

> **Disperse, ye rebels!**

—*BRITISH MAJOR JOHN PITCAIRN*
shouting at Lexington militia in the path of his soldiers marching to destroy munitions at Concord

and saving their stores—the objective of the operation. In similar previous raids, the soldiers had been trailed by armed militia and jeering crowds, but there had been no shooting. Gage assumed that secrecy and speed would give the British troops the advantage now and that the expedition would be over before the militia could organize. He hoped that capture of militia military stores would prevent any uprising from taking place. Spies in Boston discovered Gage's plan, however, and the alarm went out for the militia to muster.

Q: What is the meaning of "One if by land, two if by sea"?

A: Patriot spies organized by Dr. Joseph Warren reported that hundreds of troops were marching under cover of night from Boston Common, preparing to take boats across to the mainland. Two lanterns were lit in the steeple of Boston's North Church to indicate the troops were coming by water—"One if by land, two if by sea" were the pre-arranged lantern signals. If the troops had marched overland, across Boston Neck, one lantern would have been lit to warn the militia of their route.

Q: Was Paul Revere sent only to warn the militia to muster?

A: Dr. Warren ordered Revere to get to Concord to tell the militia to remove what stores they could save. Revere's other duty was to find Sam Adams and John Hancock, who were at Lexington, about six miles from Concord. Spies had warned that the British intended to arrest these two, and soldier horsemen were already abroad, trying to find them. Other Patriot riders, including William Dawes, were also sounding the alarm that "the regulars were coming." Adams and Hancock escaped the British dragnet, and the militia rose by the thousands to resist the expedition.

The eight hundred British troops, led by Colonel Francis Smith, encountered seventy militiamen under Captain John Parker at Lexington. The outnumbered militia had begun to disperse when a shot rang out. The regulars fired, then charged with the bayonet. Eight militiamen died, and ten were wounded, while only one British soldier was wounded.

Above: "The First Resistance" is the title of this colorful but imaginary early twentieth-century portrayal of Lexington residents confronting British regulars. Unlike these peaceable folk, the militia were actually drawn up in line of battle and carried muskets. Yet the artist has captured the spirit of the moment, as grim soldiers face off with well-dressed, prosperous New Englanders.

Left: "Paul Revere's Ride" to warn of the approaching British expedition has been celebrated ever since in verse, art, and legend. Revere was one of several couriers sent out on the night of April 18, 1775, to call the Patriot militia to arms.

Lexington and Concord

Q: Who fired first at Lexington Green?

A: The question of who fired "the shot heard round the world" on April 19, 1775, and started the war, Britisher or American, was extremely important to the people of the time. At first, each side sought to blame the other for the outbreak of armed conflict. Eventually, Americans vied for the honor of having fired that shot. The village of Concord claimed it had begun the first "forcible resistance," asserting that no one at Lexington had fired at the British. Lexington, in turn, claimed the first shots came from militia on its village green.

The feud between Lexington and Concord lasted a hundred years and was so bitter that the towns refused to participate jointly in the first centennial celebration. Legal depositions containing sworn statements by witnesses at Lexington were taken by the Massachusetts Provincial Congress immediately after the April 19 engagement. Historians have studied the claims and debated this issue for two centuries, but the evidence is inconclusive. Many believe that provocateur Sam Adams, who wanted to see a clash between militia and troops, had encouraged someone at Lexington to fire from cover on the troops confronting the militiamen. Hearing the volleys of soldier muskets from two miles' distance, Adams declared, "What a glorious morning this is! . . . For America!"

Q: How did the British troops respond to the harassment they endured during their retreat from Concord and Lexington?

A: The soldiers were counterattacked at Concord, and they began to withdraw slowly. Resistance grew hourly as

Just after sunrise on April 19, 1775, Captain John Parker and his seventy-seven militiamen faced the British advance guard on Lexington Green. "Don't fire unless fired upon," Parker ordered, but from somewhere shooting began, ending with eight militiamen dead.

hundreds, then thousands of militia arrived to fire at them. Their march became a twenty-mile running battle, and even though hundreds more troops came from Boston to reinforce them, the expedition was in danger of being wiped out.

The soldiers stood and fought from time to time, but they suffered heavy losses from concealed militiamen firing on every side. Some troops took revenge by charging into houses, barns, and inns along the way, attacking whomever they found there, armed or unarmed. Many of the ninety or so colonial casualties were incurred in this way, and many were noncombatants. Almost thirty-five hundred colonials joined in the battle. The eighteen hundred regulars engaged lost approximately two hundred and seventy killed and wounded.

Q: What famous American song became the anthem of liberty after the clashes at Lexington and Concord?

A: "Yankee Doodle." This song had humorous and vulgar verses that made fun of New Englanders—Yankees—and the British soldiers enjoyed singing it to insult and infuriate the people of Boston. "Doodle" means fool.

Yankee Doodle came to town
For to buy a firelock.
We will tar and feather him,
And so we will John Hancock.

As for their king, that John Hancock,
And Adams, if they're taken,
Their heads for signs shall hang
up high.
Upon that hill called Beacon.

—1775 BRITISH SOLDIER VERSES TO "THE YANKEE SONG," WHICH MOCKED NEW ENGLANDERS AND PATRIOT LEADERS

This iron fife from the revolutionary period was unearthed in New Jersey in 1880. Fifes are small flutes with six holes and no keys. Their high pitch made them effective for signaling troops over the din of battle.

Since the French and Indian War, the soldier verses were well known to New Englanders, who despised the song. When the British reinforcements marched out of Boston to support the expedition to Concord that was already under fire, they marched to the music of "The Yankee Song." As the engagement came to a close, with the militia triumphant, American fifes struck up the song to hurl the mockery back in the faces of the regulars.

A British officer later grumbled about "Yankee Doodle" that day, "They made us dance to it." New words were written, and the song became the anthem of the Revolution.

In our rear, they were most numerous and came on pretty close, frequently calling out 'King Hancock forever!'

—LIEUTENANT FREDERICK MACKENZIE OF THE ROYAL WELSH FUSILIERS
a participant in the Concord expedition

A Bloody British Victory

Q: Why did the Battle of Breed's Hill not take place on Bunker Hill, as originally planned by the American leaders?

A: The elderly American general Israel Putnam was a key figure in the deployment of militia forces before the battle commonly known as Bunker Hill. He and other militia leaders in the council of war decided on June 15, 1775, to occupy Bunker Hill, some 110 feet high and overlooking Boston from the Charlestown peninsula.

Bunker Hill was the highest point on the peninsula and would be more defensible than nearby Breed's Hill, which was lower and was vulnerable to British guns in the city. Just before trenches and defensive works were to be dug, Putnam and Massachusetts colonel William Prescott held a two-hour conference to determine the final positions. In the end, the war council's orders were disobeyed, and Breed's Hill, not Bunker, became the main defensive site.

British troops advance toward American positions on Breed's Hill in July 1775. They were driven back twice, then threw off their packs and charged uphill to dislodge the Patriots. With more than 1050 casualties, this was the bloodiest engagement of the war for the king's army.

Putnam, who was highly respected for his military experience and was in nominal command, is said to have called for digging the Breed's Hill earthworks. Since Breed's was closer to Boston and therefore more threatening, General Gage immediately ordered an attack to drive the militia away. The weak Breed's Hill fortification was a mistake, because Bunker Hill could have been made almost impregnable to direct assault.

Q: Was the charge of British troops straight up Breed's Hill and into the point-blank fire of American muskets simply stupidity?

A: Thomas Gage ordered the assault on the dug-in Americans, expecting they would flee at the sight of the well-disciplined scarlet and white ranks with glittering bayonets. Gage was supported by William Howe, one of three other British generals present in the city. Howe proposed a *limited* frontal attack, however, while he led another force to overwhelm and "roll up" the American left flank. The frontal attack was meant only to hold the militia in the earthworks while the more important flanking attack developed. Gage had to move quickly to cross the water from Boston before the tide ebbed. He also wanted to attack before the militia could further strengthen their position and fight off a landing by the soldiers. Despite the terrible British losses in the battle, modern historians agree that Gage's tactics would have worked if only the Americans had not resisted so stoutly—and unexpectedly—at Breed's Hill and other points on the peninsula. Experienced American officers led their men expertly in the battle, forcing the regulars to charge three times up Breed's Hill in a desperate attempt to drive the Patriots off.

Q: Did anyone "win" the Battle of Breed's Hill?

A: The Battle of Breed's or Bunker Hill was the bloodiest single engagement of the entire war. The 3,000 Americans suffered 441 casualties, including 140 killed. The 2,500 British lost more than 1,150, with almost 230 killed. The British routed the militia and captured the hill, but their shocking losses devastated the government, king, and Loyalists. The battle rallied the

rest of the colonies and convinced the Continental Congress, then in session, that only force of arms would decide the issue. Further, first Lexington and Concord, and now Breed's Hill, proved the mighty regulars could be beaten.

A detail from "The Battle of Bunker's Hill," a print after Revolutionary War artist Jonathan Trumbull's "Death of General Warren," depicts the moment when Massachusetts Patriot leader Dr. Joseph Warren was killed by the British.

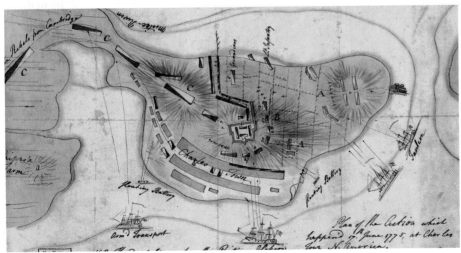

This map was drawn in pen-and-ink and watercolor by a British officer on the scene. The map is inscribed on the back: "Plan of the action, Charles Town, 17th June 1775."

> **[A]s it has been a kind of destiny, that has thrown me upon this service, I shall hope that my undertaking it is designed to answer some good purpose.**
>
> —GEORGE WASHINGTON
>
> *writing to his wife, Martha, about accepting command of the Continental forces*

Boston Under Siege

Q: Who were the three full generals in Boston along with Gage?

A: These three ambitious career officers—major generals William Howe and Henry Clinton and their junior, John Burgoyne—saw the siege of Boston as an opportunity for glory and honors. They arrived on the same vessel in May 1775, eager to attack and defeat the rebellion.

Burgoyne was a thorn in Gage's side, ever writing critical letters that found their way to the highest reaches of government. He was the least qualified of the generals, but his influence caused officials in London to demand that Gage hurry and defeat this "rabble in arms," as Burgoyne termed the militia. Clinton had recently lost his beloved wife and was still gloomy when he decided to change his surroundings and set off on a campaign against the rebels. The son of a colonial governor, he had grown up in New York, becoming commander of a militia regiment before returning to England with his father and taking up a military career. The aggressive Clinton also pushed Gage for action, but his risky plans were not accepted.

General Howe had built a brilliant reputation during the French and Indian War, and he held American colonials

Right: Washington, center, surveys the troops at Boston in July 1775. The Continental Congress adopted the army besieging Boston as the Continental Army when it appointed Washington as "General and Commander in Chief of the Army of the United Colonies," this rank symbolized by the blue sash he wears.

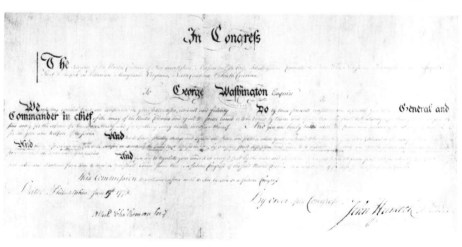

George Washington's commission from the Continental Congress as commander in chief is dated June 19, 1775. Washington formally resigned and returned this commission to Congress in December 1783, after the end of hostilities.

> **[A]t daybreak the next morning we perceived two posts upon the highest hills of Dorchester peninsula, that appeared more like majick than the work of human beings.**
>
> —*BRITISH COLONEL CHARLES STUART*
> *writing about the swift American fortification of Dorchester Heights*

in high esteem. As a Whig member of Parliament, Howe opposed the Tories' colonial policy, yet he considered it his patriotic and solemn duty when ordered to help put down the American rebels. When Gage was recalled after the slaughter at Breed's Hill, Howe became supreme British commander in America.

Q: **How did Washington win the confidence and trust of his army during the siege of Boston?**

A: When he arrived at Cambridge from Philadelphia on June 15, 1775, with Congress's commission as commander in chief, Washington found an undisciplined force of militiamen, rent by dissension and regional mistrust and unwilling to follow any officers but their own. He had to turn this motley assemblage into the Continental Army, but to do so he had to find funds, supplies, draft animals, and munitions, all of which were scarce. He also had to instill discipline, and do it by force as well as compromise.

Although Washington's army had a potential hornets' nest bottled up in Boston, he had to permit large numbers of men to go home on furlough, hoping they would return. Others had to be persuaded or cajoled to reenlist, and many had to be punished for discourtesy to officers or for fighting. At one point, the general himself broke up a brawl, lifting the troublemakers by the scruffs of their necks and shaking them like puppies. Washington's personal example of physical strength, endurance, and dignity was essential to winning the allegiance and trust of the troops. He also chose able staff officers who were highly respected by the men. These young officers included Samuel Webb of Connecticut, Nathanael Greene of Rhode Island, John Sullivan of New Hampshire, and Henry Knox of Massachusetts. These men would be with him throughout the war.

Q: **What was the importance of the Fort Ticonderoga cannon?**

A: In May 1775, forces led by Benedict Arnold of Connecticut and Ethan Allen of the Hampshire Grants surprised and captured the small British garrison at Fort Ticonderoga, on Lake Champlain. That November, the Continental Army's artillery commander, Henry Knox, began to haul sixty of Ticonderoga's cannon to Washington's army besieging Boston, three hundred miles distant. Knox arrived on January 24, 1776, and the Ticonderoga guns were positioned to bombard the city if Howe did not evacuate.

Henry Knox

Center: Self-educated as an artillerist by reading books, Henry Knox became one of Washington's most trusted commanders. Knox eventually succeeded to the rank of commander in chief.

Below: Knox's "Noble Train of Artillery" is history's enduring description of the eighty ox teams and forty-two sleds that hauled captured cannon from Fort Ticonderoga to Boston in the winter of 1775–76. Snow-covered routes and frozen rivers made possible the timely transport of 120,000 pounds of guns and mortars, which ultimately were used to drive the British from Boston.

A Great Victory for Washington

Q: **What was Washington's first great triumph—a siege that ended with almost no bloodshed?**

A: The siege of Boston, which he commanded—after Bunker Hill—from June 1775 until March 1776, must be considered one of Washington's finest victories, achieved almost bloodlessly. Even though the British would have taken the first opportunity to break out if they had detected a weakness, many historians have given Washington little credit for this victory. Perhaps, if the British had been defeated by a massive American assault, the successful siege would have stood higher in America's military annals. If Washington had failed, the Revolutionary War might have ended there. As it was, the siege was a remarkable accomplishment, driving five thousand regulars and their formidable naval forces out of Massachusetts for good.

Washington was closely advised by officers who at times disagreed with his strategy or tactics, and he willingly accepted advice that went against his plans. In February, he proposed that his sixteen thousand troops, supported by the firepower of the cannon brought from Ticonderoga, launch a surprise attack on British positions by crossing over the ice. His officers opposed this plan, and instead agreed to occupy Dorchester Heights and place the guns there, threatening the British defenders in the hope they would depart. The British soon did.

Q: **What was the British plan to break the siege, and why did it fail?**

A: When Howe saw the American guns bristling on Dorchester Heights and threatening his anchored warships, he decided upon a surprise night assault with twenty-two hundred troops crossing over in boats and attacking with the bayonet. The general's plan was called off at the last moment, however, as a fierce rainstorm rolled in.

Howe saw the American positions steadily strengthen, while his own cannon

Officers of the Continental Corps of Artillery organize the shipment of guns from New London, Connecticut, to Washington's new base of operations on Manhattan. The artillery officers are identified by the red facings and yellow buttons of their uniforms.

could not be elevated enough to fire upon them. There was no choice but for his eleven thousand army and navy personnel and a thousand Loyalists to evacuate the city, sailing away under the silent American guns.

Q: **What was Washington's strategy after his triumph at Boston?**

A: The British left Boston and sailed for Nova Scotia, where they reorganized and prepared for the next campaign.

Washington expected their strike to come at New York, the greatest seaport in the colonies and centrally located for an invasion force to move inland as it chose.

While organizing the defenses of New York City, Washington worried about a faltering expedition against Montreal and Quebec. This move was intended to occupy Canadian ports and defend them against any British move up the St. Lawrence. A strong British force in Canada could invade southward along the Lake Champlain–Hudson Valley corridor. Washington could count on more than twenty thousand volunteers in defense of New York, but he had few reinforcements to send on the Canadian campaign. His hope was to defeat Howe's expected attack on New York City, inflicting enough British casualties to force Parliament to think twice about becoming mired in a prolonged war.

If New York fell, then Washington would retreat toward Philadelphia, to defend the revolutionary government there. He had to prolong resistance until King George and Parliament lost their taste for full-scale war in America—an immensely expensive prospect, as the French and Indian War had already proven.

General William Howe, British commander in America, had captured Philadelphia and was at the height of success when this portrait was rendered in 1778.

Left: "Bunkers Hill or America's Head Dress" is the name of this satirical cartoon published in London in April 1776. The exaggerated coiffure supports redoubts, soldiers, artillery, tents, and several ships. Flags flying over the redoubts are decorated with a monkey, women, and a goose.

"Thus was this unhappy distressed town . . . relieved from a set of men whose unparalleled wickedness . . . is inexpressible."

—TIMOTHY NEWELL
Boston selectman and Patriot, on the evacuation of the city

IN CONGRESS, JULY 4, 1776.

e unanimous Declaration of the thirteen united States of America.

THE FIRST STRUGGLES

In the summer of 1775, American troops set off over Lake Champlain to attack Montreal, and soon afterward General Benedict Arnold led a force toward Quebec City. Early successes in this campaign were followed by stalemate, costing the Americans any hope of victory in Canada. Meanwhile, Washington had assembled a large army by mid-1776 to defend New York City. Bloody clashes erupted on the frontiers in this year, and a British naval attack on the southern coast was repulsed. In June, Howe invaded New York with powerful land and sea forces, and as the Declaration of Independence was being signed in Philadelphia, the stage was set for the greatest battle yet seen in North America. The subsequent American defeat in the campaign for New York almost destroyed Washington's army, but its remnants escaped across the Delaware River. Washington struck back, triumphing at Trenton and then at Princeton, giving the Patriot cause a glimmer of hope.

Above: American artillery is loaded by the light of torches into whaleboats for ferrying across New York's East River as dawn breaks, a warning that the British soon will appear.

Left: This 1776 map published in London shows New York, Staten Island, Long Island, and eastern New Jersey, the theater of operations for the New York campaign. The map was accompanied by "a particular description of the engagement on the woody heights of Long Island, between Flatbush and Brooklyn, on the 27th of August 1776."

Attack on Canada

Q: Why did the revolutionaries launch an invasion of Canada?

A: The 1775 expeditions of Benedict Arnold and Ethan Allen loosened the British grip on strategic Lake Champlain. Arnold successfully raided the British fort at St. Johns, Canada, north of the lake, capturing vessels there. The revolutionaries saw an opportunity to invade lightly defended Canada and persuade the eighty thousand French Canadians and few hundred British-born colonists to become the fourteenth colony in rebellion. If Canada remained loyal, however, the British could use Quebec and Montreal as bases for staging an invasion southward, capturing Albany and moving through the Hudson River Valley to New York City. The American offensive against Canada was intended to strike before British reinforcements arrived by sea and made the province impregnable.

Q: What were the Americans' campaign plans, and why did they ultimately fail?

A: General Philip Schuyler of New York organized an invasion force twelve hundred strong and led by General Richard Montgomery. It set off in August 1775 to capture St. Johns and nearby Fort Chambly. The garrisons there held out, however, slowing the invasion and throwing the plan off schedule. Ethan Allen tried to attack Montreal but was captured and sent in chains to England.

Meanwhile, another prong of the invasion, led by Arnold, followed the Kennebec and Chaudière rivers to Quebec City. Arnold began his "March to Quebec" through the Maine wilderness with eleven hundred men, but many turned back as supplies dwindled and cold weather set in. The expedition trekked 350 miles, crossing the St. Lawrence River in November, hoping to surprise Quebec's defenders. Canadian governor Guy Carleton was

While General Richard Montgomery's main army besieged the British at St. Johns, Canada, in September 1775, Vermonter Ethan Allen was sent ahead with a detachment of approximately one hundred men to recruit Canadian volunteers. Allen was soon surrounded and captured by a force under the command of Governor Guy Carleton.

[British control of the Hudson Valley would] stop the Intercourse between the northern and southern Colonies, upon which depends the Safety of America.

—*Washington*

preparing to counter British operations in 1776

ready, however, having gathered twelve hundred men—all volunteers except for about eighty regulars and four hundred sailors and marines. The rest of Carleton's regulars—six hundred of them—had been captured at St. Johns after Montgomery's siege brought them close to starvation.

Montgomery took Montreal without a fight and joined Arnold besieging Quebec. A surprise night assault by the Americans on December 31 cost Montgomery his life, and Arnold was wounded. The campaign was doomed. Hundreds of Americans were falling ill from exposure and smallpox, and many others went home when their enlistments expired, or simply deserted. By early spring, reinforcements increased the American army to seven thousand, but it was too late to take Quebec. The vanguard of the British fleet arrived in May with the first of thirteen thousand regulars, lifting the siege.

As the Americans retreated, many more men fell gravely ill. Of the five thousand casualties left behind in Canada, three thousand were hospital cases, most with smallpox.

Q: Who was the British hero in the defense of Canada?

A: Guy Carleton, governor of Canada since 1766, commanded the defenders. Carleton was a veteran of the French and Indian War and arguably the most qualified officer to lead British and Loyalist forces against the Americans. In June of 1775 Carleton declared martial law in Canada, forestalling any American efforts to rally against him. By making a stand at Quebec City he forced the ill-equipped and poorly supplied Americans to fight a winter campaign they could not win. When British reinforcements arrived in 1776, Carleton organized an invasion force that prepared to advance southward.

French and Indian War veteran Guy Carleton was appointed governor of Canada in 1767. Much respected in the colonies, Carleton skillfully repulsed the American invasion of 1775–76, but his counter-invasion was forced to return as winter set in. The last British commander in chief of the Revolution, Carleton turned over New York City to Washington in November of 1783.

John Trumbull, known as the "Painter of the Revolution," portrayed the January 1, 1776, death of General Richard Montgomery at Quebec. While leading an advance party through a blizzard, Montgomery died in a hail of grapeshot from the point-blank blast of a British cannon. The assault failed, and Quebec held out against the winter-long siege.

War Comes to New York

Right: This engraving of Benedict Arnold is after a portrait by John Trumbull. Arguably the most brilliant Patriot battlefield commander of the war's first years, Arnold bitterly resented being passed over for promotion. He conspired to serve the British in 1779 but was discovered and fled to occupied New York City. In America, Benedict Arnold's name became synonymous with "traitor."

Below: Risen again: The gunboat *Philadelphia*, sunk at the Battle of Valcour Island in October 1776, was brought to the surface more than two centuries later. Termed a "gundalow" (gondola), the *Philadelphia* was one of the smallest vessels in Arnold's Champlain squadron. All but five of the fifteen American vessels were lost, several of them being scuttled to prevent capture.

Q: What characteristics and experience made Benedict Arnold so able as a military leader?

A: This thirty-four-year-old Connecticut native had little formal military training, serving only briefly in the French and Indian War—from which he deserted. A druggist by profession, he became a successful merchant, sailing his own vessels to the West Indies and Canada. The harsh discipline aboard ship taught Arnold leadership. He was athletic and strong, with great stamina. He was also energetic and bold, as well as cunning. Elected captain of a militia company, he joined the 1775 siege of Boston, and Massachusetts made him a colonel. Arnold's early successes on Lake Champlain and his audacious march to Quebec earned him a reputation as one of the Americans' best field commanders.

Benedict Arnold

Q: Why was Arnold's stand at Valcour Island in Lake Champlain so important to the American cause?

A: In mid-1776, Carleton's invasion force from Canada approached Lake Champlain, the great waterway into New York and New England. His first objective was Fort Ticonderoga, at the southern end of Champlain. Hurrying to block Carleton's advance, Arnold organized New England shipwrights to build a fleet with which to oppose the British. Arnold soon had a squadron of nineteen vessels made up of gunboats and a captured sloop and schooners. Learning this, Carleton had to halt his advance in order to construct his own warships. If his troops had attempted to advance only in whaleboats, square-nosed bateaux, and canoes, the American vessels would have inflicted heavy casualties.

With far more resources than Arnold, Carleton built a fleet of much larger and more heavily armed craft and also dragged vessels up the rapids from the St. Lawrence. On October 11, Arnold brought on a battle at Valcour Island, but after a three-day running fight, most of his boats were destroyed. Although the outgunned American fleet was wiped out, Arnold had delayed the British invasion. As Carleton's flotilla reached Ticonderoga, the weather turned sharply colder, with ice appearing on the water. Carleton did not want to campaign in the winter wilderness and so turned back. Ticonderoga was saved. To the south, however, New York City had fallen.

Q: Why did Washington attempt to defend New York in 1776 against so huge an invading army?

A: While Carleton was threatening to break through from Lake Champlain, Washington faced General William Howe's thirty-two thousand troops, who had landed on Staten Island, across the bay from New York City. Howe commanded the largest expeditionary force Britain had ever sent out. In it were thousands of German mercenaries, known as Hessians, because most were from the small state of Hesse-Cassel. The American army was also impressive, numbering twenty-eight thousand, so Washington could not give up the city without a fight, or morale would suffer. Yet he did not have the vessels to counter the British fleet of thirty warships and hundreds of transports, commanded by Admiral Richard Howe, brother of the British commander in chief. The British could move men by water, landing anywhere they chose before the Americans could maneuver to stop them.

One of the best American seaports, New York was ideal as the British base and headquarters—Philadelphia and Congress were just ninety miles away. If Carleton succeeded, and Howe took New York, the two armies would unite. Washington had no choice but to fight for New York and make the British pay dearly if they won.

Albany's Peter Gansevoort wore this regimental uniform coat when he successfully defended Fort Stanwix, in the Mohawk Valley, when besieged by British and Indians in 1777. A top commander in the Albany–Saratoga region, Colonel Gansevoort was the grandfather of author Herman Melville.

" I [saw] something resembling a wood of pine trees trimmed . . . [and] the whole Bay was full of shipping as ever it could be. "

—*A New Yorker looking out his window on the morning of June 29, 1776, seeing Howe's fleet arriving*

Victories Large and Small

Q: What American victory in mid-1776 gave the rebels hope that an attack on New York might be beaten back?

A: The British seaborne expedition to capture Charleston, South Carolina, was defeated largely by well-placed and well-manned artillery on land. The nine-ship

Fort Moultrie, Charleston, is a scene of carnage and death as its defenders exchange cannon fire with the British invasion fleet in mid-1776. The fort's palmetto logs and soft earthworks absorbed the impact of the enemy's projectiles, while the rebel guns delivered a ferocious pounding that drove off the British fleet.

British invasion fleet was devastated, and British commander Henry Clinton was unable to get his twenty-five hundred troops ashore. Giving up, Clinton rejoined Howe's expedition against New York.

Q: Were most New Yorkers enthusiastic about breaking away from Great Britain?

A: No. New York City was one of the most Loyalist communities in the colonies. The city profited from trade and commerce with the empire, and war could only damage the businesses of prosperous merchants and shippers. In northern New York and the Mohawk Valley the settlers were sharply divided in their allegiance. Many former soldiers were farming in that region, and when hostilities began they disagreed with their Patriot neighbors. Most fled with their families to Canada and took up arms against the revolution. Of the fifty thousand Americans who joined the sixty-nine Loyalist regiments or militia companies, twenty-three thousand came from New York, a number estimated to be higher than the number who joined the Patriot forces.

Q: How were Washington's troops on Long Island let down by the errors of a key commander?

A: Once again, as when fortifying Breed's Hill instead of Bunker Hill, General Israel Putnam proved to be responsible for allowing the British a great advantage in the Battle of Long Island.

On August 22, eight thousand men of Washington's main army were positioned on western Long Island, at Bedford,

> [I]t was a fine sight to see with what alacrity they despatched the Rebels with their bayonets after we had surrounded them so that they could not resist.
>
> —A BRITISH OFFICER, DESCRIBING THE SLAUGHTER OF AMERICANS AT THE BATTLE OF LONG ISLAND

Flatbush, and Brooklyn Heights. They faced twenty thousand of Howe's troops, who had just come across from Staten Island. Putnam commanded the eastern wing of the army, astride Jamaica Pass, a strategic route that led to the rear of the American army. Although a brave soldier, Putnam was not up to the task of deploying his men to guard this pass. Howe ordered a night march, sending ten thousand troops through this gap to attack the American forces from the rear.

After losing a thousand men, the Americans retreated to stronger defenses at Brooklyn Heights. William Howe paused to rest his troops, thinking Washington was trapped against the East River, where Richard Howe's warships would appear to cannonade the Americans as soon as the winds were favorable. Instead, Washington organized a withdrawal by night across the river to Manhattan. With muffled oars and maintaining absolute silence, the army was ferried over by expert Massachusetts boatmen from Marblehead and Salem. Boatload after boatload of men, horses, guns, and supplies crossed the river. By morning, Howe found the American positions empty, and his victory was drained of ultimate triumph. The American army was saved to fight another day, and Washington reorganized to meet the British invasion of Manhattan.

Q: Where did the Americans first deliver a blow that proved they could stand up against British troops?

A: At Harlem Heights, in northern Manhattan, on September 16. The day before, Howe landed at Kip's Bay and rapidly advanced to bring on a general engagement. Then crack Scottish troops were ambushed near the old Dutch village of Harlem. This sharp skirmish in a buckwheat field put the few hundred Scots in danger of being surrounded, but German reinforcements arrived to allow them to withdraw. This little triumph not only boosted faltering American spirits, but it made Howe more cautious. He slowed down and built fortifications, allowing Washington another month to reorganize.

The British now occupied Manhattan, but Washington still had an army in the field, with garrisons at Fort Washington at the northern tip of the island and across the Hudson at Fort Lee.

Hard-fighting Maryland and Delaware troops withdraw across Gowanus Creek after standing firmly against the British at the Battle of Long Island in August 1776. Thanks to these regiments, Washington's outnumbered army reached a second line of defense at Brooklyn Heights and later escaped under cover of darkness.

Incendiaries and Disaster

Q: Who ordered the attempt to burn New York after the British forces occupied the city?

A: Historians do not know who ordered New York to be torched, but it could have been George Washington. At least, the general had stated that he wished the deed done, but Congress ordered him not to do it.

Just after midnight on September 21, a wooden house near the Hudson River burst into flame, and the wind pushed the blaze northward, consuming other buildings between Broadway and the river. A number of "incendiaries" were at work that night, and almost five hundred buildings were ultimately destroyed. When soldiers caught a suspected arsonist, they often beat him to death on the spot.

The troops lost many of their intended quarters and would have difficulty finding billets in the city. For Howe, this was a bad beginning to what would be an unhappy seven-year occupation of New York. Hearing about the fire, Washington stated: "Providence, or some good honest fellow, has done more for us than we were disposed to do for ourselves."

Q: What was Nathan Hale's plan, and how did he get caught?

A: This twenty-one-year-old Connecticut schoolteacher and militia captain operated as one of Washington's spies behind Howe's lines. Spying was not only dangerous, it was considered dishonorable, but the noble-minded Hale volunteered because no one else would, and Washington was desperate for intelligence.

Disguised as a Dutch schoolteacher, Hale was recognized by a Tory cousin, who had him arrested. This was the day after the city had almost burned down,

Fire sweeps through New York in September 1776, set by incendiaries determined to prevent Howe's army from being comfortably quartered there. Suspected arsonists are beaten to death by angry soldiers, as residents and their servants hurry to save what they can from the burning houses.

and Hale was accused by Howe of being an arsonist. The furious Howe decided to make an example of Hale and ordered him hanged without trial.

Awaiting execution, Hale wrote to his brother, with the immortal words: "I only regret that I have but one life to lose for my country."

Q: Why was the New York campaign of 1776 one of the greatest disasters for the revolutionaries and Washington?

A: The main revolutionary army was virtually eliminated as a fighting force by several defeats in this campaign.

In mid-October, Howe sent thirteen thousand troops against Washington's lines at White Plains, and on October 28 he skillfully outflanked the Americans. A frontal attack and a charge by dragoons forced Washington from the field. Still, Howe could not wipe the rebels out, inflicting only 150 casualties while suffering more than 300. Washington was proving resilient and tough to bring to ground. Howe next moved against Fort Washington, capturing it in mid-November along with three thousand men and precious munitions. He then attacked Fort Lee, on the New Jersey side of the Hudson, but the garrison escaped.

The New York campaign was over, with Howe taking five thousand prisoners and almost all the rebel munitions and guns. The large American force that had prepared to defend New York was broken, and morale was shattered. Some American regiments, notably the militia, melted away, many deserting, others with their enlistments up. Washington led three thousand troops in full retreat to defend Philadelphia, and Howe ordered out his triumphant regiments in pursuit.

Left: This period German engraving shows the king's troops marching triumphantly through the empty streets of New York City in September 1776. Washington's army would make another brief stand north of the city, but New York remained in British hands for the duration of the war.

The four thousand troops of General Charles Cornwallis's command land on the New Jersey shore in November 1776, preparing to cut off Fort Lee. The fort was immediately evacuated, saving the garrison to rejoin Washington's main force.

"[I]t must give your lordship pain to be sent so far on so hopeless a business."

—*BENJAMIN FRANKLIN*
refusing Howe's offer to negotiate peace during the New York campaign

Cornwallis in Pursuit

Below: These buckskin breeches were worn when the soldier was at work or perhaps on a difficult march. As overalls, they protected the white breeches of the dress uniform, which would be worn on parade or into battle.

Q: How did Washington keep his defeated army together and escape to Pennsylvania?

A: After White Plains and the loss of the two forts on the Hudson, Washington arrayed more than ten thousand troops to defend New England and the mid-Hudson Valley. These included four thousand under General Charles Lee, a former English officer, who was ordered to follow Washington southward by a different route. With three thousand troops, Washington rushed across New Jersey, the British following rapidly.

At one point, the desperate Americans had to destroy their tents and baggage to lighten their load and move faster. Their clothes were in tatters, their shoes worn through, but one day saw them march twenty miles through heavy rain on miserable roads to stay ahead of the enemy. Washington's strength of character and the admiration of his men kept them together throughout that three-week ordeal. Furthermore, with enemy troops on their heels, stragglers or deserters might be captured or killed. If the general himself were taken, he faced execution in London Tower for treason. He wrote to Martha at Mount Vernon, his plantation, that he would continue the fight in the wilderness if need be, and she could join him there.

Right: Cornwallis is pictured after the war in all his lordly splendor as a marquis. One of the best British field commanders of the Revolution, Cornwallis was instrumental in the attack that defeated Washington on Long Island in 1776, but during the New Jersey campaign of the following year he was outmaneuvered by the American commander.

Q: Which important British general led the pursuit of Washington?

A: Lord Charles Cornwallis, one of Howe's best field commanders, nearly caught Washington several times: His men entered Newark just as Washington's were leaving, and Cornwallis's advance troops caught up to the rebel rear guard at New Brunswick and prevented the destruction of a bridge over the Raritan River. Then the cautious Howe ordered Cornwallis to halt, allowing Washington to cross the Delaware unchallenged on December 7. There, the Americans prepared for the next British attack.

Many of the Rebels who were killed . . . were without shoes or Stockings . . . without any shirt or Waistcoat. . . . [T]hey must suffer terribly.

—*A British officer examining casualties from Washington's rear guard at New Brunswick*

Taken by his former subordinate: General Charles Lee is captured in Basking Ridge, New Jersey, by Lieutenant Colonel William Harcourt and troopers of the Sixteenth Light Horse. This was the same unit with which Lee had served in Portugal more than ten years earlier, when Harcourt was his junior.

Q: **Which important American officer was captured by the British during the New Jersey campaign?**

A: General Charles Lee was discovered by dragoons—men from his former regiment—while he slept at a western New Jersey inn. A few months earlier, Lee had won honors for leading troops at the defense of Charleston.

Although Washington had ordered Lee to hurry his troops to reunite their forces, Lee had lingered and delayed, making excuses. It is suspected that he was hoping for Washington to be defeated so he could take overall command of American forces. Lee had written disparagingly to friends about Washington, blaming him for the New York defeats. Some believe the capture of Lee was a blessing in disguise, for he later proved to be a dangerous adversary of Washington's. At the time, however, the loss of the general who was second in command seemed a great blow to the Americans. It was a satisfying triumph for Howe.

As another blessing, Howe now was so confident that he decided to go into winter quarters instead of pressing on across the Delaware and attacking Philadelphia.

Victory or Death

Q: What did the Hessian commander at Trenton say when advised to dig trenches because it was rumored that Washington intended to attack him?

A: "Let them come," Colonel Johann Rall said scornfully. "We want no trenches. We will go at them with the bayonet." Rall and his twelve hundred soldiers enjoyed Christmas Eve and Christmas Day 1776, drinking rum and wine and gambling, sure that the rebels—"country clowns"— would be easily defeated if they dared show themselves.

Q: Why did Washington decide to counterattack at Trenton?

A: Firstly, the cause was desperate for a victory, and he had been receiving reinforcements from his scattered detachments, including Lee's. In late December there were as many as six thousand effectives, but the end of enlistments for a large portion of his force would occur on December 31. He had to go into battle before they departed for home.

Further, Washington saw an opportunity. The overconfident Howe had placed

American infantry advance past Hessian artillerymen and infantry lying in the snow as dawn breaks over Trenton, New Jersey, in 1776. Washington's triumph on this day proved he could continue to resist the king's troops, even though they had driven him from New York and almost destroyed his army.

> **Tell General Sullivan to use the bayonet. I am determined to take Trenton.**
>
> —*Washington*
>
> *as he prepared to attack after being told his army's gunpowder had been soaked by the rains and was useless*

garrisons in several forward positions, including Trenton, that were vulnerable to surprise attack. Also, many people in New Jersey who had previously been Loyalists or neutral were now bitterly hostile to Howe, whose troops had pillaged and robbed during their pursuit of Washington. The Hessians were especially hated for brutality, and even the British camp followers had stolen from the farms and villages they passed through. A victory might inspire New Jersey folk to support the Patriots. As for Cornwallis, he was back in New York, preparing to board ship for England.

Q: How did Washington spend the night before his daring strike against the British at Trenton in 1776?

A: The general was anxious about the riskiness of his plans. He had divided his army in three, with one wing to cross the Delaware and attack the enemy garrison at Bordentown, to keep them from aiding Trenton. Another wing would move to prevent the British escape from Trenton. His main force of twenty-four hundred men had to cross the ice-choked river, with Henry Knox's cannon on board, and do so rapidly to achieve a predawn attack and assure the element of surprise. He had the Massachusetts boatmen once more, and his men were eager to get back into the fight, but Washington knew there could be only one result: "Victory or death," he wrote on a scrap of paper and tucked it away.

Q: Did the attack on the garrison at Trenton go smoothly?

A: From the start there were problems with weather and troop movements. Washington's force was crossing the river by two o'clock on the morning of December 26, but the wind picked up, bringing rain and stinging hail. The current was swift, and chunks of ice threatened to swamp the boats. Many men still lacked clothes, some with hardly anything on their feet. The crossing was painfully slow, and Washington found himself four hours behind schedule, unable to attack before dawn. More distressing was news that one detachment was unable to cross the river, and the other could not get to Trenton on time to join in the assault.

Then Washington's scouts ran into an enemy patrol and exchanged fire. He had to press on faster. At eight o'clock a Hessian outpost was surprised and driven back, and the attack began. The Trenton garrison was completely surprised, and as the men rushed into the streets, they were cut down by American cannon fire. Hessian guns were captured by a bayonet charge, and after less than two hours the mortally wounded Rall surrendered.

Hessian mercenaries surrender to General Washington after the Battle of Trenton in this German engraving from the period. Hessian commander Rall, though dying, chivalrously insisted he be brought to Washington to hand over his sword in person.

Foiling the Pride of Kings

Q: Why, after Trenton, did Washington immediately engage the British at Princeton, and what was his main goal?

A: Cornwallis canceled his trip to England and swiftly returned to New Jersey to bring Washington to battle. On January 2, 1777, the outnumbered Americans were encamped across a creek from Cornwallis's army, which apparently had them trapped. Cornwallis boasted he would "bag the fox" and was so confident that he spurned advice to attack immediately.

Having to save his army, Washington silently slipped away under darkness, leaving fires burning and a few hundred men in camp. The Americans moved in silence, their cart wheels muffled with rags so they would not rumble or squeak. Washington moved around Cornwallis's camp without being detected and aimed for hill country, where his army could spend the winter.

The general knew there was a British supply depot—and a paymaster's chest full of silver—at New Brunswick, and he hoped to make a dash for it before Cornwallis could catch up with him.

At Princeton, Washington's five thousand troops collided with the rear of Cornwallis's army, about twelve hundred men. The surprised British attempted bayonet attacks, but the Americans counterattacked and raked them with cannon fire. Defeated, the regulars fled headlong toward Trenton. By now, Washington's army was too exhausted to try for New Brunswick, but the sharp victory at Princeton added to American morale. The army hurried to Morristown and winter quarters.

Cornwallis was furious and embarrassed by Washington's escape. He would long for revenge, but would not meet Washington again until Yorktown in 1781.

The loss of General Hugh Mercer at Princeton, as seen in this Jonathan Trumbull painting, was a profound blow to his good friend General Washington. The victory was overshadowed by the death of Mercer, a Scottish-born Virginia physician and war veteran who was a leading member of Washington's officer corps.

> **We moved slow, on account of the artillery, frequently coming to a halt . . . [and] when ordered forward again, one, two or three men in each platoon would stand, with their arms supported, fast asleep. . . .**
>
> —*An American soldier, describing the nighttime escape of Washington's army from Cornwallis*

Q: **What secret was guarded by the American army wintering at Morristown?**

A: That there was almost no army left. Washington had to keep spies from slipping in to find that thousands of men had gone home now that their enlistments were up. They had returned to support their families in distant New England, New York, and in the South. A trickle of other men arrived that winter, but if Howe had known how weak Washington was, the British surely would have mounted a campaign to finish him off.

Q: **What famous writer was in Washington's army in 1776?**

A: English-born Thomas Paine had enlisted with Washington as a headquarters aide during the flight through New Jersey. A friend of Franklin's, Paine had written the anonymous forty-seven-page pamphlet *Common Sense,* published in January. Paine put into words what was on so many Patriots' minds: "In the early

ages of the world . . . there were no kings; the consequence of which, there were no wars; it is the pride of kings that throws mankind into confusion."

Paine's pamphlet was a sensation throughout the colonies and was reproduced in the hundreds of thousands. He called for American independence, saying: "'Tis time to part."

During the winter of 1776–77, Paine would write *The Crisis,* published in a series of articles in a Pennsylvania newspaper. He made little financially from the sale of these works, but Paine is remembered for several famous and inspiring passages, such as this from *The Crisis*: "These are the times that try men's souls. The summer soldier and the sunshine patriot will, in this crisis, shrink from the service of their country; but he that stands it now, deserves the thanks of man and woman. Tyranny, like hell, is not easily conquered; yet we have the consolation with us, that the harder the conflict, the more glorious the triumph."

Thomas Paine

Left: Born a Quaker in England in 1737, Thomas Paine had few successes until he came to America in 1774 on the advice of his friend Benjamin Franklin, who gave him letters of introduction in Philadelphia. A freelance journalist, Paine wrote the inflammatory pamphlet *Common Sense,* published in January 1776, calling for American independence.

the alarm was spread
That rebels risen from the dead
Were marching into town.
Some scampered here, some scampered there,
And some for action did prepare,
But soon their arms laid down.

—FROM THE PATRIOT SONG
"BATTLE OF TRENTON"

Ice creepers tied in front of the heels of shoes made it possible to walk over frozen snow and icy ground when the Revolutionary troops encamped through the hard winters of Morristown, New Jersey.

A Bleeding Frontier

Right: One of the most horrific frontier massacres of the Revolution was the 1778 raid on New York's Cherry Valley by Loyalists and Indians under the command of Walter Butler and Joseph Brant. More than thirty noncombatants, including babies, were murdered before the garrison of the nearby fort counterattacked to save many other settlers.

Q: Did all the frontier communities join the revolutionary forces?

A: No, many fought on the side of the Loyalists. The side a community chose had more to do with local alliances and enmities than with relations between colony and king. For example, Scottish settlers in the Carolinas remained fiercely loyal even though the oldest among them had been shipped to America as prisoners after a failed rebellion. They were loyal largely because neighbors they despised were Patriots and had tried forcibly to make them join the cause.

In New York's Mohawk Valley, communities were divided, this time with English and Scottish colonists remaining loyal while German and Dutch settlers were Patriots. Long-standing local conflicts and hostilities played out during the Revolution, which was America's first civil war.

The Patriots were so weak at first that few native peoples wanted to risk allying themselves with the losing side once again. As it turned out, they did just that, and their lands would be vulnerable to settlement after the war.

Loyalist Mohawk war chief Joseph Brant, or Thayendanegea, was painted from life in 1797, wearing full regalia, by Charles Willson Peale. A brilliant leader in frontier fighting, Brant after the war resettled his people in Ontario, where the Canadian city of Brantford was named for him.

Q: Why did the powerful Cherokee, Shawnee, most of the Iroquois, and other frontier nations fight against the revolutionaries?

A: After their defeat in the French and Indian War, then the failure of Pontiac's Rebellion in 1763, many nations still resented the British colonies and feared they intended to expand into Indian lands. The British government's Proclamation of 1763 and the Quebec Act of 1774 officially prohibited uncontrolled expansion into "Indian Country," placing the nations squarely on the side of the government and the Loyalists.

Q: Why was the conflict between white Loyalists and Patriots living on the frontier so bloody and bitter?

A: As matters quickened in the buildup to the war, every community, even families, had to take sides. The resulting brawls, arrests, imprisonment, whippings, and tar-and-featherings of opponents caused deep anger and hatred. There were executions also, and families and businesses were burned out or driven away once the war began. On the frontier, the British enlisted Indian allies and often used ruthless tactics to destroy Patriot settlements and farms. Patriots, in turn, could be as ruthless, driving Indian families away, torching their communities, and cutting

British opposition to the Revolutionary War's frontier bloodshed is seen in this 1780 etching that shows George III sharing a human bone with a native as others drink blood and trade for weapons.

down their orchards. While few uniformed troops operated on the frontier from New York to Georgia, there were many war parties and scouts from both sides who struck without warning and without mercy.

Q: How did Daniel Boone become a key frontiersman in the Kentucky country?

A: A native Pennsylvanian raised in frontier North Carolina, Boone had seen action as a wagoneer during the French and Indian War. He barely

Daniel Boone

escaped with his life from the doomed 1755 Braddock campaign against Fort Duquesne. After the war, Boone hunted the Kentucky country, fighting Indians and surveying land he intended to claim one day. Defying the Proclamation of 1763, he led pioneers into Kentucky country along the Wilderness Road, which he had helped trace. In 1775, he and several others established Boonesboro, a palisaded settlement that became the goal and base for waves of migration. Early in the Revolutionary War, Boone became a Patriot militia captain battling Indian and Loyalist raids and supporting Virginia's claim to the region.

Legendary frontier leader Daniel Boone is pictured in old age, after a storied career fighting Indians and Loyalists on the Virginia and Kentucky frontiers. A teamster who survived the 1755 Braddock massacre, Boone was captured by Shawnees in 1778, later escaping to warn Boonesborough of imminent attack.

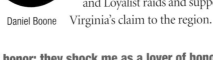

" [T]hey shock every sentiment of honor; they shock me as a lover of honorable war, and a detester of murderous barbarity. "

—*WILLIAM PITT (THE ELDER)*
in 1777, protesting in the House of Lords
against plans to unleash Indian raiding parties against Patriot farms and settlements

A Declaration by the Representatives of the UNITED STATES
OF AMERICA, in General Congress assembled.

When in the course of human events it becomes necessary for one people
dissolve the political bands which have connected them with another, and to
~~assume among the~~ ~~that~~ ~~equal~~ ~~station~~
~~sume~~ among the powers of the earth the separate and equal station to
which the laws of nature & of nature's god entitle them, a decent respect
to the opinions of mankind requires that they should declare the causes
which impel them to ~~the~~ ~~the~~ separation.

We hold these truths to be self-evident; ~~sacred & undeniable~~, that all men ~~are~~
created equal ~~& independent~~, that ~~from~~ ~~that equal creation they derive~~
they are endowed by their creator with
~~rights~~ ~~inherent~~ & inalienable, rights; that among ~~which~~ these are ~~the~~
life, & liberty, & the pursuit of happiness; that to secure these rights, go-
-vernments are instituted among men, deriving their just powers from
the consent of the governed; that whenever any form of government
~~shall~~ becomes destructive of these ends, it is the right of the people to al-
or to abolish it, & to institute new government, laying it's foundation on
such principles & organising it's powers in such form, as to them sh-
-seem most likely to effect their safety & happiness. prudence indeed
will dictate that governments long established should not be ch~~anged~~ for
light & transient causes: and accordingly all experience hath shewn tha-
mankind are more disposed to suffer while evils are sufferable, than to
right themselves by abolishing the forms to which they are accustomed. bu-
when a long train of abuses & usurpations [begun at a distinguished period
&] pursuing invariably the same object, evinces a design to ~~subject~~ reduce
them + under absolute Despotism, it is their right, it is their duty, to throw off such
+ & to provide new guards for their future security. such has
been the patient sufferance of these colonies; & such is now the necessity
which constrains them to expunge their former systems of government.
the history of ~~his~~ the present King of Great Britain is a history of [unremitting] injuries and

CHAPTER 5

DECLARING INDEPENDENCE

Throughout that sultry June of 1776, the Second Continental Congress in Philadelphia debated the volatile issue of independence from Great Britain, but many Americans were already prepared for this dramatic step. A few months previous, Thomas Paine's pamphlet, *Common Sense*, had inspired hundreds of thousands of colonials to believe in independence. The halls and inns of Philadelphia crackled with exchanges of political and social philosophy and with arguments over the economic impact of leaving the empire. The consequences of failure haunted the delegates, their proceedings overshadowed by the "ministerial army" then landing in New York. In early July, high-minded ideals and down-to-earth legal doctrine were finally joined in an empire-shaking document written by Thomas Jefferson with the advice of a drafting committee led by Benjamin Franklin and John Adams. That summer the Declaration of Independence was read aloud in hundreds of American towns, but on the battlefield the forces of Congress were reeling in defeat.

Above: The Assembly Room in Philadelphia's Independence Hall looks much as it did during the meetings of the Second Continental Congress in 1776.

Left: Thomas Jefferson's original rough draft of the Declaration of Independence shows comments by fellow drafting committee members John Adams and Benjamin Franklin. Written in June 1776, the final text was adopted by Congress on July 4, 1776.

Cutting Away the Bridge

Q: How did Congress arrive at declaring independence?

A: In July 1775, a Continental Congress committee headed by Franklin and Jefferson drew up the "Declaration of the Causes and Necessities of Taking Up Arms," which was to be read by General Washington to the troops besieging Boston. This declaration, mainly written by Pennsylvania's John Dickinson, laid the groundwork for the following year's Declaration of Independence, stating: "Our cause is just. Our union is perfect. Our internal resources are great, and, if necessary, foreign assistance is available." It also stated the delegates were "with one mind resolved to die freemen rather than to live slaves."

Such a revolutionary declaration was as close as the Americans could come to actually declaring independence. One difference between the 1775 and 1776 documents is that the "Taking Up Arms" declaration asserted that the Patriots were defending themselves against tyrannical government ministers, meaning Parliament, while that of 1776 accuses King George himself of "repeated injuries and usurpations." Further, there had been a "Declaration of Rights and Grievances" by the Stamp Act Congress of 1765, which asserted that Parliament had no right to tax the colonies. The Declaration of Independence had a direct line to these earlier declarations.

Officially, the Continental Congress declared in 1775: "We have not raised armies with the ambitious design of separating from Great Britain and establishing independent states." A year later, however, with blood spilled and the British driven from Boston and defeated at Charleston, delegates to Congress from North Carolina and Virginia were proposing that "these United Colonies are, and of right ought to be, free and independent States."

The very maturity and economic strength of the colonies made independence a logical next step after asserting the right to take up arms against the British government.

Q: Who was the most outspoken Continental Congress delegate who opposed independence?

A: The eloquent John Dickinson conceded that he would be condemned if he spoke out against independence, but he did anyway. An attorney, Dickinson was famous for his 1768 articles, *Letters from a Farmer in Pennsylvania*, which had challenged British authority to tax the colonies. He was taken seriously in 1776 when he warned Congress that independence would bring terror to the Indian frontiers and the destruction or capture of the American merchant fleet. He agreed with taking up arms in

Right: This black and white portrait of Pennsylvania delegate John Dickinson was rendered by fellow Maryland native Charles Willson Peale in 1770, when Dickinson was a radical opponent of British colonial policy. By 1775, Dickinson was against the colonies' declaring independence, and he called for a peaceful settlement of the crisis.

John Dickinson

defense, but he was against outright independence. It was too soon, he said, "like destroying our house in winter" before another had been built.

Seeing how his objections isolated him, the high-minded Dickinson enlisted as a private in the Continental Army, saying he would support "the defense and happiness of those unkind Countrymen whom I . . . esteem as fellow Citizens amidst their Fury against me." Yet he remained a delegate to Congress and eventually served in the Constitutional Convention of 1787, which created the Constitution of the United States.

There were a number of serious rifts in the thirteen congressional delegations, with some members in favor of independence and others opposed. Some colonies, like New Jersey, removed their opposition delegates and sent new ones who would back independence.

John Adams

tion of Thirteen States, independent of Parliament, Minister, and of King!" He spoke for a great many Americans, expressing "the felt necessities of the time."

"Every post and every day rolls in upon us Independence like a torrent," he wrote to a friend in Boston. To another in Baltimore, he said, "Freedom is a counterbalance for poverty, discord and war and more."

After Congress adopted the Declaration on July 4, he wrote, "The river is passed, the bridge cut away."

Left: Massachusetts delegate John Adams lobbied for an immediate declaration of independence and stood up to argue against Dickinson's formidable oration for remaining in the empire.

Below: The Second Continental Congress convened in Philadelphia at the Pennsylvania State House, which was renamed Independence Hall after the Declaration of Independence was adopted there on July 4, 1776.

Q: **Who was the most eloquent proponent of independence?**

A: John Adams was chosen to answer John Dickinson's powerful speech against independence. He electrified the delegates, according to Jefferson, with his insistence on "A Union and a confedera-

> **[The Revolution] was in the minds of the people, and in the union of the colonies, both of which were accomplished before hostilities commenced.**
>
> —*John Adams*
> *writing many years after the Revolution*

The Natural Rights of Mankind

Q: What were the main issues for and against independence?

A: In the spring of 1776, delegates to the Second Continental Congress in Philadelphia were vigorously debating independence and the formation of a confederation of states. Debate was heated, but the issue was less whether to declare independence and more about when. It was apparent the mother country would never accept American demands, and one favorable development was the apparent willingness of France to ally with America.

That May, Virginia's legislature voted for independence. In Philadelphia, Virginia radicals such as Richard Henry Lee and Thomas Jefferson allied with Sam and John Adams of Massachusetts to urge declaring independence in order to unite against British military moves. Moderates such as Pennsylvania's John Dickinson and New York's John Jay, Robert R. Livingston, and James Duane worried that it was too soon. They believed in reestablishing amicable relations with king and Parliament to avoid all-out war. South Carolina's John Rutledge wept when his own colony also passed a resolution for independence.

Parliament was the enemy, not the king, said the conservatives, who termed the regulars the "ministerial army," not the "king's troops." The new states would be weak, they argued, and some could fall victim to powerful empires such as France or Spain. John Adams objected, saying that "discipline in the army" and "a confederation of the whole" was all that could save the Americans from future British oppression. General Howe had already landed on New York's doorstep, and Governor Carleton's forces were moving down from the north. There was no choice now but independence, and there was no time to lose.

Q: Why was Jefferson chosen to write the final draft of the Declaration of Independence?

A: The delegates voted to appoint the drafting committee, and Jefferson received the most votes, one more than John Adams, who later said: "[Jefferson] brought with him a reputation for literature, science, and a happy talent of composition. Writings of his were handed about, remarkable for the peculiar felicity of expression."

This first known portrait of Thomas Jefferson was painted during his 1786 visit to London. Jefferson, in his mid-forties, was portrayed by Mather Brown, one of several young American artists then living in London.

Right: Jefferson wrote the Declaration of Independence on this portable lap desk of his own design. It has a hinged writing board, a locking drawer for papers and pens, and an inkwell.

I had rather forfeit popularity forever, than vote away the blood and happiness of my countrymen!

—*Pennsylvania delegate John Dickinson*
speaking out against independence

When Jefferson proposed that Adams write the draft, Adams declined, saying, "You are a Virginian, and a Virginian ought to appear at the head of this thing." Furthermore, Adams said, "You can write ten times better than I can."

Q: How did Jefferson work on the Declaration of Independence?

A: As a member of Congress in 1775, Jefferson had drafted several policy papers that were rejected as too anti-British, so he knew he must be more deliberate in what he wrote this time—the most important document of all. He depended on consultation with fellow committee members: Franklin, Adams, Livingston, and Connecticut's Roger Sherman. These men represented the spectrum of opinion in Congress and would weigh in on Jefferson's writing before it was presented to the entire body. Jefferson was thirty-three years of age, while Franklin was seventy, Sherman fifty-four, and Adams forty-one; Livingston, the youngest, was thirty.

For weeks, Jefferson spent much time alone, writing at his quarters or strolling in thought alongside the waterfront. He consulted no legal tracts or pamphlets. Instead, he went to the heart of the issue, pointedly and decisively, basing the justification for American independence on widely accepted modern wisdom.

Open-minded British intellectuals accepted seventeenth-century philosopher John Locke's concept of divinely ordained natural law. Locke said it was a self-evident truth that mankind possessed God-given rights to life, liberty, and property. Any government that violates those natural rights forfeits the mandate to govern. This premise would be the starting point for declaring American statehood.

Thomas Jefferson, standing, meets at his Philadelphia lodgings with Benjamin Franklin, left, and John Adams to review a draft of the Declaration of Independence. The other members of the drafting committee were Roger Sherman and Robert Livingston.

> **[John Adams] came out with a power of thought and expression that moved us from our seats.**
>
> —*JEFFERSON*
> *describing the debate over independence*

Consent of the Governed

Q: Was July 4, 1776, the day Congress voted for independence or the day it signed the Declaration of Independence?

A: Neither. Congress voted for independence on July 2. On July 4 Congress debated the drafting committee's document. Arguments were fierce, tempers as hot as the Philadelphia summer, but by the end of this day Congress amended, then adopted, the final version of the Declaration of Independence.

Official fair copies had to be made on parchment, an official American seal devised and fabricated, and the Declaration had to be printed and sent throughout the land for public readings. On July 8, the Declaration was read on the green in front of the State House before a small audience. The essence of the document was already widely known.

It was not until August 2, 1776, that delegates from the thirteen former colonies officially signed the Declaration of Independence. Six signers, not present then, later added their names.

This silver inkstand was used by members of the Second Continental Congress to sign the Declaration of Independence. Approximately seven and a half inches tall and more than ten inches long, it was made in 1752 by Philadelphia silversmith Philip Syng. The same inkstand was also used in 1787 to sign the United States Constitution.

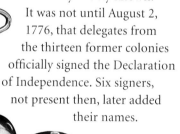

Q: What are the Declaration's salient points?

A: Fundamentally, that governments derive their powers from the "Consent of the Governed" in order to protect "certain inalienable Rights, that among these are Life, Liberty, and the Pursuit of Happiness." Thus, "whenever any Form of Government becomes destructive of these Ends, it is the Right of the People to alter or abolish it, and to institute new Government."

King George was particularly singled out for committing "a long train of Abuses and Usurpations" leading to despotism and causing the colonies to break with the mother country to "throw off such Government." The Declaration presents a litany of assertions to "a candid World" regarding the king's abuses of power, among them: He refused to approve laws passed by colonial legislatures, forbade governors to act on important matters without his direct approval, dissolved colonial legislatures repeatedly, blocked migration to the colonies, interfered with judiciaries, sent "Swarms of Officers to harass our People," made the military superior to civil powers, kept standing armies in the colonies without consent, denied trials by jury, cut off American trade with the rest of the world, abolished English law in Canada, waged war against Americans, "plundered our

With a firm reliance on the protection of divine Providence, we mutually pledge to each other our Lives, our Fortunes, and our Sacred Honour.

—CLOSING STATEMENT OF THE DECLARATION OF INDEPENDENCE

Seas, ravaged our Coasts, burnt our Towns [and transported] foreign Mercenaries to compleat the Works of Death, Desolation, and Tyranny."

Such a prince, stated the Declaration, is "unfit to be the Ruler of a free People." All appeals for redress of colonial grievances having failed, "We, Therefore, the Representatives of the UNITED STATES OF AMERICA, in GENERAL CONGRESS, Assembled, . . . solemnly Publish and Declare, That these United Colonies are, and of Right ought to be, FREE AND INDEPENDENT STATES."

All "political connection" with the "State of Great Britain" was thereby "totally dissolved."

Q: Did the Declaration address the slavery of Africans?

A: Not the final version. Although Jefferson himself owned more than eighty slaves at his plantation, Monticello, his draft to Congress contained a harsh denunciation of slavery, "this assemblage of horrors; this market where men are bought and sold!" He also accused King George of likewise enslaving all American colonists. Many delegates objected to bringing the issue of slavery into the Declaration, and it was struck out. Inalienable rights did not, according to some delegates, belong to black slaves.

The controversial issue of African slavery was unresolved by Congress in 1776, but it would flame up over the next eight decades. There would be another rebellion, this time by the southern slaveholding states, bringing on the Civil War.

This lithograph is entitled "The Tocsin of Liberty." "Tocsin" refers to an alarm signal that is rung out by a bell—in this case by the Pennsylvania State House bell, announcing the Declaration of Independence on July 4, 1776.

Below: Captain John Nixon, commander of the Philadelphia city guard, reads the Declaration of Independence from the steps of Independence Hall on July 8, 1776.

"We must hang together, gentlemen, or most assuredly we will hang separately."

—*Benjamin Franklin*
July 1776

A Desperate Conspiracy

Q: If the Revolution were defeated, what could have been the punishment for members of the Continental Congress?

A: Imprisonment for many years at least, and loss of all they possessed, as well as branding as traitors to their country. Worse, leaders such as Washington, the Adamses, and Jefferson might be deported to England and executed as examples to all who dared oppose Parliament and the king. In July of 1776 there was some chance for reconciliation, as General Howe proposed to negotiate peace terms with Congress. The Declaration of Independence, however, tore the British Empire asunder and authorized America to align with foreign allies. Now the revolutionary leaders had to prepare for a fight that might well end with defeat and death.

Frederick Lord North

Right: This portrait of British prime minister Frederick Lord North was published in England in 1780, at the height of the American Revolution, which was brought on in part by North's unswerving enforcement of oppressive colonial policies. North was considered a willing "instrument" of King George, who stubbornly tried to use force to subdue America.

mercenaries, establish a permanent standing army in America, and continue the already oppressive colonial measures that had brought on rebellion.

The agent of British oppression would be Lord George Germain, newly appointed secretary of state for the American colonies. A haughty and arrogant aristocrat, Germain was also commissioner of trade and plantations, with great power and influence. He believed that military force was needed to subdue America. At the same time, he had bad personal relations with two of the best British commanders in America, Carleton and Howe. In the coming years, Germain's interference would diminish their ability to achieve as much as they otherwise might have done.

Another key player was Frederick North,

Q: Who were the leading British statesmen whose actions served to bring on the Revolution?

A: The Tory party controlling Parliament followed the lead of King George III, who in October 1775 issued a declaration stating he intended to destroy the "desperate conspiracy" in America that sought to establish an "independent Empire." He would increase the size of the army and navy, hire thousands of

Bottom right: At six o'clock in the evening, on July 9, 1776, Washington's regiments in New York assembled to hear a reading of the newly written Declaration of Independence.

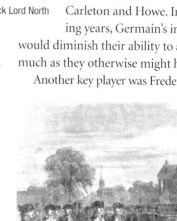

since 1770 the British prime minister. Lord North's previous government positions had involved him in the taxation policies that had inflamed America. King George saw North as the perfect ally, an instrument for the subjugation of the colonies. North supported the punishment of Boston, but as hostilities approached he at first counseled making peace. North's loyalty ultimately compelled him to support his sovereign in making the war, which he soon came to realize was a mistake. Until the bitter end he did not attempt to defuse the king's stubborn determination to defeat the American Revolution by force of arms.

Q: **How did Washington's army at New York City formally hear about the Declaration of Independence?**

A: By July 9, 1776, the Declaration was being read to regiments drawn up on parade before their various barracks and defensive works. That evening, as the British fleet filled the bay, and the lights of thousands of enemy campfires lined Staten Island's shores, Washington announced: "The General hopes this important Event will serve as a fresh incentive to every officer and soldier." He said each man must know that "the peace and safety of his Country depends (under God) solely on the success of our arms."

Q: **What did King George do on the day the Declaration of Independence was adopted by Congress?**

A: Because news was brought by ship across the ocean, King George and London would not hear about the Declaration until two months later. On July 4, 1776, the king wrote in his diary, "Nothing important happened today."

After the Declaration was read in New York City, a crowd went to the Bowling Green and tore down the equestrian statue of King George III. Made of glided lead, the statue was chopped up for molding into bullets, but the head went missing, reputedly stolen by Loyalists who smuggled it to England.

" I am well aware of the toil and blood and treasure it will cost us to maintain this declaration and support and defend these states. Yet through the gloom I can see the rays of ravishing light and glory. "

—*John Adams*
July 4, 1776

CHAPTER 6

THE FORCES OF KING AND CONGRESS

Citizen soldiers were crucial to the Patriot cause in the early campaigns of the Revolution. Although at first there were no American troops to compare with the professional British regiments, volunteer militia led by French and Indian War veterans slaughtered the king's troops in Massachusetts and stood up to them in New York and New Jersey. When armed rebellion developed into full-scale war, however, it was the trained Continental soldier who bore the brunt of the fighting. Short-term militia volunteers could briefly swell Washington's forces, but it was the long-term Continental "regular" who served to the end of the war. Thousands of colonials joined the king's forces as well, enlisting as regulars as well as in Loyalist regiments, and both sides depended on African Americans, whether as soldiers, as auxiliaries building defenses, or as officers' body servants. On the frontiers Native American fighters gave the British the advantage until Patriot forces marched against them and against the British outposts supplying the nations with firearms.

Left: General William Maxwell leads American soldiers at Brandywine, Pennsylvania, in September 1777, carrying the first national flag of the stars and stripes design. Maxwell's light infantry corps collected stragglers and wounded and withdrew in good order during the army's retreat. Although a defeat, Brandywine was noteworthy for the discipline shown by Washington's forces in conducting a fighting retreat. This painting, *The Nation Makers*, was painted by Howard Pyle in 1903, and is in the collection of the Brandywine River Museum.

Militia and Continentals

Q: How important were militia volunteers to the Patriot cause?

A: Ever since the British first settled North America in the seventeenth century, the militia system had been the main organization for defense. Once or twice a year militiamen attended "training days,"

Americans storm German guns at the Battle of Bennington in mid-August 1777, one of the most outstanding performances by militiamen during the war. Loyalists and Indians were in the "Bennington Raid," as this doomed British expedition by mainly Braunschweig, Germany, regulars was termed. During the battle there were many instances of neighbor killing neighbor.

which were social gatherings as much as military musters. In the colonial wars with France, militia were support troops for the British regulars, often garrisoning forts, running supply trains, and holding defensive positions when the regulars attacked.

Unlike regulars, who were issued firearms, equipment, and uniforms by the government, militiamen provided their own needs and weaponry and wore civilian clothes. The militiaman served only for the duration of a campaign, since he was needed back on the farm at harvest time. At the beginning of the Revolutionary War the army of Congress

was all militia, with some companies trained and equipped better than others. For the most part the militia were unreliable in battle and difficult to control. Washington started with eight thousand militia at the Battle of Long Island, but they were easily driven off, and only two thousand remained with him after the battle. This unreliability was in part because militia elected their officers, often politically popular commanders rather than qualified men who would exact strict discipline.

Yet the Patriot cause needed the thousands of militia who could, by law, be called up by their states. At times, such as in the victory at Bennington in 1777, militia were a powerful force. One British historian remarked that the American militia could not always be counted on by its friends, but neither could it be ignored by its enemies.

Approximately one hundred and forty-five thousand militia served in the Patriot cause, many of them later enlisting in Continental regiments.

Q: What was a Continental soldier?

A: The heart and soul of the American army was the Continental, a regular "line soldier," who trained hard and was expected to stand toe to toe with the British regular. The main battles of the Revolutionary War were fought between troops in conventional massed formations—lines—using similar tactics that required disciplined maneuver, the ability to give and take musket volleys, and the courage to fight with the bayonet. The battles were seldom fought by rebels concealed behind trees firing at British regulars who marched in parade in the open. Just as Americans learned to form up in ranks, to march, and fight in the open field, so did British regulars train to fight in woods and campaign in wilderness—as they had done so well during previous colonial wars.

Indeed, it was in pitched battle that the Revolution was decided. As the war progressed, Continental soldiers rapidly improved in professionalism and discipline, until the best were organized into elite units that won the respect of even the British regular. When France contributed thousands of line troops to the side of Congress, the British found themselves vastly outnumbered.

In 1775 Congress authorized the raising of more than twenty-seven thousand Continentals, organized in regiments numbering between five and eight hundred men, usually from the same state. The First Continental Infantry Regiment was from Pennsylvania. Each state was obliged to provide, in proportion to its population, a certain number of regiments to serve

Left: These Continental soldiers wear government-issue blue coats, white shirts, and buff waistcoats and breeches. The coat is folded back to show white facings, but many Continental regiments had red facings. White belts crossing over the chest carry the soldier's cartridge box and pouch.

for the duration of the war. As times of military activity alternated with times of inactivity, the number of Continentals in service varied. By the last years of the war, 1781–83, fewer than half the thirty-three thousand Continentals authorized by Congress were actually enlisted.

It is estimated that almost two hundred and thirty-eight thousand Continental soldiers served during the war, with Massachusetts providing the most: sixty-eight thousand.

Below: The spontoon was the official sidearm of junior officers in Continental regiments. This spear, or "half pike," gave the officer some protection while allowing him to keep his attention on his men. Loading and firing a musket or pistol could distract the officer from his duties in action.

> **To curry favor with the men (by whom they were chosen, and on whose smiles possibly they may think they may again rely) seems to be one of the principal objects of their attention. . . .**
>
> —*WASHINGTON*
> *complaining about New England militia,*
> *from the encampment at Cambridge, Massachusetts, 1775*

Lobsterbacks and Hessians

Q: **How were the British regiments raised and organized?**

A: In 1775 the British soldier's reputation was a proud one. The defeat of France in the Seven Years' War (1756–63) had brought the British Empire to its zenith and earned the regulars fame for their devastating bayonet charges. A regular regiment was made up of ten companies of between fifty and eighty men each. Eight "line companies" composed the core fighting formation—solidly massed ranks. One company, termed "light," was used for scouting, and another was an elite company of "grenadiers." Grenadiers were trained to hurl grenades—bombs fitted with a fuse that was lit before throwing. Grenadier companies were often detached from the regiment and operated with other grenadiers. Usually taller and stronger than average, they wore distinctive, high hats sometimes made of bearskin.

A typical regiment was founded and raised by a gentleman who helped finance it by selling officers' commissions to other gentlemen. These officers, often quite youthful, exercised authority whether or not they had military training. The regiment's founder held the rank of colonel, but it was the lieutenant colonel who led the men in battle. Officers could buy and sell their commissions, and even the colonel could sell his own commission, if he so wished.

American regiments were organized much the same way, except their commanders and leaders in battle were colonels, and officers' commissions were given by the states or Congress, not bought and sold.

Q: **Why were the British regulars called "lobsterbacks"?**

A: Their scarlet coats could well have earned them the derogatory nickname "lobsterback," but this term derived from the especially degrading, even savage, discipline the soldier endured. Specifically, the lash was used freely on soldiers' backs as punishment for major or minor infringements of regulations, drunkenness, or indiscipline. Virtually every regular had the lash's mottled scars, or stripes, on his back (perhaps shown off proudly by the longtime hardened veteran). These red

General John Burgoyne

Above: This British grenadier's bearskin cap, more than thirteen inches tall, made elite soldiers appear even more impressive and stand out on the battlefield. The bearskin is hung with a white cord tassel, and the front plate is stamped with the royal lion and "GR," meaning *Georgeus Rex*—King George.

Right: General John Burgoyne wrote a forward-thinking treatise on the duties of the officer, asserting that soldiers should be treated as human beings and not suffer degrading corporal punishment.

Though it was once the fashion of this army to treat them in the most contemptible light, they are now become a formidable enemy.

—A BRITISH LIEUTENANT COMMENTING ON AMERICAN FORCES, MARCH 1777

welts earned regulars the name "lobster-backs," which was interchangeable with the more gruesome "bloodybacks."

American regulars, too, were harshly disciplined and lashed as punishment, but never as unmercifully as the British. Independent-minded Americans did not readily bow to unfair orders or arbitrary discipline, and their defiant tempers warned off the officer who dared have them whipped without great cause. The average British regular, however, was usually a hard case who answered better to threats and curses—or so most of their commanders presumed. General John Burgoyne, on the other hand, treated his men with respect, and for that they nicknamed him fondly "Gentleman Johnny." The term "redcoats" was not commonly used for regulars until the nineteenth century.

Q: Who were the German mercenaries on the British side termed "Hessians"?

A: The immense debts from waging the Seven Years' War had persuaded the British government to keep its standing army small. In 1775 there were only forty-five thousand troops in the vast empire's "peacetime establishment." As hostilities with America developed, few British were willing to enlist to fight Americans, who were also considered to be British, so King George hired mercenaries from various German states. Generally known as "Hessians" because most came from Hesse-Cassel—perhaps also because three German commanders in chief were from there—they totaled almost thirty thousand in the course of the war. In many cases, these men had been conscripted into military service of seven or eight years and then sent to fight in America.

Britain paid almost 4.6 million pounds sterling for German mercenaries, who fought in virtually every major campaign and won a reputation as dependable troops. More than seventy-seven hundred Germans died in America, and it is estimated that as many as five thousand deserted to become Americans themselves.

Left: This nineteenth-century engraving, entitled "Conscription of German soldiers for service in America," shows German troops invading a home and arresting a young father to force him into the military. The pleas of the man's wife and children are to no avail, and he ultimately will be shipped off to fight against American revolutionaries.

Below: The Hessian lion is stamped on the brass plate of this "miter cap," worn by a soldier of the Knyphausen regiment, defeated at Trenton in 1776. The miter style, also worn by some British troops, is so named for its resemblance to a peaked headdress worn by bishops and abbots.

"These states will receive all such foreigners who shall leave the armies of his Britannic majesty in America and . . . Congress shall provide . . . 50 acres of unappropriated lands. . . ."

—*CONGRESS AUTHORIZES LAND BOUNTIES FOR HESSIAN DESERTERS, 1776*

The King's American Commanders

No Revolutionary War commander other than Washington held so important a rank for as long as did Henry Clinton. Second to Howe from 1775 to 1778, Clinton took command soon after France entered the war, which placed the British on the defensive.

Right: As militiamen from New York's Mohawk Valley marched to relieve the siege of Fort Stanwix in August 1777, they were ambushed and defeated at Oriskany by Indians and Loyalists. This six-hour hand-to-hand struggle cost the militia one hundred and sixty killed and fifty wounded out of six hundred engaged. The crown's forces suffered fewer than one hundred casualties.

Q: Who were the top British colonial military leaders?

A: A number of high-ranking British commanders in the "American establishment," as the colonial military organization was termed, had lived in America since the French and Indian War. The most prominent were overall commander Thomas Gage, Canada's governor Guy Carleton, and Swiss-born General Frederick Haldimand—second in command to Gage—all of whom by 1775 were as American as most colonists. Returning to serve against the rebellion were Henry Clinton and William Howe, both with strong ties to America. Clinton was raised as the governor's son in New York and had distinguished himself in Europe during the Seven Years' War. Howe won a stellar reputation in America's French and Indian War—in which his much-admired eldest brother, George, died serving with Rogers' Rangers at Ticonderoga in 1758. General Simon Fraser and Lieutenant Colonel Barry St. Leger, both of whom had served in America during the French

and Indian War, also returned at the start of the Revolution.

One of the most significant British colonial officers was John Montresor, who came to America in 1754 and rose to become the army's chief engineer in the colonies. Montresor returned to England in 1778, but his memoirs are important to the history of the Revolution.

Q: Who were the top Loyalist battlefield leaders?

A: Some of the most successful Loyalist commanders operated along the frontiers and were involved in the no-quarter brutality of wilderness combat. The likes of New York's John and Walter Butler and Guy Johnson shed civilian blood and destabilized the settlements of western

> **The most shocking cruelty was exercised a few nights ago, upon an old man . . . [who] was stript stark naked . . . his body covered all over with tar, then with feathers.**
>
> —*ANN HULTON OF BOSTON*
> *describing the beating of a man who defied the Sons of Liberty, 1774*

New York—the "Niagara frontier"—but their greatest successes were considered massacres rather than military victories. Britisher Banastre Tarleton, just in his mid-twenties, was an effective commander of Loyalist dragoons in the South until he was outmaneuvered and outfought at Cowpens, South Carolina, in January 1781.

Another Loyalist defeat in South Carolina, at King's Mountain, in October 1780, cost the lives of several highly regarded Loyalist commanders who might have gone on to fame and honor. They were summarily hanged after the battle. One of the most effective Loyalist ranger leaders was Connecticut native John Peters, who raised the highly regarded Peters's Corps for Burgoyne's 1777 campaign. This unit was almost wiped out by the defeat at Bennington a few weeks before Saratoga, but Peters rejoined Burgoyne, serving through the campaign and escaping just before the surrender.

Canada was largely held against the Patriots by Loyalist volunteers, particularly by the newly raised Eighty-fourth Regiment of Foot. Known as the "Royal Highland Emigrants" and composed mainly of Scottish-born colonists and their descendants, it was raised and led by Colonel Allan MacLean.

Oliver De Lancey and Henry H. Cruger, two of the most important Loyalist field commanders, were from powerful New York families. De Lancey raised a mounted legion that fought throughout the war, notably securing Jamaica Pass for Howe, which led to the victory at Long Island. A career British dragoon officer, De Lancey rose to adjutant general of the British army in America and managed the secret service. Cruger, a former New York City mayor and son of a mayor, commanded De Lancey's legion, serving with distinction in the South. Cruger won fame by successfully resisting the monthlong Patriot siege of Ninety-six, a fortified Loyalist town in South Carolina. He went on to command both British and Loyalist troops in the defense of Charleston near the end of the war, an indication of how highly he was regarded by Commander in Chief Clinton.

The most famous American ranger of all was Robert Rogers, hero of the French and Indian War. The aging Rogers was quickly arrested by Washington as a suspected Loyalist spy, but he escaped and raised the Queen's Rangers. His days as a fighter were over, however, and he played a part in few actions before dropping out of sight in 1776.

The brilliant American victory at the Battle of Cowpens, South Carolina, in January 1781 was completed by Colonel William Washington's dragoons routing the Loyalist dragoons of Banastre Tarleton. As Loyalist horsemen were chased from the field, Tarleton and Washington fought a brief duel that ended as the British officer missed with a pistol shot, then galloped away.

Can we subsist—did any State ever subsist, without exterminating traitors?

—JOSEPH HAWLEY OF MASSACHUSETTS
calling for the execution of Loyalists, 1776

Americans on Both Sides

Q: How important were Loyalist troops to the British military?

A: Many American Loyalists were able soldiers, but the British did not use them to best effect, and none became generals except for Benedict Arnold, who still was not trusted by other British officers. Arnold raised Loyalist troops and led raids in Virginia in 1781, but Loyalist line regiments were often left in garrisons and their officers were not allowed to take initiative in the war. Too late in the war, British commanders came to realize the value of Americans as fighters. They generally learned this the hard way, at the hands of Patriot forces, and the thousands of Loyalists the British might have used to good effect were in large part wasted.

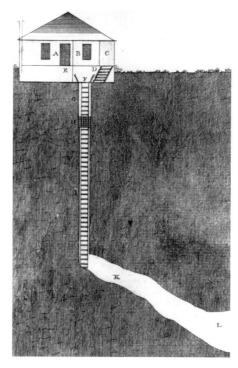

Both sides in the Revolution were guilty of cruel imprisonment of enemy captives. Loyalists prisoners were kept in Connecticut's dank, chill Simsbury mines, an underground death trap termed "Hell." This 1781 view of the guardhouse, published in London, shows a diagram of the mine shaft leading down to "Hell."

Q: How common was it for troops to change sides?

A: Prisoners were often given the opportunity to change their allegiance and fight for the side that had captured them. In many cases, those who turned their coats originally had been pressured to join up and were not enthusiastic supporters of the cause they first had been serving.

In other cases, such as in the Loyalist forces that garrisoned besieged New York, former Patriot soldiers were glad enough to do soldiers' duties for the king in return for food, wages, and decent shelter. Meanwhile, Patriot prisoners were languishing on British prison ships, dying by the hundreds of disease and starvation. Being holed up in New York's garrison was also a way to keep out of any future battles. Up to one-third of Americans wanted no part of the Revolution, nor did they want to fight on the Loyalist side.

The Patriots received recruits from the German mercenaries captured with the 1777 "Convention Army," as Burgoyne's defeated force was termed. Burgoyne did not just surrender, but he accepted terms of a "convention," which helped him save some face. This agreement required that the prisoners no longer take up arms against Congress, and they were supposed to be shipped out of America. Instead, Congress broke the agreement because it wanted to avoid having the men being deployed elsewhere to free up British troops for American service. The unfortunate prisoners were held for years under harsh conditions. As they were being marched through Pennsylvania to Virginia, most of the two thousand Germans slipped away and joined the large German community there. This was the way the Congress wanted it, since these men would not have to be fed and housed in captivity. Some even enlisted with the Patriot forces.

Q: Which Loyalist units were most famous during the war?

A: The best-known British regiment in America in 1775 was the Sixtieth Foot, formed during the French and Indian War and named the Royal Americans. Originally organized with Swiss and German officers and colonial soldiers, the regiment fought well enough against the French to win the honorific "Royal." When the Revolution broke out, the government suspected these troops would not fight other Americans, so the regiment was stationed in Florida and the West Indies to keep it out of action.

One of the most-feared Loyalist units was the British Legion, a force of American dragoons commanded by British officer Banastre Tarleton. Reputedly the best mounted troops in the British army in America, the legion fought mainly in the South as scouts and raiders, but they were routed by rebel cavalry at Cowpens, which shattered their reputation. Tarleton's dragoons were accused of

Left: An American Loyalist dragoon from Tarleton's Legion, also known as the "British Legion," prepares his mount for action. Tarleton's hard-riding dragoons were routed by William Washington's Patriot cavalry at Cowpens, South Carolina, in January 1781.

Below: The flamboyant Banastre Tarleton is pictured in England in 1782, after Cornwallis's southern campaign, which ended with surrender and capture at Yorktown. As commander of "Tarleton's Legion" of Loyalist dragoons, he was a dashing horseman but was despised by Patriots, who considered him the cold-blooded and ruthless "Bloody Tarleton."

killing prisoners, a controversial accusation still debated more than two centuries later. Other Loyalist units, such as the Royal Greens and Butler's Rangers, earned fearsome reputations as ruthless frontier fighters who unquestionably took part with Indians in horrific civilian massacres.

There were as many as sixty-nine Loyalist regiments on the British side. Some of them, such as the Royal Highland Emigrants, defenders of Quebec in 1775–76, won reputations as heroes in a lost cause.

> **Great revolutions of empire are seldom achieved without much human calamity.**
> —*New York Patriot statesman Gouverneur Morris,*
> *writing to his mother,*
> *a Loyalist, in 1776; his half-brother, Staats L. Morris,*
> *was a general in the British army, a career officer who did not serve in America*

Patriot Battlefield Leaders

Q: Who were the top American battlefield commanders?

A: Even the most senior generals could be found in the heat of a battle, but it was the junior field commanders—usually lieutenant colonels or colonels—who ultimately led the troops to victory or defeat.

Artilleryman Henry Knox of Massachusetts was instrumental in battle after battle, especially at Monmouth, where even the British praised his handling of the guns. Massachusetts militia commander William Prescott was the hero of Breed's (Bunker) Hill, although it was his only battle of distinction before retiring in 1777. Among the most successful commanders was Benedict Arnold, who helped capture Ticonderoga in 1775 and delayed Carleton's invasion in 1776. In the 1777 Saratoga campaign, Arnold turned back the British-Indian invasion of the Mohawk Valley and led decisive attacks against Burgoyne to win the final battles. New Hampshire's John Stark won at Bennington in 1777 and led the force that cut off Burgoyne's retreat from Saratoga.

Virginia frontiersman Daniel Morgan proved a forceful leader in Arnold's 1775 march to Quebec, and he later raised a body of sharpshooters who distinguished themselves against Burgoyne and in General Nathanael Greene's southern campaigns. Morgan won an important battle at Cowpens, South Carolina, in 1781, and with him was Virginia dragoon commander William Washington, who served throughout the war, honored for exploits in the South.

South Carolina's Francis Marion was a mounted raider so elusive that he earned the name "Swamp Fox," and William Moultrie was instrumental in the successful defense of Charleston in 1776. Pennsylvanian "Mad" Anthony Wayne earned his nickname by leading fierce bayonet attacks, while Maryland's William Smallwood won fame when his regiment held its ground at Long Island while the army crumbled around it. Generals Philip van Cortlandt and Richard Montgomery of New York, and New Hampshire's John Sullivan were excellent battlefield commanders, as was Virginia's George Rogers Clark, who led an expedition to capture forts in the Old Northwest, breaking British power on the frontier.

Q: Who were the most famous European officers who joined the American cause?

A: A number of Europeans were in Congress's service, most notably Friedrich von Steuben of Prussia, who trained Washington's infantry and led them in battle. Poland's Thaddeus Kosciuszko won accolades as a cavalry leader, as did

Right: This portrait of frontier leader Daniel Morgan was probably painted in 1794 by Charles Willson Peale in Philadelphia. Injuries had forced Morgan to retire to his Virginia home after the 1781 victory at Cowpens. He returned to active military service in 1794, leading Virginia militia to put down the Whiskey Rebellion—a short-lived uprising against the federal tax on liquor.

Daniel Morgan

his countryman, Casimir Pulaski, killed at Savannah in 1779. Bavarian Johann Kalb, an experienced soldier, came to America to be hired as a general; he died at Camden in 1780. Delaware's Irish-born Colonel John Haslet distinguished himself in the 1776 New York campaign but was killed at Princeton. Scottish-born John Paul Jones triumphed on the high seas, and another Scot, French and Indian War veteran Arthur St. Clair, skillfully withdrew from doomed Fort Ticonderoga in 1777, saving the army from Burgoyne to fight again.

The most famous foreigner was France's Marquis de Lafayette, who began as an aide to Washington. Later taking a command in the South, Lafayette harried Cornwallis's army all the way to Yorktown in 1781.

Q: Which battle is said to have given birth to the "regular" American army?

A: The Battle of Monmouth, New Jersey, in 1778. By now the disciplined training of Baron von Steuben and experience in battle had produced elite units of American infantry. More than once at Monmouth they charged the British with only the bayonet and came out on top. Wayne's Light Infantry, a twelve-hundred-man force, stood up to a dragoon charge and shattered it, then joined an artillery battery to stop an infantry assault, and later repulsed a desperate attack by British grenadiers, elite shock troops. This battle was considered a draw, but it is said that the regular American army was born on this day because of the high performance of the troops. A few weeks later, Wayne's men captured the fort at Stony Point, New York, with a daring night assault, using the bayonet.

Above: Washington commissioned Charles Willson Peale to paint this portrait of the Marquis de Lafayette in 1779; before sending the finished three-quarter-length painting to Washington, Peale painted this bust-length replica for his own collection.

Left: After intensive training in winter quarters at Valley Forge, the American army was eager to go into action that spring, when Washington attacked Clinton's army at Monmouth, New Jersey. General Charles Lee, recently released from British captivity, lacked confidence, however, and retreated until stopped by Washington himself.

" The boy cannot escape me! "

—*CORNWALLIS*

boasting in 1781 that he soon would defeat and capture twenty-four-year-old General Lafayette, which he failed to do before withdrawing to Yorktown

The Revolution Divides All Peoples

Right: Black troops served in several eighteenth-century European armies, as seen in this depiction of Spanish forces assaulting British Fort George at Pensacola, Florida, which fell in May 1780. Among the attackers, in red coat and leather cap, is a soldier from the Company of Free Blacks of Havana.

Q: How important were black troops to the Patriot side?

A: From the start of hostilities black colonists volunteered for the revolutionary ranks, and many a gentleman, from North and South, had a black body servant who joined him on campaigns. Well-dressed and educated, these servants were known for acts of heroism and personal devotion to their masters.

Thousands of blacks served in the ranks, and others were in the American navy or aboard privateers. After the 1777 battle of Hubbardton, Vermont, the British were surprised by how many blacks and Indians were in the New England forces. American blacks also fought with the Loyalists, served British officers, and were employed in construction and road building.

Washington's forces had an average of fifty blacks in every battalion of five hundred men. Rhode Island raised a mostly

black regiment, officered by whites, that distinguished itself at Newport in 1778, and other black units were raised in New England. The majority in Congress wanted to enlist thousands of black soldiers, but southerners were generally opposed, fearing the consequences of weapons in the hands of freedmen or slaves. By 1781, however, Maryland had enlisted 750 blacks to serve in her regiments.

Southern resistance to black soldiers was steadily being eroded, and had hostilities continued, the institution of slavery would have been compromised by the need for black manpower. Virginia freed all her slaves who had fought for the Patriot cause.

The British promised liberty to former slaves who served as Loyalists, and in this way won recruits. Actual British practice was starkly different, however, as slaves became booty of war. Slaves were rounded up by the thousands and sold in the West Indies, making a fortune for British

This French engraving portrays Lafayette after Yorktown in 1781. With him is James Armistead, honored for having served as a spy against Cornwallis. Armistead, who even deceived turncoat Benedict Arnold, then fighting for the British in Virginia, was later emancipated in gratitude for his service, and took Lafayette as his surname.

commanders. When the British evacuated Charleston at the close of the Revolution, they took with them five thousand slaves as the spoils of war.

Q: What part did the Indian nations have in the fighting?

A: French traders had traditionally traded native peoples firearms and ammunition for furs, so during the colonial wars, most Indians fought on the French side. The Iroquois, for the most part, kept out of these struggles, and their homeland on the New York frontier was a buffer between the hostile nations and British communities. When the British took over the French forts and trading posts in 1763, they continued trading much-needed firearms for furs.

When the Revolution began, most Indian nations decided the sensible alliance was with the government against the rebels. The Iroquois were led by Thayendanegea, the mission-school educated Mohawk whose sister became the mistress of Sir William Johnson, colonial Indian affairs administrator. Known to whites as Joseph Brant, Thayendanegea allied with Loyalist raiders who set the New York frontier ablaze. The leading Northwest nations were the Chippewa, Miami, and Shawnee; in the South they were the Cherokee, Creek, and Seminole; and on the Niagara frontier were

the Six Nations, or Iroquois. One of the six, the Oneida, allied with the rebels.

Congress tried to persuade the Indians to stay out of this "family quarrel between us and Old England," but the native peoples knew the Americans would threaten them if the British were defeated. Before the war ended, the Iroquois were driven from their homeland, withdrawing to Canada, and the Creek and Cherokee also were badly defeated by expeditions sent against them. The next phase of the struggle for Indian territory was set by the Revolution.

Virginia's George Rogers Clark confers with Indian leaders during his 1778 expedition against British posts in the Northwest. Clark offers a choice: the white wampum belt of peace with his expedition, or the red belt of war. The Indians chose white, neutrality, and Clark went on to defeat and capture the region's British commander.

" I am just returned from a most fatiguing pursuit of the enemy, and . . . any of them that [escaped] will have tales only of horror to relate. "
—*NEW YORK COLONEL MARINUS WILLETT*
reporting on a decisive defeat of Loyalists and Indians in 1781

Leaders

T hroughout this volume, portraits of most of the important military and political leaders are seen in relation to events that directly involved them. Here are portraits of other, often equally important, individuals who were prominent during the war.

Victory has many fathers, and America was indebted to hundreds of military commanders and political figures who risked everything to give birth to a new nation out of the Revolution's turmoil. Some leaders, such as Montgomery and Warren, gave their lives. Others, such as Livingston and Madison, helped establish the foundations of American liberty.

Few British, Loyalist, or German leaders won lasting fame as a result of the war. Some, such as Admiral Howe and Lord Percy, earned American respect by refusing to continue serving against Americans. German generals von Riedesel and Knyphausen were soon forgotten, but they were effective commanders whose troops almost turned the tide against the revolutionaries. Johnson spread terror with his frontier raids and was hated by Patriot settlers, but he was a hero to his own kind, fighting for survival.

In the tumultuous and uncertain years of the American War of Independence, these opposing leaders fought for the causes they believed in. This struggle bound their destinies together in a crucible of revolution and war that produced a new republic and a new world order.

ETHAN ALLEN

Patriots

ETHAN ALLEN
Leader of frontier militia in the Green Mountains of future Vermont. With Benedict Arnold, he and his "Green Mountain Boys" took Ticonderoga in 1775. Captured before Montreal, imprisoned a year, and later paroled.

United States flags (left to right): "Colonial Red Ensign," "Betsy Ross" flag, "Grand Union" flag

British & Loyalists

Royal Coat of Arms of King George III

PATRICK FERGUSON
Scottish officer, served as ranger commander and sharpshooter. Declined to shoot an officer, who was almost certainly Washington, from behind at Brandywine, where Ferguson was later wounded. Died leading loyalists at King's Mountain in 1780.

ROBERT R. LIVINGSTON
Member of Congress from New York and the most prominent member of a distinguished family. Relatively conservative, he helped draft the Declaration of Independence but wished to postpone its issue, hoping for reconciliation.

JAMES MADISON
Member of Congress from Virginia, influential in guaranteeing freedom of religion, establishing trade policy, and framing the Bill of Rights. Fourth president of the United States, 1809–17.

RICHARD MONTGOMERY
Irish-born general and a professional soldier, he served in the French and Indian War. He settled in the Hudson Valley, marrying the daughter of Robert Livingston. Killed leading the 1775 invasion of Canada.

RICHARD HOWE
British admiral, brother of General William Howe, supreme commander in America, and of George Howe, killed during the French and Indian War. The admiral favored peace and resigned in 1778 rather than fight against Americans.

SIMON FRASER
Scottish general killed by a sharpshooter at Saratoga. He had served in the French and Indian War and later in Europe. Returned to America with Burgoyne in 1776 and commanded the advance corps in the Saratoga campaign.

Patriots

J. PETER MUHLENBERG
Continental general and Lutheran clergyman raised in Pennsylvania, sent to Germany for education; absconded to join Royal Americans, settled in Virginia. Served in the field from Brandywine to Yorktown and through the last years of the war.

JAMES OTIS
Massachusetts politician, attorney, and militia commander. His orations against British colonial policy inspired revolutionaries such as John Adams, who quoted him as saying, "Taxation without representation is tyranny."

> **There is a time for all things—a time to preach and a time to pray; but there is also a time to fight, and that time has now come.**
> —J. PETER MUHLENBERG
> *tossing aside minister's robes, revealing his uniform, and calling on the congregation to enlist*

British & Loyalists

WILLIAM PITT
The Earl of Chatham, British statesman and leader of the Whig opposition. A fierce opponent of the Tory government's American policies and the war, he died in the House of Lords in 1778 while protesting that policy.

JOHN JOHNSON
New York Loyalist leader, knighted in 1765 after fighting in frontier wars. The son of Sir William Johnson, Indian commissioner in the Mohawk Valley, he led raids that ravaged the valley; settled in Canada.

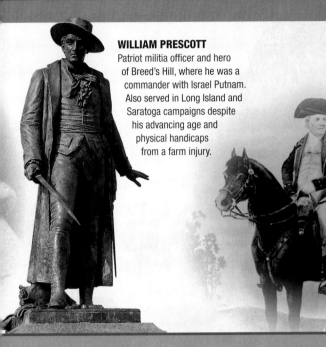

WILLIAM PRESCOTT

Patriot militia officer and hero of Breed's Hill, where he was a commander with Israel Putnam. Also served in Long Island and Saratoga campaigns despite his advancing age and physical handicaps from a farm injury.

ISRAEL PUTNAM

Aging hero of the French and Indian War, during which he served with Rogers' Rangers. Commanding general at Breed's Hill and the siege of Boston; defeated on Long Island in 1776. Retired after a stroke in 1779.

PAUL REVERE

Patriot leader and militia officer from Boston, he rode out to alert the militia before Lexington and Concord. A silversmith and engraver by trade, Revere was contracted to be the first printer of Continental money.

ROBERT ROGERS

Legendary leader of rangers in the French and Indian War, raised in New Hampshire. Founded Loyalist regiment the Queen's Rangers, but the British deprived him of command. He dropped out of sight until fleeing to England in 1780.

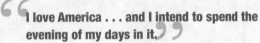

"I love America . . . and I intend to spend the evening of my days in it."

—ROBERT ROGERS TO WASHINGTON
before the general arrested him as a spy in 1776

JOHN SIMCOE

British commander of Loyalist regiment the Queen's Rangers. He came to America in 1771 with the Thirty-fifth Foot. Served in New York, New Jersey, and in the South, where he was captured at Yorktown. Later served as first lieutenant-governor of Upper Canada.

Patriots

WILLIAM SMALLWOOD
Continental general from Maryland; served as a soldier in the French and Indian War. Raised a regiment for the Revolutionary War that distinguished itself for courage and discipline. Served until the end of the war.

JOHN SULLIVAN
Continental general from New Hampshire; commanded troops from 1775 in Canada to Newport in 1778, with mixed success. Led the 1779 expedition to drive the Iroquois from New York, devastating their villages and farms.

ARTEMAS WARD
A French and Indian War veteran, he was named second in command to Washington in 1775. Kept besieging army together until Washington arrived at Boston. Constantly at odds with the commander in chief, Ward had no further important service.

British & Loyalists

BARON WILHELM VON KNYPHAUSEN
Prussian general who commanded German mercenaries; his own black-uniformed "Regiment Knyphausen" was captured at Trenton—he was not present. He became commander in chief of German forces in 1778 until illness forced retirement in 1782.

British Royal Seal

BARRY ST. LEGER
Cambridge-educated British colonel skilled in frontier warfare; led a failed expedition from Canada intended to join Burgoyne in 1777. Afterward commanded rangers and met with disgruntled Vermonters considering reconciliation with the British.

JOSEPH WARREN

Physician and Patriot leader active in anti-British movement in Boston before the war. Sent Paul Revere out from Boston to warn militia before Lexington and Concord. Killed as a volunteer fighting at Breed's Hill.

WILLIAM WASHINGTON

Continental dragoon officer from Virginia, a distant relative of George Washington; served in the North through the Philadelphia campaign. A key commander in the South from 1780 until wounded and captured at Eutaw Springs in 1781.

> **Lieut. Col. Washington, having been informed that Tarleton was cutting down our riflemen on the left, pushed forward and charged them with such firmness that [they] broke and fled.**
>
> —*Daniel Morgan*
> *describing William Washington's decisive assault at Cowpens, South Carolina, in 1781.*

> **Not a stone wall from whence the rebels did not fire at us!**
> —*Percy describes the British retreat at Lexington and Concord*

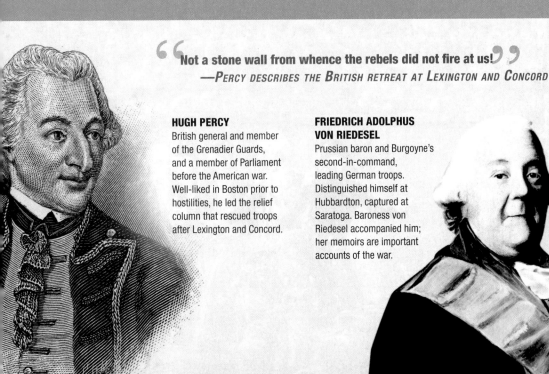

HUGH PERCY

British general and member of the Grenadier Guards, and a member of Parliament before the American war. Well-liked in Boston prior to hostilities, he led the relief column that rescued troops after Lexington and Concord.

FRIEDRICH ADOLPHUS VON RIEDESEL

Prussian baron and Burgoyne's second-in-command, leading German troops. Distinguished himself at Hubbardton, captured at Saratoga. Baroness von Riedesel accompanied him; her memoirs are important accounts of the war.

Major Campaigns

After their defeat in the April 1775 Battles of Lexington and Concord, the king's troops under Gage were besieged in Boston by a Patriot army led by Washington. Meanwhile, British posts in the Hudson River–Lake Champlain corridor were captured by revolutionaries who next invaded Canada, took Montreal, and laid siege to Quebec.

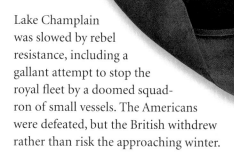

Tricorne hat

NORTHERN CAMPAIGNS

The British were forced to evacuate Boston in early 1776, withdrawing by sea to Nova Scotia. The American campaign in Canada, however, turned into defeat when thousands of British troops arrived by sea. Washington occupied New York to defend it against another large British force, under Howe, which landed on Staten Island in July. By August Howe had beaten Washington in the Battle of Long Island, soon forcing him to abandon New York. In this same time, a British invasion down Lake Champlain was slowed by rebel resistance, including a gallant attempt to stop the royal fleet by a doomed squadron of small vessels. The Americans were defeated, but the British withdrew rather than risk the approaching winter.

CROSSING THE DELAWARE

By now, Washington was retreating across New Jersey, with the king's troops close behind. Against the odds, he counterattacked on Christmas Day and captured the Hessian garrison at Trenton. Then his little army fought its way into the hills and winter quarters at Morristown.

Benedict Arnold leads Patriot forces at Saratoga

VICTORY AT SARATOGA

In 1777, a powerful army led by Burgoyne invaded over Lake Champlain toward Albany. Howe then moved by sea against Philadelphia—although Burgoyne had expected him instead to advance northward to Albany, in coordination with his own invasion. That fall Washington was defeated by Howe at Brandywine, and Philadelphia fell. Washington's counterattack at Germantown also failed. The outnumbered Burgoyne, however, was surrounded and captured at Saratoga in October. Washington wintered in hunger-plagued Valley Forge.

FIGHT TO A DRAW

In 1778 France entered the war on the American side. Howe was replaced by Clinton, who was ordered to evacuate Philadelphia. In June, as Clinton's army marched overland toward New York, it was attacked by Washington at Monmouth, New Jersey. The battle was indecisive but proved the Continental Army was rapidly improving. The British now turned their efforts to the South, capturing Savannah in December.

Siege of Charleston

WAR IN THE SOUTH

The year 1779 saw action on the western frontier and a few minor engagements in the East. By December a botched Franco-American attack on Savannah resulted in a major British victory.

In April 1780 the British captured Charleston and attempted to win control of the South. Loyalist and Patriot frontiersmen fought at the Battle of King's Mountain, South

Combination knife and fork used by Hessian soldiers

Carolina, in October, resulting in a Patriot victory that shattered British plans to dominate the southern frontier country.

THE FINAL CAMPAIGN

The next year, 1781, saw a series of clashes in the South while the main British army was besieged in New York. Cornwallis led the royal troops to battlefield successes, but as the summer drew to a close he was in dire need of supplies and reinforcements. Moving to Yorktown, on the Virginia coast, he expected support from the Royal Navy. Instead, Washington's army and French forces under Rochambeau laid siege to Yorktown, while the French navy fought off the British fleet in the Chesapeake Bay.

Cornwallis surrendered on October 19, 1781, closing the last campaign of the War of American Independence.

Battle of the Virginia Capes, off Yorktown

Weaponry

Firearms and artillery were not greatly improved from the French and Indian War, and battle-field tactics were similar: firing lines, massed ranks, bayonet attacks, and maneuvers in line and column. America's forests and hills usually erased the advantage of horseman over infantryman, and the movement of artillery and supply trains was impeded by woods and the lack of roads. As ever, this was an infantryman's war, with many actions won by the army that marched faster and hit where the enemy was least prepared.

One American advantage that dismayed the British was the ability to throw up earthworks quickly, as they did in besieging Boston. After the slaughter of regulars attacking Breed's Hill, the British dreaded being forced to assault dug-in Americans. At times, this resulted in British armies being burdened with slow-moving artillery trains that commanders deemed essential to rooting out the Americans.

War-making in eighteenth-century America was dominated by European chivalry, regimental honor, and gentlemen commanders, and the foot soldier was no more than a pawn. The Revolutionary War, however, began to change some conventions, because the independent-minded American soldier

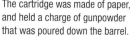

The cartridge was made of paper, and held a charge of gunpowder that was poured down the barrel.

Hand-made lead bullets came in different sizes and seldom were molded perfectly to fit the rifle or musket.

Cartridges were kept in cases, such as this dragoon's cartridge box, which was worn around the waist.

This primitive bullet mold, carved from soapstone, is held together with four wooden sticks.

wanted to know the reasoning behind a command. While training Continental troops at Valley Forge, von Steuben complained that the American soldier asked "Why?" when the European simply obeyed.

Yet von Steuben learned that combining American individualism with a training system that the soldier believed in could achieve near miracles, as it did after Valley Forge.

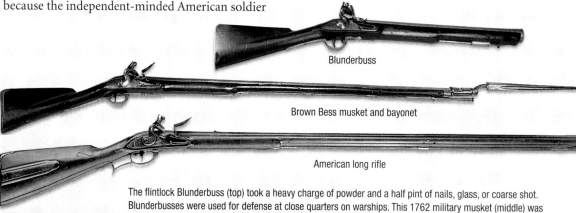

Blunderbuss

Brown Bess musket and bayonet

American long rifle

The flintlock Blunderbuss (top) took a heavy charge of powder and a half pint of nails, glass, or coarse shot. Blunderbusses were used for defense at close quarters on warships. This 1762 military musket (middle) was known as the Brown Bess, likely because of its color. This 1760 American long rifle (bottom) had a sixty-inch, grooved barrel, which made the ball spin and become more accurate than a bullet from a smoothbore musket.

The flintlock musket was the most prevalent firearm carried by Revolutionary War soldiers. In order to load and fire when ordered they were taught the manual of arms (above). Massed troops unleashing a volley from fifty yards or less could shatter an opposing line. The best troops held their fire, bravely received the first volley, and then fired when the enemy came in close.

This is a link from the West Point Chain that was strung across the Hudson River at West Point to keep the British fleet striking northward from New York City.

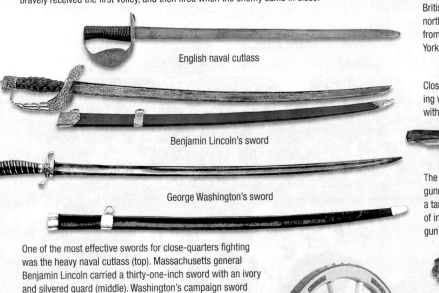

English naval cutlass

Benjamin Lincoln's sword

George Washington's sword

Close combat could involve fighting with daggers, such as this one with a ten-inch iron blade.

The artillery gauge was employed by gunners to calculate the distance to a target and the angle of inclination of the gun's barrel.

One of the most effective swords for close-quarters fighting was the heavy naval cutlass (top). Massachusetts general Benjamin Lincoln carried a thirty-one-inch sword with an ivory and silvered guard (middle). Washington's campaign sword (bottom) was more than thirty-six inches long. He bequeathed it to nephew Samuel T. Washington, admonishing him to unsheath it "only in defense of country and its rights."

This British field gun was captured in Burgoyne's 1777 defeat at Saratoga. The Americans had little artillery—ordnance—and most of what they had was taken from British forts and ships. This gun is inscribed with "SURRENDERED/BY THE/CONVENTION/OF/SARATOGA/OCTR. 17 1777."

Chronology

The Revolutionary War's theaters of action assumed a definite pattern, as seen from year to year in the sequence of battles and campaigns. During the first years of the war, the major battles took place in the North, beginning with operations against the British army at Boston. A more calculated military effort sent revolutionary forces to Canada to attack the next most powerful British force in America.

With the 1776 evacuation of Boston and the arrival of more British troops, New York became the main theater of war. The defeat of Washington that summer brought the war to New Jersey and to the doorstep of Philadelphia. That winter, Washington's unexpected victories forced the British to withdraw to New York City.

In 1777, the major actions were still in the North-east, with Burgoyne's defeat and Howe's capture of Philadelphia. In 1778 France's entry into the war compelled the evacuation of Philadelphia, and the siege of New York became more intense. British strategy in 1779 moved major operations to the South, where the conflict continued through the final battle at Yorktown in late 1781. The last two years saw intensive political action and negotiations, but no major battles.

1775

APRIL Battles of Lexington and Concord

MAY The Second Continental Congress convenes in Philadelphia and elects John Hancock president of Congress • Fort Ticonderoga is captured

JUNE Battle of Breed's Hill • Congress names George Washington commander in chief of the Continental army • Siege of Boston begins

The capture of Fort Ticonderoga

JULY George Washington assumes command of the Continental army • The Continental Congress sends the Olive Branch Petition to King George III, expressing hope for reconciliation

AUGUST King George III refuses to look at the Olive Branch Petition and issues a proclamation declaring the American colonies are in open rebellion

SEPTEMBER American forces under Richard Montgomery and Benedict Arnold begin invasions of Canada

NOVEMBER Congress establishes a Continental navy

DECEMBER King George III issues a proclamation suspending all commerce and trade to the Colonies as of March 1776

1776

JANUARY Thomas Paine's *Common Sense* is published • Henry Knox brings Fort Ticonderoga's guns by ox-drawn sled to Cambridge, Massachusetts

FEBRUARY Loyalist forces fall at the Battle of Moore's Creek Bridge, North Carolina

MARCH British forces evacuate Boston

MAY France sends arms and ammunition to America • American forces begin to retreat from Canada

JUNE Siege of Charleston, South Carolina

JULY The Declaration of Independence is approved by Congress • The British fleet led by General William Howe arrives in New York harbor

AUGUST The Declaration of Independence is officially signed • Battle of Long Island; Washington retreats by night and avoids surrender

SEPTEMBER Battle of Harlem Heights • Much of New York City is destroyed by fire • Nathan Hale is executed • The submarine *Turtle* fails to attach explosives to a British warship in New York harbor

OCTOBER Most of the Continental navy is obliterated at the Battle of Valcour Island • Battle of White Plains, New York

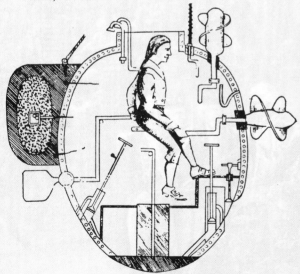

The submarine *Turtle*

NOVEMBER Fort Washington and Fort Lee fall to the British • Washington retreats across New Jersey

DECEMBER The Continental Congress abandons Philadelphia for Baltimore • Battle of Trenton • Benjamin Franklin sails to France

1777

JANUARY Battle of Princeton

FEBRUARY Washington's army dwindles due to death and desertion at Morristown, New Jersey

JUNE Congress mandates a flag of thirteen stars and thirteen stripes • British General John Burgoyne leads an invasion from Canada

JULY Burgoyne recaptures Fort Ticonderoga • Battle of Hubbardton, Vermont • Young Marquis de Lafayette volunteers for the Continental army

AUGUST Battle of Oriskany • Battle of Bennington

SEPTEMBER Battle of Brandywine • Howe's forces occupy Philadelphia • Congress relocates to Lancaster, Pennsylvania

OCTOBER Battle of Germantown • Burgoyne surrenders his army of 5,700 men after defeat at the Second Battle of Saratoga

NOVEMBER Adoption of the Articles of Confederation, declaring Congress the sole governmental authority for the new United States of America

1778

JANUARY Hunger, disease, and supply problems plague American forces at Valley Forge

FEBRUARY American and French representatives in Paris sign a Treaty of Amity and Commerce and a Treaty of Alliance • Baron von Steuben of Prussia arrives at Valley Forge

MAY General Henry Clinton replaces General Howe as commander of all British forces in America

JUNE British Forces withdraw from Philadelphia • Battle of Monmouth, New Jersey • George Rogers Clark begins his wilderness campaign

JULY Congress returns to Philadelphia • Loyalist and Iroquois raiders massacre settlers in Wyoming Valley, Pennsylvania • Washington sets up headquarters at West Point, New York • France declares war on Britain

AUGUST American and French forces fail their attempted siege of Newport, Rhode Island

Iroquois warrior

NOVEMBER Loyalist and Seneca forces massacre more than forty settlers at Cherry Valley, New York

DECEMBER British forces capture Savannah, Georgia

1779

FEBRUARY George Rogers Clark captures Vincennes

APRIL American forces attack Chickamauga Indian villages in Tennessee

JUNE 6,000 British troops travel up the Hudson River toward West Point • Spain declares war on Britain

JULY Battle of Stony Point, New York

AUGUST Congress proposes a peace plan stipulating independence, British evacuation, and free navigation on the Mississippi River

SEPTEMBER Captain John Paul Jones's ship *Bonhomme Richard* captures the HMS *Serapis*

OCTOBER Siege of Savannah • Washington's army sets up camp at Morristown for the most severe winter of the eighteenth century

1780

MARCH Siege of Charleston begins

MAY General Henry Clinton captures Charleston in the worst American defeat of the war

JUNE Congress chooses General Horatio Gates to command the Southern Continental army

JULY Comte de Rochambeau and 5,000 French troops arrive at Newport, Rhode Island • Benedict Arnold covertly offers to surrender West Point

AUGUST Cornwallis defeats General Gates's army at Camden, North Carolina

West Point in 1780

SEPTEMBER John André is captured • Benedict Arnold flees to the British ship HMS *Vulture*

OCTOBER John André is hanged • Battle of King's Mountain • General Nathanael Green replaces Gates as commander of the Southern Continental army

1781

JANUARY Mutiny of the Pennsylvania and New Jersey Lines • Battle of Cowpens, South Carolina

FEBRUARY Marquis de Lafayette begins his Virginia Campaign

MARCH The Articles of Confederation are ratified • Battle of Guilford Court House, North Carolina

MAY The Spanish take control of Pensacola, Florida

JUNE Congress appoints Benjamin Franklin, Thomas Jefferson, and John Jay as peace commissioners to Great Britain alongside John Adams

AUGUST Washington and Rochambeau coordinate a plan of attack on Yorktown, Virginia • French Admiral Comte de Grasse's fleet arrives off Yorktown

SEPTEMBER De Grasse defeats the British navy in the Battle of the Virginia Capes • De Grasse blockades Yorktown, trapping Cornwallis on land • Battle of Eutaw Springs, South Carolina • Siege of Yorktown begins

OCTOBER Cornwallis surrenders at Yorktown

1782

JANUARY Loyalists begin leaving America for Nova Scotia and New Brunswick

MARCH British Prime minister Lord North resigns; his successor, Lord Rockingham, seeks immediate negotiations with the Americans

APRIL Sir Guy Carleton becomes commander of British forces in America • Washington sets up headquarters at Newburgh, New York

JUNE British evacuate Savannah

AUGUST Battle of Combahee Ferry, South Carolina

NOVEMBER The last battle of the war is fought between American, Loyalist, and Shawnee forces in the Ohio territory • Preliminary peace treaty signed between Britain and the United States

DECEMBER British forces evacuate Charleston

1783

FEBRUARY Spain officially recognizes the United States of America

JUNE The Continental army is disbanded

SEPTEMBER The Treaty of Paris is signed by the United States, Great Britain, France, Spain, and the Netherlands

NOVEMBER British forces evacuate New York City • Washington enters the city on November 25

DECEMBER George Washington resigns his command of the Continental army

Washington resigns his commission

Theaters of War

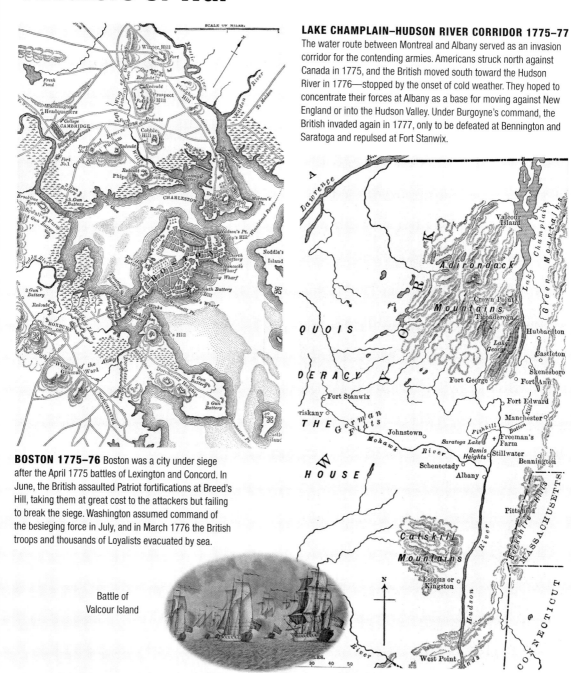

LAKE CHAMPLAIN–HUDSON RIVER CORRIDOR 1775–77

The water route between Montreal and Albany served as an invasion corridor for the contending armies. Americans struck north against Canada in 1775, and the British moved south toward the Hudson River in 1776—stopped by the onset of cold weather. They hoped to concentrate their forces at Albany as a base for moving against New England or into the Hudson Valley. Under Burgoyne's command, the British invaded again in 1777, only to be defeated at Bennington and Saratoga and repulsed at Fort Stanwix.

BOSTON 1775–76 Boston was a city under siege after the April 1775 battles of Lexington and Concord. In June, the British assaulted Patriot fortifications at Breed's Hill, taking them at great cost to the attackers but failing to break the siege. Washington assumed command of the besieging force in July, and in March 1776 the British troops and thousands of Loyalists evacuated by sea.

Battle of
Valcour Island

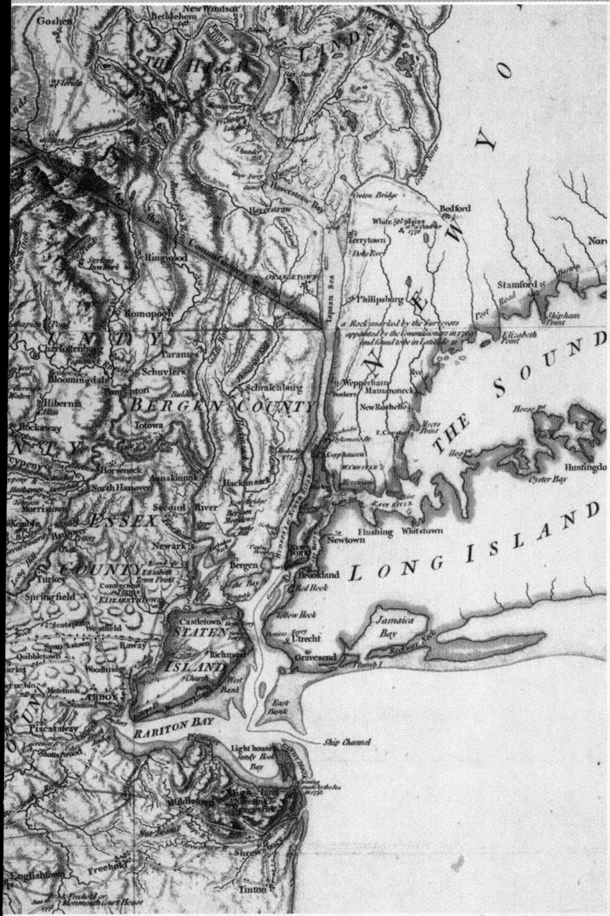

NEW YORK AND NEW JERSEY 1776

Washington was unsuccessful in defending New York against Howe's overwhelming invasion force, which landed on Staten Island in mid-1776. Soundly defeated on Long Island, Washington withdrew to Manhattan, only to be driven out and again defeated at White Plains. The Patriot army then divided, part to defend New England and the rest to retreat with Washington through New Jersey toward Philadelphia with Cornwallis close on his heels.

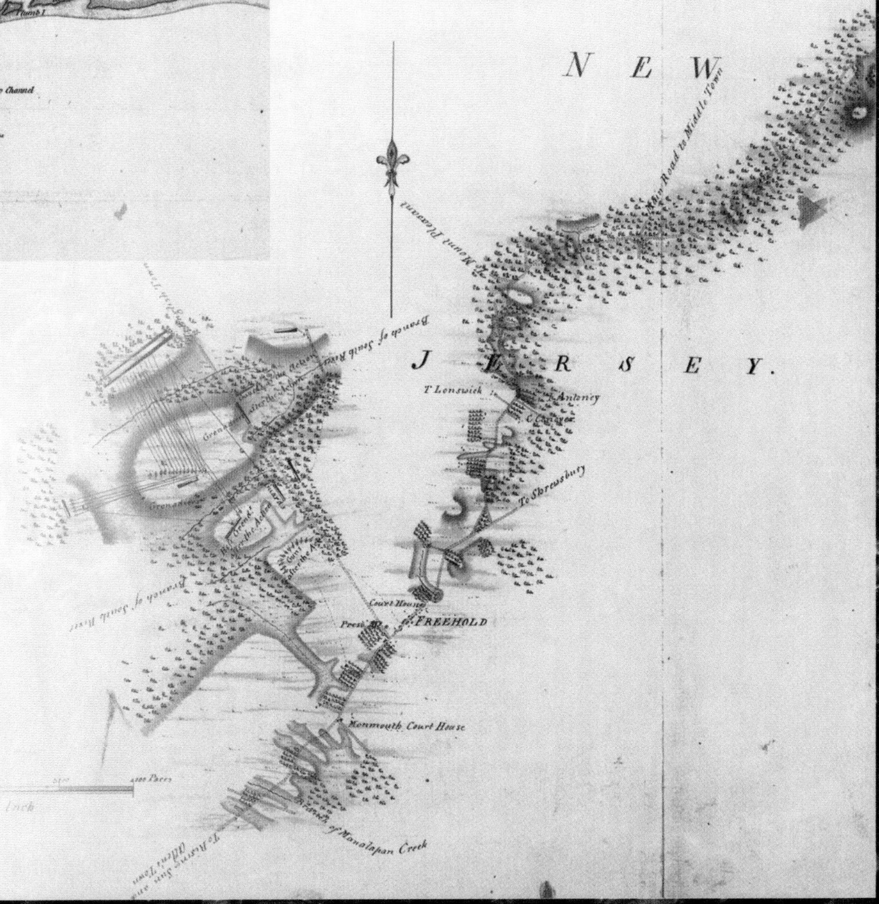

PHILADELPHIA AND MONMOUTH 1777–78

Washington's unexpected victories at Trenton (shown at right) and Princeton in late 1776 and early 1777 shocked the British, who withdrew most of their garrisons in New Jersey. Later that year Howe led a massive seaborne expedition that captured Philadelphia, in between defeating Washington at Brandywine and again at Germantown. In 1778, as the British evacuated Philadelphia to avoid being trapped by a French naval blockade, Washington left quarters at Valley Forge and struck the enemy's rear guard at Monmouth.

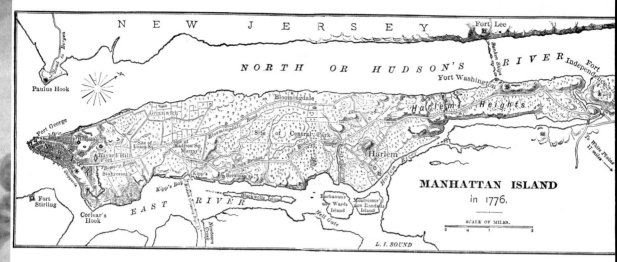

MANHATTAN ISLAND
in 1776.

WESTERN THEATER George Rogers Clark led expeditions through this territory, where small British garrisons held strategic trading posts such as Vincennes and Kaskaskia. The main British stronghold was Fort Detroit, linked to Fort Niagara by water routes over Lake Erie and too powerful to attack. Clark's bold exploits persuaded many Indians and French in the region to remain neutral during the war. Further, his conquests established American claims to the Northwest after hostilities ended.

NEW YORK UNDER SIEGE British and Loyalist forces were bottled up in New York for most of the war, as Washington's Continental Army and local Patriot militia kept close watch from New Jersey and the Hudson Valley. The region between the lines was a dangerous no-man's-land known as the Neutral Ground, where raids and counterraids took place. Even when Washington and the French were marching to Yorktown, the British in New York were reluctant to launch their own attack, knowing they would be swarmed by thousands of militia.

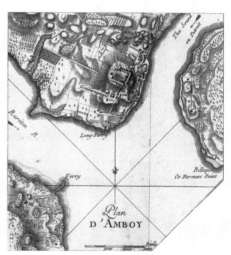

SOUTHERN CAMPAIGNS 1778–83 The British southern strategy began with the capture of Savannah in late 1778 and involved sieges and small battles that were decisive in keeping the Loyalists down. British campaigning in 1781 involved fast-moving bodies of troops that attempted without success to destroy Nathanael Greene's elusive main army. After Cornwallis's defeat at Yorktown that year, the British held only Charleston (shown above), Savannah, and Wilmington.

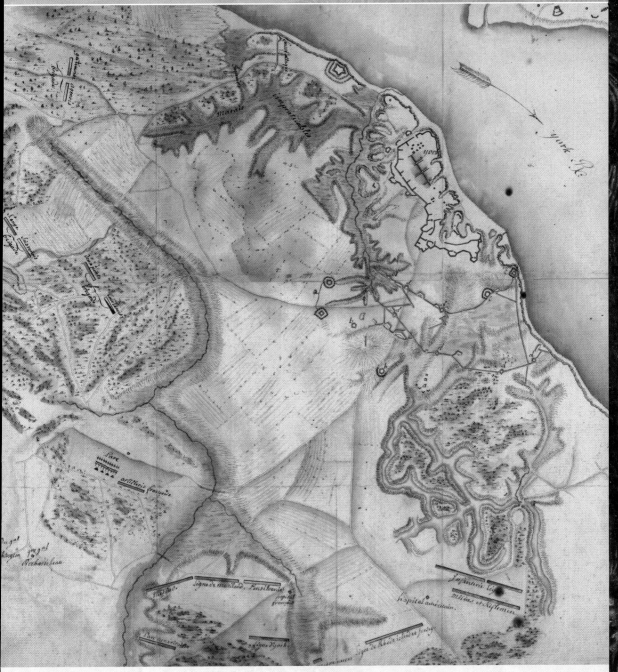

SIEGE OF YORKTOWN American and French forces numbering seventeen thousand men surrounded Cornwallis's beleaguered eight-thousand-strong army at the York River's outlet to the Chesapeake Bay. The French fleet blockaded the bay, preventing British vessels from getting through to Cornwallis, fortified at Yorktown and Gloucester. Digging trenches at night, the Allies moved steadily closer to Yorktown, attacking strong points and moving up artillery until the steady bombardment forced Cornwallis to surrender.

CHAPTER 7

HEROISM, LEGEND, AND LORE

The campaign season of 1777 opened with General John Burgoyne's powerful force moving southward from Canada. Lake Champlain's impressive Fort Ticonderoga was indefensible without thousands of troops, which American general Arthur St. Clair did not have. St. Clair abandoned Ticonderoga, at great cost to his reputation, but he saved his army for upcoming battles. Regional commander General Philip Schuyler of Albany mustered what men he could to delay Burgoyne's invasion, destroying bridges and blocking forest trails. Reinforcements trickled in, and small battles were fought, as every day made Patriot forces a bit stronger. Meanwhile, Howe's army in New York embarked for Philadelphia, where Washington waited after detaching much-needed troops to oppose Burgoyne. Heroism on both sides was plentiful in these campaigns and in the coming operations in the South and Northwest. New legends were born—about the flag and about Washington—and tales shared around campfires and embroidered upon by storytellers became American lore and tradition, rich and colorful, whether true or not.

George Washington's 1787 portrait by Charles Willson Peale provided the artist's younger brother James Peale with a source for this c. 1790 portrait of the general. The picture commemorates victory at the battle of Yorktown, and in the background are French soldiers.

The Turning Point

Right: The surrender of
Burgoyne at Saratoga in
1777, portrayed by John
Trumbull, was commis-
sioned for the Capitol
Rotunda in 1817. The
central figure is American
general Horatio Gates,
who permits Burgoyne
to keep his sword—a
gesture of respect for a
defeated foe. The figures
are officers from the campaign, except Benedict
Arnold, whose treason led
to his role in the victory
being downplayed.

Q: **Which campaign is considered the Revolutionary War's turning point—when the tide began to run in favor of the revolutionaries?**

A: General Burgoyne's 1777 Saratoga campaign—sometimes termed Burgoyne's Offensive—resulted in one of history's most resounding and unexpected defeats for British arms, and was in retrospect considered the turning point of the war. After the failure the previous year of the British naval invasion over Lake Champlain, Burgoyne won the backing, from King George himself, to lead the seven-thousand-strong Northern Army toward Albany, New York, and the Hudson Valley. General Howe was expected to advance northward from New York City and meet Burgoyne at Albany, while a third force, under Colonel Barry St. Leger, moved toward Albany from the west.

St. Leger was stopped at Fort Stanwix, however, Howe moved against Philadelphia instead of Albany, and Burgoyne found himself facing overwhelming numbers with his supply line threatened. In the two Battles of Saratoga between September 19 and October 7, Burgoyne suffered heavily and was cut off from his base at the northern end of Champlain. The American army was led by General Horatio Gates, but other

commanders actually won the battle, particularly Benedict Arnold, Benjamin Lincoln, Enoch Poor, and John Glover.

Burgoyne's surrender convinced the French that the revolutionaries were worth supporting, and the government of young King Louis XVI decided to recognize American independence. A French alliance was essential to American victory.

Q: **What almost unknown engagement of this campaign proved to British regulars that Americans were willing and able to fight them in the open field?**

A: The July 1777 Battle of Hubbardton, now in Vermont, demonstrated the stiffening American resistance. Burgoyne had just captured Fort Ticonderoga, abandoned without a fight by the American army, and his advance troops were rushing along forest trails to attack the rear guard under Colonel Seth Warner of New Hampshire. The Americans fought off the pursuers and even counterattacked,

Above: This sketch is
believed to show the
American order of battle
at Saratoga. Saratoga
signaled that the revolu-
tionaries were capable of
winning victories and was
decisive in France's joining the Americans. French
funds and war matériel
flowed generously to the
American cause.

killing fifteen officers and sixty rank and file, wounding one hundred and fifty. The Americans lost forty-one killed and two hundred captured. This was the first of several setbacks for Burgoyne, as resistance mounted to slow down his invasion.

Q: Why did Burgoyne detach many of his German troops and send them on a mission that resulted in their destruction and ultimately his defeat?

A: Burgoyne hoped to capture desperately needed supplies and also horses—many of his Germans were dragoons campaigning on foot. The Brunswickers who made up the bulk of Burgoyne's three thousand German troops had won his confidence by proving themselves in the capture of Ticonderoga and at Hubbardton.

Burgoyne ordered eight hundred men, including four hundred Germans and many Loyalists, to march eastward and find enemy supply bases, perhaps even continue operating as a separate wing of his army. This first detachment was ambushed by General John Stark's rebels at Hoosick, New York, close to Bennington (in the future Vermont). Burgoyne sent six hundred and fifty German reinforcements, who were too late to prevent a rout and themselves were badly mauled.

The Battle of Bennington cost Burgoyne more than two hundred dead and seven hundred taken prisoner.

Although his luck was running out, and despite this devastating loss, Burgoyne chose to keep advancing toward Albany.

Q: What was "The Year of the Bloody Sevens"?

A: This was the name given the year 1777 by New York's Mohawk Valley settlers, who suffered savage attacks from British regulars, Loyalists, and Indians during Burgoyne's Offensive. Heavy militia losses at Oriskany in August took the lives or wounded more than two hundred settlers.

This dramatic but fanciful depiction portrays the capture of Brunswick soldiers after their disastrous defeat at Bennington in 1777. Many Brunswickers were dragoons, but they had no mounts and therefore did not go into this expedition wearing full regalia, including riding boots, which would not have served for tramping over forest trails.

Philadelphia Captures Howe

Q: Which battle is considered General William Howe's most brilliant victory?

A: The Battle of Brandywine, Pennsylvania, on September 11, 1777, was a great triumph for the British commander. Although Howe's victory on Long Island in 1776 was also highly commended, at Brandywine he did not have such an overwhelming advantage in numbers, and Washington's army was more experienced.

Howe's fleet of 260 warships and transports landed fifteen thousand troops from Chesapeake Bay. Washington made a stand at Brandywine Creek as Howe advanced on Philadelphia, seat of Congress and the revolutionary government. Howe's frontal attack held Washington's ten thousand–man army in place while Cornwallis led a flanking march around the Patriot right wing and struck from behind. The Americans were driven back, but they withdrew stubbornly, proving themselves unafraid of Howe's regulars.

Congress had to flee Philadelphia, which was occupied by Howe, who stayed there through the winter of 1777–78.

Top Right: Lafayette falls, wounded, at the Battle of Brandywine in 1777. This French nobleman was just nineteen when, a few months before the battle, he joined Washington, offering to serve at his own expense. This was before France had entered the war. Lafayette returned to action and rose to be a Continental general.

fog, fired on each other, causing more confusion. The British rallied and counter-attacked, holding the field as the Americans withdrew.

The exhausted British made no attempt to pursue Washington, who moved his army to Valley Forge, Pennsylvania, within striking distance of Philadelphia.

Q: Which major battle saw victory just elude Washington?

A: At Germantown, Pennsylvania, on October 4, 1777, Washington's forces surprised the British encampments at dawn and drove the enemy to the brink of a rout. When 120 British regulars held out inside a stone mansion, they stalled the American attack. Misfortune struck when American units, concealed by a thick

Bottom Right: The desperate British defense of this stone mansion belonging to Loyalist Benjamin Chew foiled the American assault at Germantown in 1777. Instead of bypassing the 120 men in the house, the Americans tried to take it, suffering great loss. The delay allowed the main British force to rally and successfully counterattack.

Q: What British officer had Washington in his rifle sights during the Philadelphia campaign?

A: While scouting in the lead-up to Brandywine, Major Patrick Ferguson, a Scotsman and a career officer skilled at wilderness fighting, was lying in bushes when he saw a handsome horse and rider canter past. He knew this was a Patriot officer, but, as he said later, "It was not pleasant to fire at the back of an un-offending individual who was acquitting himself very coolly of his duty, so I left him alone." He also told his men to hold their fire. Soon discovered by American scouts, Ferguson was badly wounded in the arm but escaped.

Ferguson would win a place in history for inventing a breech-loading rifle that had a high rate of fire and was extremely accurate. He was unsuccessful, however, in trying to persuade British generals to supply their troops with this unconventional weapon, even though it was far superior to the standard muzzle-loading smoothbore musket. A breechloader would have given the British regulars an insurmountable advantage in battle.

Returning to service after his wound, Ferguson went to the Carolina mountains to raise Loyalist forces from the Scottish emigrants there. He was killed leading them at King's Mountain, South Carolina.

Casting lead shot—or bullets—required a pot to melt the lead and a ladle to pour the molten lead from the pot into the bullet mold. Excess lead was cut with the closing of the mold and then remelted.

Q: Who, upon hearing that Howe had captured Philadelphia, remarked, "No, Philadelphia has captured Howe"?

A: Benjamin Franklin, in Paris at the time to negotiate a treaty of alliance with France, made this famous witticism. Franklin knew Howe's occupation of Philadelphia would not end the Revolution but instead would draw British forces away from New York, a much more important city and seaport. With the impending entry of France into the war, Howe's main army in Philadelphia would be needed in New York, which was soon to be menaced by the French navy.

" Awful was the scene to behold—such a number of fellow beings lying together severely wounded and some mortally. "

—*Quaker Joseph Townsend*
joining other civilians to aid the wounded on the battlefield at Brandywine

An Army Is Born at Valley Forge

General Washington, left, and the newly arrived French nobleman Marie Joseph du Motier, the Marquis de Lafayette, ride out to visit the troops at Valley Forge. Washington reviews the men to see how well they are keeping warm and dry, and also that they are alert and on guard, like the sentry at attention before him.

Q: What American leader accused the Continental Congress of "having little feeling for the naked and distressed soldiers" at Valley Forge?

A: General George Washington. In late fall of 1777 Washington needed winter quarters that allowed observation of the British in Philadelphia without risking surprise attack. In December he led ten thousand men into Valley Forge, Pennsylvania, where they suffered through a severe winter. Food was in short supply, housing was overcrowded, and soldiers were poorly clothed. Illness kept many from duty, and nearly twenty-five hundred died of disease in the first months. Washington blamed the Continental Congress for failing to provide for the army. At times, supplies were stockpiled elsewhere but did not reach the troops because of administrative incompetence.

As the supply situation improved, strict training during that winter brought great improvement in discipline and organization, which would lead to final victory.

During the colonial period, cattle horns were used by woodsmen and by soldiers for storing gunpowder in a safe, dry place. The horns also became decorative objects.

Q: Who wrote the first training manual for the Continental Army?

A: The Continental Army lacked a uniform system of training and discipline, so when former Prussian officer Friedrich Wilhelm von Steuben arrived at Valley Forge in February 1778, Washington assigned him to be drillmaster. Steuben,

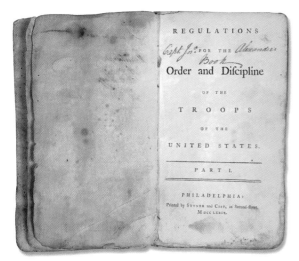

The Baron Friedrich Wilhelm von Steuben wrote the *Regulations For Order And Discipline* in his native language, German. The book was translated into English and used to train the men at Valley Forge.

who had served in Frederick the Great's army, developed an infantry manual, *Regulations for the Order and Discipline of the Troops of the United States.* Published in 1779, it remained the basic American infantry manual for the next twenty-five years.

Steuben simplified the loading and firing procedure, training the soldiers to lay down a more effective "field of fire" instead of following the time-consuming "aim-and-fire" method. The men learned to load and fire three rounds a minute and then to use the bayonet for hand-to-hand combat. Steuben's rigorous drilling of battlefield tactics gave Washington's regiments much-improved maneuverability in action.

Q: Which "lady" stayed with the soldiers during the winter at Valley Forge, lifting the spirits of the army?

A: Martha Washington joined her husband at Valley Forge in February 1778. She was adored by the officers and did all she could to help relieve the suffering of ordinary soldiers. One eye-witness wrote: "I never in my life knew a woman so busy from early morning until late at night as was Lady Washington, providing comforts for the sick soldiers . . . She might be seen, with basket in hand . . . going among the huts seeking the keenest and most needy sufferer, and giving all the comforts to them in her power."

Martha Washington sat for Charles Willson Peale to paint this portrait in 1795. Peale first painted Lady Washington's portrait in 1772, and had painted a miniature in 1791 for one of her granddaughters. Peale's familiarity with the Washingtons led him to propose this new portrait when he met General Washington in Philadelphia one day and remarked that Mrs. Washington looked so well that her portrait must again be painted. Washington agreed.

" The unfortunate soldiers were in want of everything; they had neither coats nor hats, nor shirts, nor shoes. Their feet and their legs froze until they were black, and it was often necessary to amputate them. "

—*THE MARQUIS DE LAFAYETTE*

British Retreat from Philadelphia

Q: **Why did the British evacuate Philadelphia in 1778?**

A: Harshly criticized by his government for failing to destroy Washington's army in the Philadelphia campaign, General Howe was replaced by General Henry Clinton. As Howe's second-in-command, Clinton had disagreed at the start with the expedition against Philadelphia. He believed the main British base should be New York and that Washington surely would strike there once he was strong enough. Further, with the recent entry of France into the war, French warships were already threatening New York and could blockade Philadelphia's access to the sea.

The British government had ordered Clinton to begin major operations in the South and to be prepared to detach large numbers of troops to oppose the French in the Caribbean. It was apparent that before long Clinton would not have the strength to take on Washington's army if it received French reinforcements. Intending to concentrate British strength at New York, Clinton ordered Philadelphia evacuated and his army to march across New Jersey. The march would be risky, but if Washington dared attack, he might be drawn into an all-out battle on terms that would favor the British.

Q: **The Battle of Monmouth was considered a draw. Why were the Americans so proud of the result?**

A: The Monmouth campaign of June–July 1778 showed how much progress Washington's troops had made during their months of training at Valley Forge. One proof of improvement was their rapid movements to outrun the British column and gain a position for a major attack on the rear guard.

Clinton and ten thousand men fought Washington's more than thirteen thou-

The French fleet under Comte d'Estaing conducted ineffective and inconclusive operations against the British fleet in American waters in 1778. Originally an army officer, d'Estaing failed in several engagements after France entered the war. French warships were mainly based at Newport, Rhode Island, and the British were at New York.

Sir, these troops are not able to meet British grenadiers!

—*General Charles Lee*

explaining to Washington why he was retreating at Monmouth

sand, but the British regiments included many of the army's best troops. In their maneuvering for battle, the Americans had to remain disciplined and organized, especially since Clinton would have defeated them separately had they attacked in uncoordinated formations. The high performance of the troops, particularly their successful bayonet charges and their breaking up of a mounted dragoon charge, was a source of pride and confidence.

Most encouraging of all was the recovery of the five thousand men whom General Charles Lee had ordered to retreat in the face of a British counter-attack. When Washington rallied those men, exhausted as they were from the hundred-degree heat, they drove back Clinton's assaults (a key one led by Cornwallis). The effects of ferocious heat and the coming of darkness finally ended the battle, and Clinton slipped away in the night toward New York. He had maintained his army through a difficult retreat and so could well claim success at Monmouth.

Q: What is the "Molly Pitcher Legend"?

A: The nickname Molly Pitcher was used for women who carried water to the troops, especially on campaign. Some of these women even served during battles. These "camp followers," who moved with the army, were usually married to soldiers, and sometimes had children. The war

gave rise to several stories of the heroism of these Molly Pitchers under fire, including Pennsylvanian Margaret Cochran Corbin, who took her mortally wounded husband's place serving a cannon at Fort Washington in 1776. She, too, was badly wounded but survived and eventually received a government pension. Known as Captain Molly, she was buried at West Point.

The most famous Molly Pitcher was Mary Ludwig Hays, also a Pennsylvanian, whose artilleryman husband fell, wounded, at Monmouth. Ludwig set down her water jug and took his place, wielding a rammer to help keep the gun firing. Washington himself remarked on her performance and commended her courage. Ludwig's husband died soon after the war, and she was left to fend for herself, but could not prevail on Congress to give her a pension.

With her husband lying mortally wounded, Mary Ludwig Hays—nicknamed Molly Pitcher—takes his place in a gun crew at the 1778 Battle of Monmouth. The Americans fought the British rearguard—General Clinton's elite troops—to a standoff in sweltering hundred-degree heat at Monmouth.

Sir, they are able, and by God they shall do it!
—WASHINGTON'S ANSWER TO LEE

The War Moves South

Q: Why did the British strategists believe their best opportunity for eventual victory lay in occupying the South?

A: The entry of France into the war in 1778, and later Spain and the Netherlands, put Britain on the defensive around the world, so large numbers of troops were not available for major American campaigns. The powerful French navy menaced British troop transports and also operated against merchant shipping to and from British-occupied seaports such as New York, Montreal, and Newport, Rhode Island. In this year, the British government decided to leave New England relatively unmolested except for holding on to Newport. Strategy called for even New York to be abandoned if French pressure became too strong.

On the other hand, the relatively lightly defended Southern seaports of Savannah, Georgia, and Charleston, South Carolina, would be good bases for Royal Navy operations against French, Spanish, and Dutch colonies. In addition, it was be-

lieved that powerful Loyalist forces in the South would rise up if British troops were there to support them.

The British fought off an American and French attempt to take Newport in the summer of 1778, and in December the king's forces captured Savannah, beginning five years of conflict in the South that would end at Yorktown in 1783.

Benjamin Lincoln

Q: What was the worst defeat of the war for combined American and French arms?

A: The combined French and American campaign against Savannah in the fall of 1779 depended on the French admiral Comte d'Estaing, who had already proven to be inept in aborted expeditions against New York City and Newport. Further complicating matters, the American commander, General Benjamin Lincoln of Massachusetts, was unable to raise large numbers of fighting men needed to conduct a prolonged siege,

The failed siege of Savannah in 1779 cost American and French forces dearly, with more than half the allied attackers at the bitter Spring Hill clash falling in action. The allies suffered heavily from British artillery, which caught them in the open as they were maneuvering into position.

because virtually all of Georgia was under British control. D'Estaing, with thirty-three warships and four thousand white-coated French regulars, treated Lincoln and his small force of two thousand Patriots with open disrespect.

The French admiral's sluggish buildup to the offensive gave the British time to fortify Savannah and defy demands for surrender—which d'Estaing made in the name of France, ignoring Congress and Lincoln. British commander General Augustine Prevost had thirty-two hundred British, German, and Loyalist troops and many civilian allies. They endured heavy bombardments from hundreds of d'Estaing's naval guns, knowing time was on their side.

D'Estaing dreaded the imminent onset of hurricane season and had only a few weeks in which to force the British surrender. Hurried allied attacks were beaten back, and Prevost counterattacked. The allies suffered more than a thousand casualties, while Prevost lost only one hundred and fifty men. Among the defenders were troops from the Sixtieth Foot, the "Royal Americans," who were instrumental in the British victory.

After the failed attacks, Lincoln pleaded with d'Estaing to continue the siege, which had lasted about a month, but the French fleet sailed away, leaving a bitter taste to the new alliance. In New York, Clinton was elated, declaring, "[This is] the greatest event that has happened in the whole war."

Q: Which American hero died at Savannah while carrying out a dangerous task that he had carried out successfully in a previous battle?

A: Sergeant William Jasper of South Carolina was killed while planting the colors of the Second South Carolina Continentals on a captured redoubt. In the defense of Charleston in 1776 Jasper had successfully risked enemy fire to replace a flag that had been shot off the parapet of Fort Sullivan. A monument was later erected to Jasper at Savannah.

American cast-iron cannonballs

To Charleston with fear,
The rebels repair;
D'Estaing scampers back
  to his boats, sir;
Each blaming the other,
Each cursing his brother,
And—may they cut
  each other's throats, sir.

    —Loyalist 1779 ballad, mocking the
    American and French defeat at Savannah

1780: Defeat and Victory

Q: At which defeat did one of Washington's most reliable generals lose an entire army?

A: The British siege of Charleston, from March to May 1780, ended in disaster for the Americans. General Benjamin Lincoln, who had served the Patriot cause since 1775 at the siege of Boston, and who had been unsuccessful at Savannah the previous fall, was forced to surrender his army of 5,600 men and vast military stores to Sir Henry Clinton, whose 12,500 invading troops suffered only 250 casualties.

Lincoln had been trapped in the city by superior land and sea forces, with little choice but to stand and fight, since most of his men were local militia and armed citizens determined to defend their homes. Because Lincoln was a northerner, it is unlikely he would have been obeyed if he had ordered the South Carolinians to abandon their city to fight another day.

Right: At the August 1780 Battle of Camden, South Carolina, General Johann de Kalb made a last stand in hand-to-hand combat that allowed much of Horatio Gates's defeated army to retreat. Gates, who had taken over the army from De Kalb a few weeks earlier, fled the battlefield, leaving his men to fend for themselves, many of whom died alongside De Kalb.

In 1780, before Baron De Kalb left Philadelphia for South Carolina, he commissioned Charles Willson Peale to paint two portraits. After De Kalb's death at Camden, Peale completed the works and shipped them to the baron's family in Europe. De Kalb wears a gold medal, the Knight's Cross of the Order of Military Merit for Swiss and German Protestant officers in the French service.

Q: What bizarre event at the Charleston surrender dealt the British a serious setback in their attempts to raise Loyalist fighters in the South?

A: Thousands of captured American muskets intended for distribution to Loyalist fighters were destroyed in an accidental explosion when gunpowder in the storehouse that held them was ignited. The explosion hurled shattered muskets and bayonets into the air to land on roofs of houses and rain down on the streets. More British artillerymen were killed and wounded by this explosion than were lost in the siege. In the resulting fire, loaded

muskets continued to explode for several more hours. Making matters worse for the British, one of their transports had just sunk with four thousand muskets, also intended for Loyalist forces.

Q: At which defeat did one of the most honored American generals prove to be an incompetent field commander?

A: The Battle of Camden, South Carolina, in August 1780 is considered one of history's most disastrous and total defeats of an American army. The commander, General Horatio Gates, had taken all the credit he could for the resounding victory at Saratoga in 1777, and he was politicking to replace Washington as commander in chief. In 1780 Gates took command of three thousand Patriot troops in North Carolina but deluded himself that he actually had seven thousand with which to take on Cornwallis's two thousand veteran regulars and Loyalists.

Cornwallis not only routed Gates, but he wiped out his army and killed the able German volunteer, General Johann de Kalb. Unlike Gates, De Kalb stood and fought to the end, giving many Americans the chance to flee. Leading the pack in retreat was Gates himself, who galloped to safety while his troops were far behind. Although Congress exonerated Gates for the defeat, he never escaped the cloud of cowardice that hung over him for the rest of the war.

Q: **Which battle, fought largely by Americans against Americans, changed the course of the war in the South?**

A: The Battle of King's Mountain, North Carolina, in October 1780 was such a decisive defeat of back-country Loyalists that it gave revolutionary forces much-needed new hope after so many setbacks in the South. For the Patriot militias of the southern states, King's Mountain was their greatest

victory, and it was the most terrible defeat for the Loyalists.

Cornwallis had hoped to win thousands of Loyalist recruits to his banner when he dispatched Major Patrick Ferguson of the Seventy-first Highlanders into the Carolina mountains to rally and arm supporters. Ferguson brought as many as fifty-five hundred men to the king's colors, many of them of Scottish heritage, like himself. At the same time, this rising prompted Patriot militia— "Over Mountain Men" from the Blue Ridge Mountains—to assemble and move against Ferguson. Led by North Carolina's Colonel Isaac Shelby, seventeen hundred Patriot militiamen surrounded and wiped out Ferguson, who was killed, and nine hundred Loyalists at King's Mountain.

This painting depicts the gathering of the Over Mountain Men before the October 1780 Battle of King's Mountain, South Carolina. These "Back Water Men," as they were also termed, came from beyond the Blue Ridge Mountains to fight Loyalist forces being massed in the Carolinas. These frontiersmen were instrumental in the victory, but took little part in subsequent operations.

"[King's Mountain] was the first link of a chain of evils that followed each other in regular succession until they at last ended in the total loss of America."

—SIR HENRY CLINTON

Heroism

Q: Who were Washington's most outstanding aides during the war?

A: Intelligence, education, and personal bravery were the hallmarks of the young aides who served with Washington during the war.

Among the most important members of the commander in chief's "military family," as aides were termed, was David Humphreys of Connecticut. An accomplished poet, Humphreys was given the honor of carrying captured enemy flags to Congress after Yorktown. Alexander Hamilton of New York was a headquarters aide until his impatient desire for a field command caused him to argue with Washington and then resign; Hamilton went on to lead troops courageously at Yorktown. Tench Tilghman, of Maryland and Pennsylvania, is credited with leading the dejected Washington to safety as the general sat on horseback, contemplating his defeat at New York in 1776. Tilghman's father was a Loyalist.

Another early aide was Samuel B. Webb of Connecticut, who was wounded at Breed's Hill, White Plains, and Trenton, and was captured and imprisoned for a year before being exchanged. He returned to the service and rose to become a general. Alexander Scammell of Massachusetts served Washington as aide-de-camp in 1776, and then led troops against Burgoyne. Returning to Washington's military family until

John Laurens, of South Carolina, was one of Washington's favorite aides. Laurens fought in the Philadelphia and Monmouth campaigns. In 1779 he was captured during the British siege of Charleston. After release, Laurens went to France to assist in raising funds, then returned to fight at Yorktown. He was killed in action in South Carolina at the age of twenty-seven.

John Laurens

early in 1781, Scammell commanded a light infantry unit at Yorktown and was extremely popular with the troops. While on a scout in this campaign, he was killed by Tarleton's Legion.

One of Washington's closest aides was John Laurens of South Carolina, son of Henry Laurens, former president of the Continental Congress and a commissioner to European powers. Young Laurens joined his father in France, then returned to Washington with a chest of hard cash from the French to support the Revolution. Laurens negotiated the surrender of Cornwallis and then returned home to fight in the Carolinas. He was killed there in a skirmish in mid-1782, a heartbreaking loss to Washington.

Q: Which daring frontier campaign established the future United States claim to the vast region known as the Northwest Territory?

A: George Rogers Clark led just two hundred men on forced marches in 1778 and 1779 to win crucial victories over the British in the Illinois territory. Clark's operations against posts at Vincennes, Kaskaskia, and Cahokia climaxed with his capture of Colonel Henry Hamilton, governor and commander of British forces in the region. Clark's boldness intimidated the native peoples and French settlers, who dared not take up arms against him. Had

Left: "Colonel Clark, where is your army?" asked the dismayed Colonel Henry Hamilton as he surrendered Fort Vincennes to George Rogers Clark late in February 1779. By marching his men back and forth, but showing the fort's defenders only flags and banners, Clark deceived the British into thinking a massive force was soon to attack them.

Below: Continental general William Alexander, who claimed the Scottish title Lord Stirling, was a mathematician and astronomer before the war. His best moment was at the 1776 Battle of Long Island, where he was captured fighting a critical delaying action. Exchanged, Alexander rejoined the army and fought in many campaigns before dying of illness in Albany, New York, in 1783.

they opposed Clark, his tiny force likely would have been wiped out, but his brazen fearlessness and the fearsome reputation of his "Longknives," as Virginia backwoodsmen were termed, won the day.

Although the 1783 peace agreement ending the war gave the United States claim to this region northwest of the Ohio River and up the Mississippi, the British held on to important posts for another thirty years. The War of 1812 finally settled possession in favor of the United States.

Q: Who were the most impressive—and doomed—American troops on the Long Island battlefield in 1776?

A: The First Maryland Regiment, under Colonel William Smallwood, had been handpicked by Smallwood from "men of honor, family, and fortune," according to their major, Mordecai Gist, who was in command of the Marylanders during much of the Battle of Long Island. Smallwood was off on other duty as the American army reeled from Cornwallis's attack.

Gist commanded two hundred and fifty men of the regiment on a counterattack led by General Alexander Stirling. This courageous and fatal offensive gave the bulk of Washington's army time to escape—aided by Smallwood, who appeared with reinforcements and artillery to cover the retreat. Of Gist's two hundred and fifty men, only he and nine others escaped the overwhelming British counterassault. Stirling himself was surrounded and captured.

> He has been a zealous servant and slave to the public, and a faithful assistant to me for nearly five years, a great part of which time he refused to receive pay.
>
> —*WASHINGTON*
>
> *praising Tench Tilghman and requesting that he be commissioned a lieutenant colonel*

Flag Lore and Legend

This nineteenth-century painting by A. M. Willard shows three patriots marching with drums and fife, leading troops into battle. Originally named by the artist "Yankee Doodle," the picture eventually came to be known as "The Spirit of '76." The model for the elderly figure in the center served in the Saratoga campaign.

Q: What was the first flag flown by American troops marching into a captured foreign city?

A: The "red flag of revolution" was carried by Patriot troops marching into Montreal in 1775. At the time there were many regimental flags, along with the rattlesnake flag ("Don't tread on me"), the New England pine tree flag, various colonial flags, and a "Continental" flag that had thirteen stripes with, in one corner, the British Union Flag of 1606 (the red cross of England and the diagonal white cross of Scotland on a blue ground). This Continental flag was also known as the Grand Union Flag, the Congress Flag, or the Colors of the United Colonies. But it was a plain red flag, traditional symbol of revolt, that was first carried in the triumphant American entry into Montreal.

Q: Did Betsy Ross really design and make the first truly American flag?

A: On June 14, 1777, Congress passed the "Flag Resolution," which prescribed the official design of its flag to be thirteen red and white stripes, with a union of thirteen white stars (representing the American states) on a dark blue field. How those stars were to be arranged—in a circle, in rows, or even in a star forma-

tion—was not prescribed. Across the new United States of America in the months immediately following, many flags were made, including one by the recently widowed Philadelphia seamstress, Elizabeth Griscom Ross.

In 1870, Ross's descendants made public the family tradition that in 1777 "Betsy" had been personally requested by Washington—who often used her seamstress services—and by congressional delegates to make the "first" Stars and Stripes.

Ross apparently did sew flags, and at least one had the famous circle of

> " In compliment to the United Colonies. "
>
> —*WASHINGTON*
> *as he ordered the raising of the Continental flag at Cambridge on New Year's Day, 1776*

five-pointed stars on the blue background, now known as the Betsy Ross Flag and the one most associated with the Revolutionary War. Ross sewed flags for the military, as indicated in the minutes of the State Navy Board of Pennsylvania for May 29, 1777, which record "an order on William Webb to Elizabeth Ross for fourteen pounds twelve shillings, and two pence, for making ship's colours, &c." Yet there is no evidence to prove Betsy Ross designed and sewed the very first official Stars and Stripes.

Q: Where was the Stars and Stripes first flown by troops on campaign?

A: As with who made and designed the first Stars and Stripes, historians do not know where the first official American flag was flown in action. It was once believed it flew over Fort Stanwix, in New York's Mohawk Valley, soon after Congress designated the design in June 1777. Later research indicates this actually was the "Continental" flag with thirteen alternating red and white stripes and the British Union Flag in the corner—the flag Washington raised at Cambridge, Massachusetts, during the siege of Boston. Another flag thought to be the first Stars and Stripes in action was the so-called Bennington Flag, with "'76" and eleven seven-pointed stars on its blue field. This flag has since been proven to be of much later manufacture. No one has definitively proven where the first Stars and Stripes was flown by the military.

Q: Which foreign country gave the Stars and Stripes its first salute by the firing of cannons?

A: The Stars and Stripes design was first saluted by the French off the south coast of Brittany in 1777. The first known salute to the Grand Union Flag (the Continental flag that Washington raised at Cambridge) was given in late October 1776 to an American merchant schooner. The salute was fired by the Danish garrison at Fort Frederik at St. Croix in the Caribbean. That November the first salute to an American warship was given by the Dutch at St. Eustatius, also in the Caribbean. On a voyage to obtain munitions and other military supplies at St. Eustatius, the brig *Andrea Doria* fired a salute as it approached the harbor and received the reply that was the first salute to an American flag on board an American warship entering a foreign port.

Fabled maker of Stars and Stripes, the Betsy Ross of legend demonstrates to delegates to Congress in Philadelphia, including George Washington seated at left, how she cuts stars for the new American flag.

George Washington Lore and Legend

Q: What is the "Indian Prophecy"?

A: In several battles during the Revolutionary War, Washington was in extreme danger: A bullet struck his sword at Trenton, and at Princeton he rode, unharmed, through the crossfire of the opposing firing lines, inspiring his men to attack. Likewise, he had narrow escapes at Germantown and Monmouth, and at Yorktown he stood exposed as cannonballs bounced around him. During the Philadelphia campaign British sharpshooter Patrick Ferguson declined to fire at him. The general's apparent invulnerability had been foretold by a sachem, or high chieftain, of the Northwest Indians when Washington was journeying to the Kanawha River in 1770. Washington's camp was approached by a party of Indians, who included this venerable chief, who was "of lofty stature, and of dignified and imposing appearance," according to a Washington biographer. The visitors were invited to join Washington's camp, and the sachem seemed to treat "Colonel Washington with the most reverential deference."

After some time, and a meal of which the sachem did not partake, he addressed the company through an interpreter, explaining that he was known to the peoples between "the great lakes [and] the far blue mountains." He said he had led warriors at the defeat of Braddock in 1755 and had seen Washington in action. During

In 1795, seventeen-year-old Rembrandt Peale painted a life portrait of George Washington, then in his second term as president. This rare opportunity had been arranged by the artist's father, Charles Willson Peale. The Peales alternated with portraitist Gilbert Stuart for sittings with Washington. The Peales painted Washington one day and Stuart worked the next.

the battle, the chief had told his men to shoot down "yon tall and daring warrior . . . who hath an Indian's wisdom."

Seeing that no bullet could harm Washington, the chief said to his men, "He cannot die in battle . . . The Great Spirit protects that man, and guides his destinies—he will become chief of nations, and a people yet unborn will hail him as founder of a mighty empire."

Years later, during the Revolutionary War, comrades in arms who had been with Washington in that camp recalled the sachem's prophecy, and it gave them great hope.

Q: Is it true Washington suffered from teeth problems?

A: Yes, almost all his adult life he had pain or discomfort, and by the Revolutionary War there were few teeth left in his mouth. He used a set of spring-loaded false teeth, but no teeth were made of wood, as some legends claim. Instead, they were a combination of ivory, hippopotamus bone, cow's tooth, and gold.

Q: Did Washington throw a silver dollar across the Potomac River, as legends say?

A: Not likely, especially not near his Mount Vernon plantation, where the river is a mile wide. Some legends say he threw a silver coin across Virginia's Rappahannock River, site of his childhood home, while others say it was the

Delaware, between Pennsylvania and New Jersey. Whether or wherever he threw anything across a river, there were no silver dollars in those days.

Q: What was Washington's promise to his country?

A: Washington swore he would not leave the army until the last British soldier had sailed away from the United States. Even after the victory at Yorktown, when many a general of his day would have gone home to rest and recuperate, Washington stayed with his army. He remained with the men during two more winters near Newburgh, New York, and at last headed home only after the last British occupation force evacuated New York City in November 1783.

Left: Washington wore this uniform from 1789 until his death in 1799. It is similar to the uniform he wore in 1775 when commissioned as commander in chief of the Continental Army. The coat is of blue and buff wool, and the waistcoat and breeches are matching buff wool.

Bottom Left: Washington usually slept and dined in the homes of the well-to-do, but in the field he used this camp chest, made of pine covered in leather. The chest has a green wool lining and iron hinges, facings, and handles and contains a cooking stove, folding pots, utensils, plates, platters, bottles, and other cooking items.

" Never mind the enemy, they can not kill him, and while he lives, our cause will never die. "

—*Dr. James Craik*

Revolutionary War surgeon and a companion on Washington's 1770 journey to the Kanawha

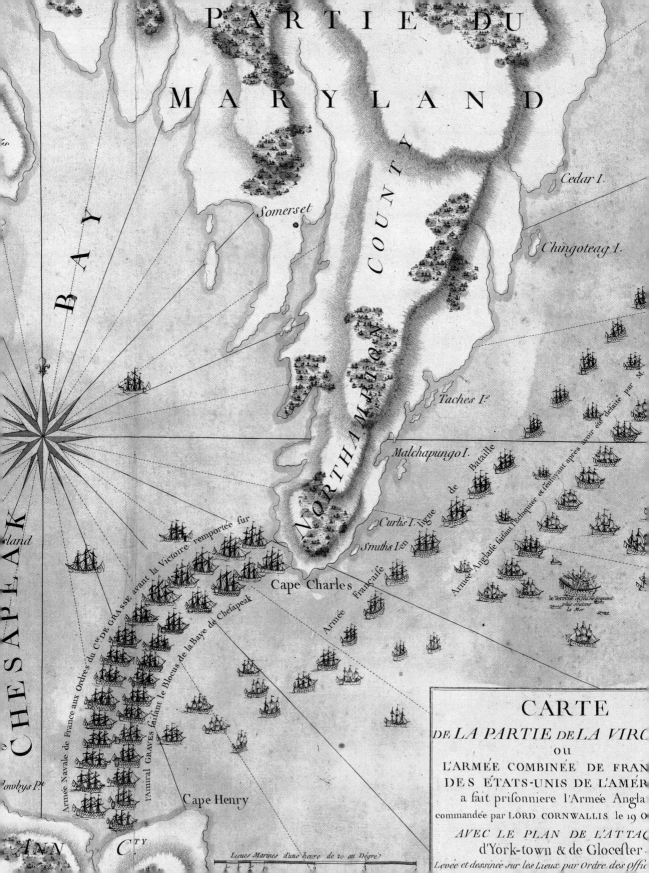

PARTIE DU

MARYLAND

Cedar I.

Chingoteag I.

B A Y

Somerset

NORTHAMPTON COUNTY

Taches Is.

Malchapungo I.

Bataille

Curtis I. *Vigne*

Smiths Ien

Armée Anglaise faisant le chiquier et se sauvant après avoir été désaite par M.

Victoire remportée sur

Cape Charles

Française

le Terrible qui s'est rompant plus s'couleur la Mer

CHESAPEAK

Armée Navale de France aux Ordres du C.te DE GRASSE avant la

l'Amiral GRAVES faisant le Blocus de la Baye de Chesapeak

Armée

land

owbys P.t

Cape Henry

ANN   C.TY

Laeues Marines d'une heure de 20 au Dégre.

CARTE

DE *LA PARTIE DE LA VIRG*
OU
L'ARMÉE COMBINÉE DE FRAN
DES ÉTATS-UNIS DE L'AMÉR
a fait prisonniere l'Armée Angla
commandée par LORD CORNWALLIS le 19 O

AVEC LE PLAN DE L'ATTAQ
d'York-town & de Glocester.
Levée et dessinée sur les Lieux par Ordre des Offic

CHAPTER 8

FRANCE AND THE WAR AT SEA

Not only did the Revolutionary War bring Americans from various regions together for the first time, but before the war was over, the French became America's firm friends and allies.

After defeat in the Seven Years' War, France had been eager to take revenge against the British, so when American revolutionaries went looking for allies, France was willing and able. France had lost New France, and now she might help Britain to lose her American colonies. French troops made the difference at Yorktown in 1781, but from 1778 to the end of the war, the French navy was instrumental in bleeding the British Empire.

A French commodore wrote, "The surest way of conquering the English is to attack them through their trade." This is what French warships did, especially in the Caribbean, the world's richest trading region.

Also, French ports served American "commerce raiders" and Continental Navy warships that attacked and captured British merchant shipping. French support changed the course of the American War of Independence in favor of the hard-pressed revolutionaries.

The history of French sea power had few more monumental triumphs than the September–October 1781 blockade of Cornwallis's army at Yorktown by Admiral de Grasse. This detail from a contemporary French plan of the battle shows de Grasse's warships arrayed across the mouth of Chesapeake Bay. The British fleet cannot break through to rescue the doomed Cornwallis.

France's Secret War

Q: How did France become involved in the American conflict even before an official state of war with Great Britain was declared?

A: As early as November 1775 an undercover French agent was clandestinely meeting with Benjamin Franklin and Congress's Committee of Secret Correspondence. The agent learned that not only were the Americans seeking foreign loans, but their resolve to fight Britain was very strong. The French had already arranged shipments of war supplies through a private merchant company. Since the spring of 1776, the trading firm of Hortalez and Cie, using a French loan of one million livres in gold coin and an equal loan from Spain, shipped war matériel to America. These shipments made possible the victories at Trenton and Princeton, and most of the equipment used by Americans at Saratoga was supplied by France.

Many in Congress, including John Adams, opposed collaboration with France, but Franklin and others worked quietly to establish relations. In October 1776, Congress sent Franklin to France to win her full support. France supported the revolutionaries but did not yet want to bring on war with Britain. By mid-1777, a dozen French vessels were carrying supplies to America. One convoy landed three million livres worth of matériel, including two hundred field guns, several thousand muskets, gunpowder, and clothing for twenty-five thousand men.

French financier and playwright Pierre Augustine Caron de Beaumarchais arranged for one of the first major shipments of firearms and ammunition—200 cannon and 25,000 muskets—to the American revolutionaries. Beaumarchais also satirized French authorities with plays such as *The Barber of Seville* and *The Marriage of Figaro.*

Q: Who led American efforts to bring the French in on the American side?

A: Franklin, although seventy years old, was the key, not only because of his diplomatic ability, but also because he was one of the world's most famous men. His scientific experiments were much admired, and his writings were translated and widely read. Franklin was welcomed as a celebrity to King Louis's court at Versailles and became a popular guest in the salons of Paris.

Arthur Lee, of Virginia, was an early agent for America. While living in London in 1775 Lee was asked by the Committee of Secret Correspondence to serve as a spy. He later joined Franklin and Silas Deane, a Connecticut attorney and delegate to Congress, as American agents in France.

Q: Who were the key French diplomats in favor of backing the American Revolution?

A: The French foreign minister, Charles Gravier, the comte de Vergennes, was central to efforts to supply America's fight against Britain. Vergennes arranged for secret aid, collaborating with Pierre-Augustin Caron, better known as the playwright Beaumarchais, author of *The Barber of Seville* and *The Marriage of Figaro.* Vergennes coordinated French diplomatic and military efforts to prepare for war against Britain. Beaumarchais managed the acquisition of matériel and the shipments to America.

The plainly dressed Benjamin Franklin receives a laurel wreath during a reception at the French court in 1778. In the picture are Queen Marie-Antoinette, seated, Louis XVI, and Princess Elizabeth. Franklin consciously dressed the part of the rustic philosopher, knowing this was how the French imagined him— although he well knew how to dress fashionably.

Q: Why was France's entry into the Revolution the start of a global war?

A: The British and French empires spanned the globe, and when they again went to war in 1778 their colonies became military objectives. France's alliance with Spain and Britain's with Portugal brought those nations and their empires into play. The Dutch were among the first to give the revolutionaries financial support. Once France entered into an alliance with America, the British Empire was in grave peril. The old order was changing, and the British Empire would be drastically diminished by the loss of most of its North American colonies.

Q: Why did American military successes at first cause France her greatest fear?

A: The French worried that the British might make peace with the American colonies, and then France would be isolated and attacked. When, after the bottles of Saratoga and Germantown, British agents were known to be in secret discussions with Franklin, Vergennes feared that his secret support of America would fall apart. This prodded France ever closer to declaring war and securing an alliance with America before matters favored the British.

" Press for the immediate and explicit declaration of France in our Favour, upon a Suggestion that a Re-union with Britain may be the Consequence of a delay. "

—*Instructions to Franklin from Congress*

The Franco-American Alliance

Q: Which American defeat persuaded the French government that the American rebellion was worth supporting?

A: Even though the stunning American victory at Saratoga in the fall of 1777 indicated that the British had a long and difficult war facing them in America, it was Germantown that sealed France's decision. Fought in October, Germantown showed that Americans could recover even after the major defeat at Brandywine and the loss of Philadelphia. Although Washington gave up the field at Germantown, French observers could see he

had almost won another devastating victory over the British.

The American revolutionary spirit appeared undaunted and strong, even in adversity. And Washington's army was becoming ever more formidable. The French government gambled that an American ally would be dependable in a protracted war against the British Empire. Although the British learned early on of French intrigues, little could be done to stop those intrigues short of declaring war, which was an undesirable option in the face of American military improvement.

Q: Who had the stronger navy, Britain or France?

A: France. Both the French and the British navies had suffered great losses in the Seven Years' War that ended in 1763, but the French were swifter to rebuild. The corrupt and inefficient British Admiralty had allowed ships to fall into disrepair, and crewmen left the navy in droves (sixty thousand deserted or died from disease between 1774 and 1780). British shipyards languished for lack of funds and leadership. French shipyards, in contrast, hummed with construction as the nation looked to take revenge for its defeats. The French maritime ministry built magnificent vessels, while new British ships were consistently of inferior quality.

This French silver-hilted small sword, with silvered guard and knuckle bow, was the type of sword commonly used by both French and American officers during the American Revolution. Many French-made armaments, from edged-weapons to artillery, were regular-issue for American forces.

The development of the American war into a major conflict prompted the British war department to rebuild its navy, which was needed to blockade American ports and prevent munitions and supplies from reaching the revolutionary armies. British forces depended on supply lines that crossed the oceans, and these routes were protected by the Royal Navy.

The Americans on their own had no fleet capable of protecting merchant vessels or defeating British warships. The British could delay making peace and might hold on to valuable port cities such as New York, Savannah, and Charleston, which were difficult to attack from land-ward. The powerful French navy could change all that.

Q: Were all American revolutionaries immediately cooperative with the French and happy to be their allies?

A: No. After centuries of war between the British and French colonies in America, there was deep-seated hatred of the French—especially in New England, which had suffered most from the frontier bloodshed. These colonials at first believed a French alliance was far more repugnant than British rule. Early in the alliance there were clashes between French crews and New Englanders when French vessels put into port. The result was some-times riots and killings.

In time, the French alliance became appreciated, and after France had for some years based her operations at Newport, Rhode Island, relations be-tween New Englanders and the French military were quite warm.

Q: Which other countries entered the war on the American side?

A: Spain declared war on Britain in June 1779. The Spanish hoped to recover the strategic fortress at Gibraltar, which commanded the en-trance to the Mediterranean Sea. Though Britain lost the Revolutionary War, Spain never did recover Gibraltar.

In December 1780 Britain declared war on the Netherlands, which had been providing loans and shipping supplies to America.

One of the most popular Frenchmen in Revolutionary America, Anne-César, chevalier de la Luzerne, was the French minister to the United States. Headquartered in Philadelphia, Luzerne was highly effective in working with Americans, even giving advice in the draft-ing of some Congressional documents.

> "Americans may be reduced by the fleet, but never can be by the army."
> —BRITISH SECRETARY AT WAR VISCOUNT BARRINGTON

The French Commanders

Charles Willson Peale probably painted Comte de Rochambeau's portrait during the Rochambeau's visit to Philadelphia in the summer of 1782. Rochambeau wears the elegant dress of a French courtier, including the Grand Croix of the Order of St. Louis, received for his service in the Seven Years' War.

Below: An excited Washington uncharacteristically waves and hops about as Rochambeau's vessel comes into sight near Chester, Pennsylvania, in 1781. Washington is eager to report that Admiral de Grasse's fleet was in Chesapeake Bay.

Q: Who was the most important French commander during the Revolutionary War?

A: One of the best and most important was Jean-Baptiste-Donatien de Vimeur, the comte de Rochambeau, overall commander of French forces in North America. With more than seven thousand troops at his command and the French navy awaiting his summons, Rochambeau could have been haughty and arrogant. Instead, he was one of Washington's greatest admirers, and in matters of leadership he almost always deferred to Washington's wishes. One of the few instances in which Rochambeau openly disagreed with Washington was whether to make an assault on British-occupied New York in 1781.

Washington favored moving on New York with the combined armies of America and France as the French fleet took up position to blockade New York harbor. Instead, Rochambeau proposed going after Cornwallis, who had taken post at Yorktown, Virginia. Rochambeau said if the French fleet appeared off Yorktown to prevent British

Rochambeau

reinforcement or resupply, Cornwallis could be captured. Washington accepted the Frenchman's plan, and their armies hurried down to Virginia.

By the time they arrived, however, many of Washington's men were disgruntled about serving in the South, especially because they were owed back pay that they desperately wanted to send home in case they died. Washington, unfortunately, had no funds with which to pay them, and on the eve of the Yorktown siege he faced the real threat of wholesale desertion. Now Rochambeau opened his own army's war chest, full of silver and gold coin, and told Washington that half was at his disposal.

Thus did France's General Rochambeau save the American Revolution at a most crucial hour.

Q: How did French naval strategy bring on the Yorktown campaign?

A: The powerful fleet of the Admiral François-Joseph Paul, the comte de Grasse, had been operating against the British in the West Indies and escorting French convoys. De Grasse's twenty warships were convoying one hundred and fifty vessels to West Indies ports in mid-1783, when he was ordered to send half his warships back to France. Before he could obey, he received a dispatch from Rochambeau, requesting his aid for operations against either New York City or the Chesapeake Bay. De Grasse ignored the orders to break up his fleet and instead assembled thirty-four warships. In August, after borrowing three thousand troops from the Haiti garrison and raising 1.5 million livres from wealthy anti-British colonists in Havana, he sailed for the Chesapeake. This move was conveyed to Washington and Rochambeau, who marched against the unsuspecting Cornwallis.

Early in September, de Grasse made contact with the Marquis de Lafayette and began landing his troops to reinforce the American and French army organizing for the siege of Yorktown. The money contributed by the colonists in Cuba was donated to the American cause.

Q: Who won the last great naval battle of the war?

A: Despite the victory of de Grasse in the Battle of the Chesapeake Capes off Yorktown, most major naval actions went against France. Yet the French navy maintained its strength. Its tactics in combat differed sharply from those of the British, who believed in fighting ship to ship, to the bitter end. The French preferred to save their ships from damage, to shoot up the enemy's sails and rigging and so prevent pursuit, enabling themselves to sail away to capture more merchant vessels. Looting Britain's colonial trade was, from the start, the

French admiral Comte de Grasse resigns his sword to British admiral Rodney after being defeated at the Battle of the Saintes in the West Indies in April 1782. This was the last great naval action of the war and cost de Grasse five vessels, including his great flagship, the *Ville de Paris*.

object of French admirals and captains, who shared in any booty taken.

As the war drew to a close, elderly British admiral George B. Rodney defeated de Grasse in the April 1782 Battle of the Saintes in the West Indies. De Grasse himself was captured and his flagship taken. After humiliation campaigning in America, the British took some comfort from this late victory at sea, even though peace negotiations were under way.

> " Sir Samuel . . . really knows not what to say in the truly lamentable state we have brought ourselves. "
>
> —British admiral Samuel Hood
>
> *when asked for orders upon finding Yorktown blockaded by the French fleet*

The Birth of the American Navy

This period engraving portrays Rhode Island's Esek Hopkins, first commander of the Continental Navy. Hopkins's main expedition, in 1776, raided Nassau in the Bahamas, but he had no further successes and was unjustly dismissed. Congress had absurdly ordered him to drive away the Royal Navy from the Carolinas to Rhode Island.

The Continental Navy's *Lexington* was originally the brigantine *Wild Duck,* purchased by Congress and renamed in 1776. Under Irish-born John Barry, she avoided the British blockade of Delaware Bay and reached the open sea. In April the *Lexington* captured the Royal Navy sloop *Edward,* with a crew of twenty-nine. This was the Continental Navy's first capture of an enemy warship in battle.

Q: How was the first United Colonies navy established?

A: During the siege of Boston in 1775 Washington lost no time organizing a fleet of small vessels to harass British shipping. Although not officially an American navy, these craft captured thirty-five enemy supply vessels, and the booty was of great value to the impoverished American army besieging the city.

Late that year Congress authorized the construction of thirteen frigates as the cornerstone of the Continental Navy. A frigate was a relatively small, fast warship, designed to support the much larger ships of the line—major warships that would be arrayed in a line of battle. Esek Hopkins of Rhode Island, an experienced sea captain and privateer, was the first commander in chief of the Continental Navy. In March 1776, Hopkins commanded a Continental Navy squadron that set out to attack British naval positions and capture merchant vessels. Sailing under a flag emblazoned with a rattlesnake, the squadron numbered eight vessels, none carrying more than twenty-four guns. One of the squadron's lieutenants was twenty-year-old John Paul Jones.

This little fleet carried a total of 110 guns, while the Royal Navy in American waters numbered seventy-eight ships carrying more than two thousand guns. Hopkins successfully raided Nassau in the Bahamas, acquiring valuable military sup-

plies. This exploit would, however, be the only operation of the Continental Navy.

Lack of a strong central government and a shortage of funds made it impossible for the Continental Navy to build powerful warships. Furthermore, there was more profit to be made in privateering, and since many influential Americans eagerly invested in privateers in order to share the prize money, little political will existed to build a national navy instead.

Q: What is a privateer, and which was the most famous of the American privateers?

A: Privateers were privately owned commerce raiders given authorization by a government to capture enemy vessels. They were not officially part of any navy. Privateering was dangerous, but also extremely profitable. These vessels acted virtually as pirate ships, but they were

> **You may depend no public ship will ever be manned while there is a privateer fitting out.**
> —*WILLIAM WHIPPLE OF CONGRESS'S MARINE COMMITTEE*

recognized internationally as legitimate vessels of war. Congress issued licenses, termed "letters of marque and reprisal," to individuals who would then fit out an armed vessel to cruise as a privateer. When "prizes"—captured vessels and cargo—were sold, the officers and crew divided up the proceeds in proportion to their rank. This also was the custom for naval vessels that took enemy prizes.

Since America had many fast merchant vessels, privateering was an effective weapon for destroying British merchant shipping and disrupting trade. Congress and individual states authorized some two thousand vessels as privateers, which inflicted more than $18 million in British losses. The most successful privateer was the *Rattlesnake,* which cruised the Baltic and on one trip took $1 million in prizes.

Q: How effective were the first American warships?

A: A total of fifty-three warships served in the Continental Navy, and another seventy or so were fitted out by states for their own navies. By 1783, only two Continental vessels were still in action, the others having been lost or captured. The Royal Navy grew during the war from 270 ships to 468, many carrying three times the number of cannon found on the largest American frigate. Still, the British suffered heavy maritime losses. American vessels sank or captured almost two hundred British ships, while privateers accounted for six hundred more.

There were many American naval exploits to be proud of, but also disastrous defeats. In 1779 a nineteen-vessel Massachusetts navy expedition carrying three thousand militia and sailors against a British fort on the Maine coast was wiped out or captured to the last ship, costing the state $7 million.

The Revolutionary War privateer *Rattlesnake* was built in Plymouth, Massachusetts, in 1779–80 in the style of a miniature frigate. Armed with up to twenty guns, she had a complement of eighty-five men. New Englanders were considered among the world's best shipbuilders, and Yankee seamen were highly regarded. The *Rattlesnake* was captured by the British in 1781.

America's First Great Captain

Q: Who was the "Father of the American Navy"?

A: Scottish-born John Paul Jones, a Virginia resident, was a highly successful commander who attacked British commerce and occasionally fought Royal Navy warships. Jones was commissioned a Continental Navy lieutenant in 1775, earned his own command in 1776, and in one cruise that year captured sixteen prizes.

Jones's success persuaded Congress to make him a captain, and in 1777 he was ordered to Europe to take command of a frigate then being built in Amsterdam for the Continental Navy. When Jones arrived, however, he found the American commissioners to Paris had given the warship to France in return for military aid and loans received. In April 1778 Jones set off from the French port of Brest with his sloop, *Ranger*, to raid the Scottish coast. In this expedition he defeated and captured a British sloop and took seven prizes and many prisoners.

This daring adventure caused much worry along the British coast, which already was anxious about a combined French and Spanish invasion. Jones rose further in repute, and France publicly honored him.

John Paul Jones may have sat for this portrait by Charles Willson Peale in 1781. Jones would have recently returned from France, after being awarded the French Cross of the Institution of Military Merit. Jones lived in France after the Revolution, where he was regarded as a dashing, romantic character.

John Paul Jones

Q: How did John Paul Jones win his greatest fame as a naval commander?

A: After the summer of 1778, with France now an American ally, the French navy fitted out a fleet of seven vessels for Jones. He named his flagship *Bonhomme Richard*, in honor of Franklin's famous *Poor Richard's Almanac*.

When Jones put out to sea in August 1779, most of his officers were Frenchmen, many of whom resented being under Jones and flying the American flag. He sailed around the British Isles, capturing seventeen prizes and threatening seaports. That September, Jones took on the *Serapis*, a Royal Navy warship of forty-four guns. The *Bonhomme Richard* was so badly shot up that it lost its flag, causing the *Serapis* commander to ask whether Jones was surrendering.

"I have not yet begun to fight!" Jones is said to have answered, and after two more ferocious hours of battle in bright moonlight, the *Serapis* gave up.

An infuriated King George declared Jones a pirate, but America and France lauded him as the first naval hero of the young United States. Although jealous older naval officers blocked Jones's promotion to admiral when he returned

> **Why don't you haul down your pendant?**
> —SERAPIS OFFICER TO JOHN PAUL JONES

Left: As the crippled *Bonhomme Richard* began to sink, Jones ordered a boarding party onto the *Serapis*, defeating the British crew in hand-to-hand combat and taking over the ship.

Right: The *Bonhomme Richard* and the HMS *Serapis* were lashed together for most their thunderous battle.

to America in February 1781, he did receive command of the *America*, then under construction at Newport, Rhode Island. This vessel would be the largest ship in the Continental Navy, carrying seventy-six guns. Once again, however, it was turned over to France instead.

Jones finished his American naval career serving with a French fleet in the West Indies.

Q: Did Jones retire in the United States, his adopted homeland?

A: No. The Continental Navy was disbanded after the war because it required too great an expense for the government. Jones was authorized to go to Europe to collect money owed him as his share of the sale of the prizes he had taken. When he returned to America in 1787, Congress awarded him the only gold medal given to a naval officer. Eager to return to sea as a naval commander, Jones soon left for Russia and served in her navy, winning honors against the Turks. Again he was faced with jealous superiors who undermined him, although he received the Order of St. Anne for his service to the empire.

Jones left Russia in 1789 and moved to Paris, where he died in 1792, at the age of forty-seven.

In 1899 his long-forgotten grave was located, and in 1905 his remains were brought to America by naval squadron. Jones was interred at the United States Naval Academy at Annapolis.

> ❝ Aye, aye, we'll do that when we can fight no longer, but . . . Yankees do not haul down their colours till they are fairly beaten. ❞
> —*JONES, AS QUOTED BY AMERICAN MIDSHIPMAN NATHANIEL FANNING*

Marines and Navies

Q: When was the United States Marine Corps established?

A: In November 1775, just after Congress had authorized the building of the Continental Navy, two battalions of Continental Marines were authorized to serve aboard the ships. Marines acted as shipboard military police who would also defend a vessel and take part in amphibious assaults. In 1740, American provincial marines fought in the West Indies, and American marines served on privateers in the French and Indian War.

At the start of the Revolutionary War several state navies organized their own marines. Eight Connecticut marines participated in the capture of Fort Ticonderoga in 1775. These men are known to the United States Marine Corps as the "Original Eight."

About two hundred marines under Captain Samuel Nicholas led the 1776 raid that captured Nassau in the Bahamas, and marines attacked that port again in 1778. The 1776 raid—the first amphibious action for American marines as a unit—captured Fort Montagu and more than one hundred artillery pieces. This ordnance was desperately needed by Washington, who was fortifying New York City. The raid even captured the British governor of the Bahamas.

The first recorded detachment of Continental Marines was the seventeen men who served aboard the Continental Navy frigate *Enterprise*, beginning in May 1775. These were Massachusetts men who also took part in the 1776 battle at Valcour Island, where an improvised American fleet opposed the British advance over Lake Champlain. Marines served in Washington's 1776–77 campaigns and participated in Hudson Valley and coastal actions in New England and the South. Marines also were on western waters, some with George Rogers Clark's expeditions. A marine company was with Clark as late as fall 1782.

Virtually every American naval battle on the high seas involved marines, who served with the Continental Navy, state navies, and privateers—including with John Paul Jones, when he landed on the British coast in a daring raid.

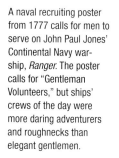

A naval recruiting poster from 1777 calls for men to serve on John Paul Jones' Continental Navy warship, *Ranger.* The poster calls for "Gentleman Volunteers," but ships' crews of the day were more daring adventurers and roughnecks than elegant gentlemen.

Q: When was the first time the "Stars and Stripes" flew over a captured foreign fortress?

A: On January 27, 1778, marines and sailors from the Continental Navy sloop *Providence* landed at Nassau and took the fortifications without the loss of a man. The Stars and Stripes were raised at Nassau. Led by the sloop's captain, John P. Rathbun of Rhode Island, the expedition held the city for three days, liberating thirty American prisoners and capturing four vessels and military supplies. Rathbun went on to considerable personal success as a naval commander, in one cruise joining two other vessels in the capture of eleven rich prizes.

Q: How important were the state navies during the Revolutionary War?

A: Eleven former colonies had volunteer navies organized similarly to their militia establishments—that is, the seamen could be called up in time of emergencies. State navies had many of the same shortcomings in war as did the militias: Independent-minded officers often chose to go their own ways rather than be commanded by men from other state navies, and there was a chronic shortage of war matériel.

The state navies served their own governments, patrolling rivers and harbors and fighting off enemy privateers. This meant they were not available to support the Continental Navy and drew away naval resources that might have been concentrated under a central control. Still, state navies often served the revolutionary cause well. Connecticut's navy, for example, carried sulfur from the West Indies with which to manufacture gunpowder. Two substantial state navies—those of South Carolina and Virginia—were destroyed or lost as a result of British operations in their states.

The Continental and state navies were so weak by 1782 that Philadelphia merchants fitted out the sixteen-gun *Hyder Ally* to protect their vessels in the Chesapeake Bay and Delaware River. The *Hyder Ally's* captain, Joshua Barney, was one of the most active revolutionary sailors. Though just in his early twenties, Barney was captured three times by the British. He was exchanged twice and escaped once.

Charles Willson Peale painted this portrait of Pennsylvania captain Joshua Barney in 1784, during one of Barney's visits to Philadelphia. Barney is just twenty-five years old, handsomely dressed in his captain's uniform.

The boarding axe was an effective and lethal weapon in close combat, but it was more important as a tool to clear the decks of downed lines, hot shot, and timbers shattered by cannon fire.

CHAPTER 9

THE HOME FRONT AND BEHIND THE LINES

Congress had difficulty supplying the army, and foreign assistance was needed to keep troops in the field. Life was hard for the impoverished soldiers, but back home matters were often worse for their families. Many communities were deeply divided, as old animosities spawned violence and pillaging that tormented the weak and drove many away.

In southern New York, the revolutionary government called upon everyone to swear an oath of allegiance, but one-third of the residents flatly refused. This region was a no-man's-land plagued by robbers and fought over by American militia and British raiders. Patriot militias tried to prevent farmers and merchants from trading with the British, who paid with precious hard cash while Americans gave almost-worthless paper money. Despite the risk of harsh punishment, this "London trade" continued throughout the war. Propaganda from both sides tried to persuade soldiers to desert and turn their coats, and spies seemed to be everywhere.

Rebecca Motte, center, offers arrows to Patriot commanders Francis Marion, left, and Henry Lee, urging that they set them aflame to set fire to her home on South Carolina's Congaree River and drive out British soldiers occupying the place. Members of her household look on.

America's First Civil War

Q: Why did virtually all major combat in the Northeast stop after 1779?

A: As the British applied their military resources to the worldwide war with France and Spain, too few troops were available for the war in America. The Royal Navy abandoned its base at Newport, allowing the French to move in there. It became impossible to mount a major invasion of New England or New York State, where there were strong militias. The center of British military power in America was New York City, but other than a few thrusts up the Hudson and into north Jersey, commanding general Clinton did not have enough troops to take and hold territory.

Although major conflict had ended in the Northeast, continuous trouble and small-scale fighting persisted around New York City, mostly between Patriot and Loyalist militias, with occasional forays of regulars from the British lines.

By now British hopes of retaining American cities and land depended on campaigns in the South, which got under way in late 1778 with the capture of Savannah. After several promising victories, however, British operations in the South were just small-scale expeditions to rally Loyalists to the king's standard. Loyalist uprisings seldom amounted to much because revolutionary forces quickly mustered to defeat them.

After Cornwallis was captured at Yorktown in 1781, British hopes of holding on to any part of the former thirteen colonies were almost gone.

Q: What was the most important meeting place in most communities?

A: Even the smallest crossroads hamlet usually had at least one tavern or inn, known as a "public house." These had one large room that served as a meeting place, whether for scheduled gatherings to discuss public matters and community business, or for friends to drink and eat and read scarce copies of newspapers.

Large cities had coffeehouses, which were often hotbeds of political discourse and argument, where ideas were exchanged and debated. Even more interesting than the local newspaper were publications from Britain or perhaps from territory that was currently occupied by the enemy.

Philadelphia's handsome City Tavern was just a year old when John Adams arrived in August 1774 for the First Continental Congress. Greeted by leading citizens, Adams was immediately taken to the tavern, which he would later describe as "the most genteel" in America. City Tavern was a favorite of the delegates to Congress and also popular with British officers during their brief 1777–78 occupation.

A cup of strong coffee and a clay pipe comforted many an American public house patron scouring periodicals for information about the war, perhaps about his abandoned home, or about the latest shipping arrivals and departures. News was hungrily devoured, even if it had arrived after a months-long ocean voyage.

Often there was espionage in public houses, where agents of Congress and king listened to conversations, clandestinely met with co-conspirators, and tried to determine who else in the room was spying for the other side.

Q: What did the British public think about the War for American Independence?

A: The British at first were unwilling to enlist to fight the Americans, who were considered family living in the provinces. There was little patriotic inspiration to make war against other British subjects. Even important senior British commanders refused to serve against the Americans. Lord Jeffrey Amherst, who had been commander in chief during the French and Indian War, resigned rather than serve against the Americans.

Of the 2.35 million British males of military age, only thirty thousand fought in the Revolutionary War. By contrast, more than three hundred thousand had served against France in the Seven Years' War.

The dismaying defeat of Burgoyne in 1777 improved recruiting, which was further stimulated by France's entry into the war. Still, there never were enough British recruits needed for the American war, not even when paupers were forced to serve and prisoners were released if they agreed to enlist.

> War's rude alarms disturbed
>   last year;
>   Our country bled and wept
>   around us;
> But this each honest heart shall
>   cheer,
>   And peace and plenty shall
>   surround us.
>
> —*From "The Old Year and the New: A Prophecy," written at New Year's 1779–80 by Loyalist poet Jonathan Odell*

Top: This long-stemmed English clay pipe was a comfortable companion to patrons of America's public houses and inns. Customers could rent a pipe from the innkeeper's rack, cutting off the stem's end for a fresh start.

Above: This wartime English print satirizes Prime Minister Lord North and another government minister, who are experiencing a vision of the atrocities committed against America. Corruption holds a cup of poison from which Britannia has drunk; a figure with mutilated breast and wearing a feathered headdress represents America.

Home Fires and Bounties

Q: How difficult was life for families of American soldiers who were away at war?

A: For average families who depended on a male to work the land or carry on a trade such as blacksmithing or tailoring, the absence of menfolk was a great hardship. Soldiers were gone much of the year, although many were allowed furloughs in winter, so that the army would not have to feed and shelter them.

The American soldier had little to give to his family in the way of money, because Congress was always behind in payments and often did not pay at all. Most officers financed their service by taking loans, and many went deeply into debt that cost them their homes and possessions. Congress's promise to pay its troops in full was not met until long after the war. The folk at home had to fend for themselves, and life could be

This weathered, handsomely uniformed private of the Third New York line regiment was on the lowest rung of the Continental army, receiving scant rations and seldom paid. Yet such soldiers were the heart and soul of the Revolutionary War. This regiment was stationed at Fort Stanwix and gallantly repulsed a siege during Burgoyne's 1777 campaign.

extremely hard and hungry.

Most American overseas trade had been cut off by the British blockade, and goods and foodstuffs that had been common in the colonies became scarce in the newly independent states. During the war it was difficult to find molasses and indigo from the Caribbean, tea and rice from the Far East, and manufactured goods from Europe. Yet even if those wares had been available, few Americans could have afforded them during the war.

Q: How were American soldiers paid?

A: Soldiers were promised a flat sum, or bounty, for joining up, and they were supposed to receive regular wages while in service. They were required to pay out of their wages for rations, uniforms, and equipment.

Once the early fervor of rebellion was dulled by the hard reality of military service, there were few volunteers for the Continental Army. To raise troops, Congress increased the cash bounty and promised a future land grant of a hundred or a hundred and fifty acres. Early in 1776, Congress paid a bounty of $6.66 to short-term enlistees who had firearms, a bayonet, and other gear. That bounty soon was raised to $10 for men who enlisted for three years. By late that year a bounty of $20 and a hundred acres was promised to those who served for the entire war.

Bounties steadily increased as recruitment became more difficult. By 1777 state regiments were offering close to

This 1789 print shows a sawmill belonging to Loyalist Philip Skene and the blockhouse at Fort Anne on the northern New York frontier. Both were burned by American forces retreating before the advance of the British army under Burgoyne. The loss of such an important sawmill was a blow to any owner, but even more so on the sparsely settled frontier, where rebuilding war-devastated communities and farms required milled lumber.

$100 for a recruit, thus limiting potential enlistment in the Continental regiments, which offered smaller bounties. By 1779, Congress increased bounties to $200, but states offered $250 and land. By 1780, New Jersey was offering a bounty of $1,000 to enlistees, a sum higher than Continental officers were paid.

Rations, too, were considered pay. Enlisted men received one ration—three meals a day—and officers were entitled to more. Captains and majors received one and a half rations, lieutenant colonels received two rations, a brigadier general received four, and a major general five. In the case of an officer being accompanied by members of his family, the extra rations were a worthwhile payment. It was seldom, however, that the army had enough supplies for its scale of rations to be met.

Firewood, too, was issued to officers and men according to the rationing system, as were candles, spruce beer, and soap.

Q: Where was it dangerous for civilians during the war?

A: The most difficult home life was in regions where Patriot and Loyalist militias were raiding and counterraiding. Homes and villages were pillaged and burned, males killed or captured, and families were left homeless and destitute. The worst of this was in the Carolinas and around besieged New York City.

> **I hope your Honour will Pardon me for not writing to your Honour before this it is owing to me being full of Business and my familie so distressed by the Burning of my house Barn and all my effects by the Enemie.**
>
> —JOHN MAURITSIUS
> *Goetschius, New Jersey, militia officer to Washington in 1780*

Neutral Ground

Q: Which state was the "Crossroads of the Revolutionary War"?

A: New Jersey, located between British-held New York City and the revolutionary capital, Philadelphia, had that unlucky distinction, as armies crossed and re-crossed the state in many campaigns. New Jersey was also known as the "cockpit of the Revolution" for the thousands of battles, raids, skirmishes, and ambushes that took place there. In 1776, Washington retreated through New Jersey after his defeat in New York. After his 1777 victories at Trenton and Princeton, he made Morristown his main base to watch the British in New York and Staten Island. The next state with the most engagements was South Carolina.

The New Jersey militia were effective in helping maintain the siege of New York. At first, New Jersey had many war opponents, termed "disaffected." Then, when British and German troops pillaged, looted, and raped their way across the state as they chased Washington, many furious residents became revolutionaries. The militia rose against the British, who found themselves unable to move in the state to forage or even purchase food. They could venture out only in large numbers—and even then they were attacked.

This map was drawn from a 1769 survey made of the "Province of New Jersey," which was divided into East Jersey and West Jersey and commonly called the Jerseys. Published in London in 1777, it shows the region around New York known as the "Neutral Ground."

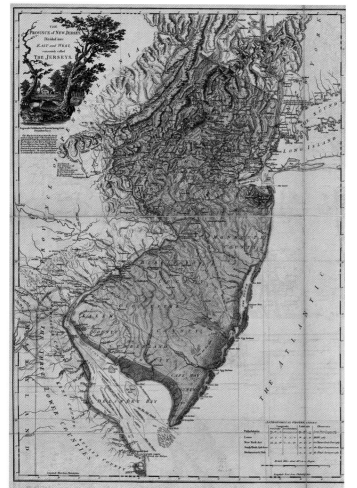

Q: What was the "Neutral Ground"?

A: The region from southern New York, along the lower Hudson River, and across to Sandy Hook on the Jersey coast was called the Neutral Ground. This once-prosperous region was not controlled by either army. The Americans could not prevent all raids by British and Loyalist forces from New York City, and the British were unable to occupy this region permanently.

The British needed the crops and cattle that were raised here, but the inhabitants were warned by Patriots not to sell to the occupying forces. Collaborators suffered punishment by the revolutionaries. When royal forces could not purchase foodstuffs from the Westchester or New Jersey markets, they attacked and pillaged and drove off what they could. Such raids stirred up the local militia, however, and foraging parties were in danger. As the war dragged on, foragers had to number in the hundreds and even thousands if they expected to get back to the city alive.

The civil strife was most severe in Bergen County, New Jersey, where it was intensified by longstanding bitter hatreds. For decades the inhabitants had been at odds because of religious differences that split the mostly Dutch Protestant churches. When the Revolutionary War began, these prevailing divisions shaped the Loyalist and Patriot camps and fostered an ever-worsening spiral of attack and counterattack. Imprisonment, murders, executions, and destruction of property instilled hatred that endured for decades afterward. This spiteful and brutal conflict forced many Loyalists into New York City, while those who remained in their communities were ever in danger of surprise attack.

350

Q: Who were the "Cowboys" and "Skinners"?

A: These were criminal bands that mercilessly preyed on civilians and sometimes ambushed small military units. Making the strife around New York City

even worse, these robbers sometimes pretended to be authorized military units as they preyed on the helpless. They took advantage of the absence of male family members, looting farms and attacking womenfolk. New York's Westchester and Dutchess counties suffered greatly from Cowboys and Skinners who stole crops, horses, and cattle to sell to New York.

This volatile combination of militia patrols looking for Loyalists, of Loyalist and British raiders foraying out from the city, and of opportunistic brigands rustling, ambushing, and murdering caused Neutral Ground families deep despair. Trouble persisted even as military campaigns were moving south by 1779.

British troops plunder a home during a foraging operation; foodstuffs, livestock, and fodder were what the army was after, but soldiers often took the opportunity to steal. In many cases, especially in northern Virginia late in the war, the British were vindictively destructive, laying waste to almost every farm or hamlet where they stopped to rest or forage.

> **What can you not achieve with such small bands who have learned to fight dispersed . . . and who retreat as quickly when attacked as they advance again . . . Never have I seen these maneuvers performed better than by the American Militia, and especially that of the Province of New Jersey.**
>
> —*Hessian officer Johann Ewald, memoirs*

Women Endure the War

Q: **What particular burdens did women have to bear?**

A: Countrywomen whose men were in the army or imprisoned had an especially difficult time. Not only did they have to raise their children without the fathers and older brothers, but they had to work longer hours planting, tilling, and harvesting. Then crops had to be sold or traded, and this duty, too, fell to the women. Often they were at risk of thievery from military foragers or roving brigands.

In the worst situations, when there was no money or the soldier's pay in continentals was refused by merchants, families suffered from hunger. One mob of a thousand women rioted and stormed their town's shops when a church turned down their desperate request for bread.

Illness, too, had to be dealt with, whether it was children or the elderly who became sick. If the mother fell ill, young children were sometimes the only ones to tend her. Communities pulled together, but families on lonely farms were far from help in times of crisis.

In 1781 Rebecca Motte of South Carolina and her children were forced from their handsome home by British soldiers, who took over the estate for quarters. When guerrilla leader Francis Marion attacked the place, Rebecca urged him to burn the enemy out. Even though it was her own home, she provided the fire arrows to destroy it.

This early twentieth-century painting, "Mrs. Murray's Strategy," illustrates a popular legend of questionable authenticity, which says the 1776 British invasion of Manhattan was delayed when General Henry Clinton dallied "quaffing wine" with Mrs. Robert Murray. For one thing, Mrs. Murray was a respected Quaker lady with twelve children, and for another Clinton was too good a field commander to be so irresponsible.

If it were a palace, it should go.

—SOUTH CAROLINA'S REBECCA MOTTE

proud of burning down her own home to evict enemy soldiers

During Burgoyne's 1777 Saratoga campaign, the British took the ripe crops from the bountiful fields of the upper Hudson River. Their foragers moved toward the mansion and farm of Patriot general Philip Schuyler, whose wife, Catherine, had stayed behind while he campaigned. Rather than allow the enemy to take the crops, Catherine called on her workers and servants to help her set fire to the fields. The furious British retaliated by burning down the mansion.

Q: What foodstuffs were the hardest to find?

A: The scarcity of sugar and coffee was especially galling—particularly to those who could afford them. And when such items were available, they were priced infuriatingly high. In 1777 one wealthy Boston merchant hid his sugar and coffee, refusing to sell until the price was even more outrageous. For several weeks in the summer Bostonians complained publicly about this practice, to no avail. Then a hundred angry women gathered in a shopping district to protest. Some had carts and hand trucks for carrying away the goods they were after. The subsequent riot was known as the Boston Coffee Party. As their men looked on in amazement, the women pushed their way into shops, forcing open some that were closed, and insisted sugar and coffee be sold.

The stingiest merchant still refused, so the women seized him by the neck and threw him into a handcart, demanding the keys to his warehouse. Frightened, he surrendered the keys, and the women flipped him out of the cart. Coffee and sugar were soon loaded in and taken away for sale to the public.

Q: How large were the groups of camp followers who accompanied Washington's army?

A: This depended on the size of his army, which ranged from a few thousand to seventeen thousand. One mob of American camp followers numbered more than twenty thousand, many of them miserably poor. These included soldiers' families as well as merchants and tradesmen who did business with the army. Washington often required the unruly camp followers to take a route different from that of the army in order not to disturb local inhabitants. Farms and towns, no matter their allegiance, often were robbed by camp followers.

Above: A typical British army camp follower of the Revolutionary War period, depicted by artist Don Troiani, carries an all-purpose basket and wears flowing skirt and aprons, a straw hat over her mobcap, and sturdy shoes.

Left: This woman's etui, or case, from Guilford Court House, North Carolina, contains tools for daily use: scissors, pencil, fork, knife, corkscrew, bodkin, tweezers, ear pick, and an ivory writing board. The case is about four inches long.

The Problems of Finance

Q: Other than fighting the enemy, what was the greatest difficulty faced by American revolutionaries?

A: The most enduring problem was financing the war, which included feeding, equipping, and sheltering the troops and fitting out naval vessels.

Although there were many wealthy speculators willing to invest money in a privateer in the hope of future gain, few Americans were willing to loan Congress the funds or extend it the credit necessary to pay the immense sums required to carry out the war. French financial backing was crucial, and a few individual Americans with connections to European private wealth could arrange credit for Congress. One of these was Haym Salomon, a Polish Jew who had immigrated to New York in 1772.

Salomon was successful in finance and speculation, and his reputation was high in Manhattan, where he remained after the British began their occupation in 1776. Suspected as a spy for Washington, Salomon was arrested and sentenced to death. He escaped and fled to Philadelphia, where he resumed his brokerage business. There he became a reliable source of credit to Congress and also to its individual members, including Jefferson and James Madison. The trusted Salomon was the intermediary for Dutch and French funds and letters of credit for

Congress and in support of French forces in America.

Q: Who was the most important administrative figure managing American finances during the war?

A: The key financial officer of the United Colonies was the English-born Robert Morris of Pennsylvania, Congress's superintendent of finance. More than any other official, Morris labored mightily to negotiate loans, acquire hard money, and provide for Washington's war chest. These feats were not always possible, however, and troops often went hungry before the entry of France into the war.

A delegate to Congress until 1779, Morris was appointed superintendent of finances in 1781—he was nominated by Alexander Hamilton—and began to earn the title "Financier of the Revolution." Morris battled against the financially irresponsible behavior of Congress and also established the Bank of North America to back the revolutionary cause. As a real bank, it accepted cash deposits, and Morris asked wealthy individuals to contribute. He himself was a leading depositor. Also, he arranged for the bank to serve as middleman for the sale of goods and agricultural products that state governments were desperate to market for hard cash.

Polish-born Jewish financier Haym Salomon was the broker for desperately needed European loans to the Continental Congress. When Solomon died in 1785, he left a wife and four young children with debts larger than the value of his estate. When the family petitioned to recover funds owed by the government, Congress refused to recognize the claims. Solomon's brother-in-law, Colonel Isaac Franks, served on Washington's staff.

Haym Salomon

Robert Morris

the war after 1782.

After the war, Morris built a financial empire, but he became overextended and it collapsed. He was in debtors' prison from 1798 to 1801 and died in poverty in 1806, virtually forgotten by the country he had been instrumental in creating.

Q: **Which foreigners were prime lenders to Congress?**

A: The French and Spanish governments and private Dutch bankers were the leading lenders, providing more than $7.83 million to finance the American struggle.

Left: British artist Robert Edge Pine painted this portrait of the banker and financier Robert Morris, in the mid-1780s. Without Morris's efforts to raise funds and put Congress on a solid financial footing, the war might have ended in America's defeat for lack of a functioning monetary system.

Below: This 1758 Spanish gold coin was typical of the various types of "hard money" circulating in the American colonies at the time of the Revolutionary War. Cash was in such short supply, with not enough in circulation to accommodate the booming commerce of the Americas, that coins often were cut into quarters and eighths.

These arrangements, however, produced little in the way of "specie," meaning gold or silver coin. That was temporarily resolved by the $200,000 in specie given by the French in 1781 and deposited in the Bank of North America. Morris and his bank were now in business, but matters still required him at times to use his own personal credit to finance the war. A major Dutch loan arranged by John Adams was crucial to prosecuting

“ **Goods are 200 per cent dearer than they were in Virginia when I left it. I was obliged to buy a hat . . . and paid 18 dollars for one of an inferior kind.** ”

—*JOSEPH EGGLESTON JR.*
writing home from Philadelphia in 1777

Poverty and Inspiration

Q: What is the meaning of the phrase "Not worth a continental"?

A: A key difficulty in paying troops was that the Continental dollar issued by Congress was almost worthless. In 1775 Congress had approved the issue of $2 million in bills of credit to pay for the war. Since Congress had no taxing authority, the Continental dollar had no real backing. By 1779, it had dropped 75 percent in face value. If a merchant were willing to sell, a pair of shoes cost twenty-five dollars that year, and fishhooks were fifty cents apiece. In 1780, Bostonians had to pay ten dollars for a pound of beef. Continental currency did the soldier little good, for shopkeepers declined to accept it. The British and German troops, on the other hand, were paid in hard cash, so their money was eagerly accepted.

The complaint "Not worth a continental" came into use when referring to something that was of no value.

To make things worse, British and Americans both printed counterfeit continentals, further diminishing their worth. Congress tried to force acceptance of the continental at face value but was unsuccessful, and in early 1781 the currency collapsed completely. Only hard cash was accepted from then on.

Q: Where did hard cash come from?

A: Since there was not enough specie available to meet the needs of buying and selling in America, the inhabitants turned to the use of foreign coins, including those of Holland and Spain. These coins were sometimes cut into pieces, enabling more cash to be in circulation. The gold Spanish dollar was cut into eight pie-shaped pieces— "pieces of eight."

Q: Was Continental paper currency ever redeemed after the war?

A: Yes, but for very little. In 1790 Congress agreed to accept the old Continental money—also nicknamed "shinplasters," since they were useless for anything better—at a rate of one hundred to one, redeemable in United States bonds. Some ambitious men then wandered throughout the country buying up continentals at a price even lower than the government's redemption rate. Later, these dollars were redeemed for a handsome profit.

The thirty-dollar note was the highest denomination issued during the first three years of Continental currency. There were also three-, four-, six-, and eight-dollar bills, bills worth fractions of a dollar, and the one-dollar coin, shown here. The first dollar coins were minted in pewter, because there was not enough silver available to Congress. Paper bills typically split in half and were often sewn back together.

Q: What was "Firecake"?

A: Hungry, penniless soldiers who found themselves on the road without cooking utensils and short of rations often made firecake from a flour-and-water batter poured onto hot stones. Firecake would be eaten with the hands, or a knife, or a piece of wood fashioned into a utensil.

Q: What was the most inspiring American song of the Revolutionary War?

A: "Chester," a solemn hymn written in 1778 by William Billings, became one of the most widely sung patriotic songs of the war. Billings, a New England music master, had composed a book of psalms for religious singing, but his "Chester" was more warlike than reverent. The war-weary American spirit was sure to triumph, championed by New England's deity.

Let tyrants shake their iron rod,
  And slavery clank her galling chains;
We fear them not, we trust in God—
  New England's God for ever reigns.

Howe and Burgoyne, and Clinton, too,
  With Prescott and Cornwallis joined;
Together plot our overthrow,
  In one infernal league combined.

When God inspired us for the fight,
  Their ranks were broke, their lines were forced;
Their ships were shattered in our sight,
  Or swiftly driven from our coast.

Although "Yankee Doodle" was the American anthem of revolution, "Chester" was the solemn hymn to invoke a martial spirit. Sung in camps, on the march, and at home, "Chester" inspired Americans in need of faith that victory would be theirs, no matter how difficult and dark the struggle.

Firecake would have been welcome fare to the thousands of hungry Continental soldiers who suffered through the starving time at Valley Forge in the winter of 1777–78. For part of the winter many troops had little shelter, but the American supply department was overhauled and the men were better fed and housed by spring.

❝ I do not like your rebel money!❞
—*COMPLAINT OF A TAVERN KEEPER JUST BEFORE WASHINGTON ORDERED HIM ARRESTED FOR REFUSING TO ACCEPT CONTINENTALS*

The Loyalists' War

Q: Which famous Patriot leader's son was a high-ranking Loyalist?

A: Benjamin Franklin. His illegitimate son William Franklin, who had been his close associate in colonial political affairs and scientific experimentation, became governor of New Jersey in 1763. Will Franklin supported the Loyalist cause at the outbreak of hostilities, alienating him from his father. The elder Franklin called his duty-bound son "a thorough government man."

The governor was arrested in mid-1776 and incarcerated in infamous Connecticut prisons, where he was badly treated. Exchanged in October 1778, Franklin went to New York City, where he became a leader of Loyalists. In 1782 he left for England, giving up his extensive estates and personal wealth for a life in exile. His natural son, William Temple Franklin, served as secretary to his grandfather and eventually edited Benjamin Franklin's writings.

Q: Which Americans were strongest in Loyalist sympathies?

A: Generally the most influential Loyalists came from the major cities, where the prosperous classes wanted no part of a revolution against the government. One group that particularly remained loyal was the Anglican clergy and their leading parishioners; another was, naturally, made up of crown officials. Other groups of Loyalists came from minorities—social, religious, or cultural—that objected to oppression from the dominant group in their regions. This was the situation along the southern backcountry, where former Scottish rebels remained loyal because of longstanding conflict with neighbors. There was even a regiment raised among devoted Loyalists from Jamaica, who served around New York.

Too often British strategy anticipated

This pre–Revolutionary War panorama of waterfronts and quays is titled "An exact prospect of Charlestown: the metropolis of the province of South Carolina." The port city's fall to Clinton in May 1780 gave Loyalists in the region hopes of rallying.

> **My heart warms up when our country is the subject.**
>
> —*Exiled Loyalist Peter van Schaack*
> *writing to longtime friend John Jay from London in 1782*

an uprising of Loyalists when the army came through. This seldom happened, and when it did the uprising was not strong enough to make a difference in the war. Attempting to defend Loyalist communities often forced the British to spread their troops too thinly, especially in the South. This led to defeats that made the Loyalists even more reluctant to take up arms for the king.

Loyalists fled to cities in British control, such as New York and Charleston. Of the fifty thousand Loyalists who fought for the British, fifteen thousand enlisted in the regular army. When the British evacuated New York City in 1783, they took with them seven thousand Loyalists. It is estimated that as many as one hundred thousand Loyalists left during the war, most for Canada, some to Britain. In Canada they became a cornerstone for building the country. They lost most of their possessions in this exodus, but some were compensated by the British government, which by 1790 had paid out almost 3.3 million pounds sterling.

Q: Who wrote the only major history of the Revolution from the Loyalist point of view?

A: New Yorker Thomas Jones, a Yale graduate, attorney, and a highly respected judge before the war, wrote the two-volume *History of New York During the Revolutionary War,* which was not published until 1879. In mid-1776, Jones was harassed by Patriot gangs who arrested and imprisoned him for six months. Released, he went home and over the following three years compiled the history, until again arrested. After being exchanged for a captured Patriot general who had been his friend, Jones went into exile in England.

For years after the American War of Independence, stories about the conflict were told, often by Americans who had suffered profoundly. Each side had a prejudiced view of what had happened. From the victorious Patriot point of view, Loyalists and lobsterbacks were painted as vandals and cowards, while Patriots were valorous and high-minded. Except for the work of Thomas Jones, the Loyalist perspective was buried with defeat. The best histories, however, reveal the conflict as a painful civil war.

Left: Rangers from Leake's, Jessup's or Peter's corps of Loyalists would have worn uniforms much like this, ideal for campaigning in the back country. Their high leggings, short coat, and broad-brimmed hat were practical accoutrements and at the same time were worn with pride, the recognized uniforms of effective scouts and skilled riflemen.

Above: Loyalist historian and former prominent New York judge Thomas Jones was pictured on the frontispiece of the first volume of his *History of New York During the Revolutionary War,* published in 1879. Jones died in 1792, in his early sixties.

" Be assured that John Jay did not cease to be a friend to Peter Van Schaak. "

—*JAY*

from Paris, to Van Schaack in 1782

Misfortunes of War

Q: How were prisoners treated?

A: Both sides generally treated prisoners badly, and capture meant almost certain death unless the prisoner was exchanged. Captives were taken on the battlefield and also dragged from their homes, accused of favoring the other side. Loyalists were thrown in chains into Connecticut copper mines, which the inmates named "Hell." Thousands of Patriot prisoners were confined to rotting prison ships tied up in New York harbor, where they were mistreated and left to die. In charge of the New York prisoners was William Cunningham, provost marshal and one of the war's most brutal characters.

Previously, Cunningham had charge of wounded Americans captured in the Breed's Hill fortifications, and he cruelly left them in a Boston jail, untended and unfed for days. Many died of their wounds or illness, and of those who had limbs amputated, none survived. During his notorious career, Cunningham is said to have starved two thousand prisoners to death and hanged two hundred and fifty more without trial.

Q: How were the captured troops exchanged?

A: Fortunate prisoners were released if they gave their promise—their parole—not to fight again until an enemy captive was exchanged for them. Usually, exchanges were of one equal rank for another—a general for a general, a major for a major, and so on. In 1779 an exchange rate was agreed upon. One sergeant was worth 2 privates, for example, an ensign was worth 4, a major 28, a colonel 100, and a lieutenant general 1,044.

Yet exchanges usually involved only officers because enlisted men were kept in such terrible prison conditions that they were half dead. Useless as fighting men, they were not exchanged.

Q: How important a factor was desertion from the Revolutionary War armies?

A: Desertion was a problem for George Washington from the start. Early in the 1775–76 siege of Boston, soldiers and officers freely came and went from

The interior of the *Jersey*, a rotting British prison ship, was illustrated in an 1855 book along with the caption: "I found myself in a loathsome prison . . . inhaling an impure atmosphere, exposed to contagion, and surrounded with the horrors of sickness and death. Here, thought I, must I linger out the morning of my life in tedious days and sleepless nights . . . until death shall put an end to my sufferings, and no friend will know of my departure."

Washington's lines. As he tightened up discipline—punishable by execution or at least severe lashings—desertions diminished, but thousands of men went home after the disaster at Long Island and New York in 1776.

Some of his commanders called for the beheading of captured deserters, but Washington opposed it. Still, in 1778 three captured deserters were forced by the officer who caught them to draw lots, and the loser was beheaded. His companions were forced to carry his head, on a pole, back to their regiment. Washington wrote the officer to say he regretted such a severe step, which gave "an appearance of inhumanity."

The recruits who joined the army were often young men looking for adventure or just glad to get off the farm. When they came to realize the difficulties of soldiering, they sometimes went home—especially during the winter. Others deserted and took the "king's shilling"—enlisting with the enemy. In 1778 the British boasted that three thousand former rebels joined them during the first five months of the year.

Desertions could also injure the British cause, and early in the war Jefferson and Franklin worked to encourage German mercenaries to quit their regiments and settle in America. Franklin fabricated a letter purportedly from a German prince who complained that too many of his wounded mercenaries were being kept alive. He preferred they should die because the British remunerated him more for dead soldiers than for wounded. This propaganda was said to have persuaded many German troops in America to desert.

German desertions numbered several thousand, but most were prisoners who escaped captivity. German mass desertion occurred when prisoners taken at Saratoga were allowed to escape while being marched through Pennsylvania. The German families in that region welcomed the fugitives and gave them shelter. The American government was pleased to be rid of the cost of their imprisonment.

Oath of allegiance certificate for John Mathias, 1778: Every officer was required to subscribe to the oath of allegiance to the independent United States. These oaths were administered by the commander in chief, major generals, or brigadier generals.

"You will . . . have the body buried lest it fall into the enemy's hands."

—*WASHINGTON*

worried that the corpse of a beheaded deserter would serve British propaganda

Spies and Spymasters

Q: Who was America's leading "spy-master" during the Revolutionary War?

A: George Washington was a spymaster who directed a number of secret agents in the New York City area, where he needed to know British plans in case a surprise expedition moved against his forces. Washington had a network of spies in the city and on Long Island during the course of the war, one of whom was Nathan Hale, caught and executed in 1776.

Q: Why do we not hear much about Washington's spies?

A: The story of Revolutionary War espionage has remained virtually unknown because spying was considered dishonorable, a betrayal of friends and associates who trusted the spy. Even those for whom a spy was working often felt revulsion, and therefore the identities of agents were kept absolutely secret, even after the war was long over.

Identification of key Patriot spies in New York City is mostly speculative, but one is thought to have been Samuel Fraunces, whose popular tavern near the waterfront was believed to be a hotbed of intrigue—both by Patriots and Loyalists. After the war, Fraunces became President Washington's household steward and moved with him to Philadelphia.

Another prominent New Yorker who was one of Washington's secret agents was printer and publisher James Rivington. Rivington's *New York Gazette* was a strident voice against the revolutionaries, but

This lithograph published in the mid-nineteenth century by Currier and Ives, is titled "Execution of Nathan Hale on the Site of East Broadway, corner of Market Street, New York."

Q: **Who were key British espionage agents?**

A: One of the first British spies was Massachusetts physician Dr. Benjamin Church, a trusted Patriot leader. Church secretly corresponded with General Gage, and when discovered he was imprisoned for a year. Church left America upon his release, never to be heard from again.

A leading figure in the British spy network was Major Nicholas Dietrich, known as Baron Ottendorf, a German mercenary who started out on the side of the Americans. After Washington relieved him of duty in 1777, Ottendorf joined the British and served as spymaster for Clinton in New York. One of his agents was a woman known as "Miss Jenny," who infiltrated the French lines. Nothing is known of Miss Jenny's personal life, but her spying informed Clinton of allied troop movements in 1781.

The silk guidon, or flag, of the Second Regiment of Continental Light Dragoons, bears the Latin motto, "The country calls and her sons respond in tones of thunder." This regiment was led by Benjamin Tallmadge, a key figure in Washington's espionage operations in and around British-occupied New York City.

Patience Lovell Wright of Bordentown, New Jersey, was a highly regarded American sculptor living in England during the Revolutionary War. It is said that she rendered service to the Americans by reporting on British plans and preparations.

after 1781 he was sending secret information to Washington. It is said that one of the general's first deeds after entering New York at the close of the war was to visit Rivington to personally pay for his services with gold. Rivington's secret status could not protect him from the threats of returning Patriots. His publishing business was boycotted and collapsed.

Another alleged agent was Irish-born tailor Hercules Mulligan, whose shop was patronized by British officers. Mulligan picked up intelligence about troop movements during their visits and fittings—interpreting whether their regiments were headed north or south, for example, by the weight of the cloth for new uniforms they ordered. Washington bought a suit of clothes from Mulligan at the end of the war, entitling the tailor to hang out a sign stating: "Clothier to Genl. Washington."

> **There is nothing more necessary than good intelligence to frustrate a designing enemy, & nothing requires greater pains to obtain.**
>
> —*George Washington*

Arnold's Treason

Q: Which officer was most essential to Washington's espionage network?

A: Major Benjamin Tallmadge organized and gathered intelligence in southern New York, in the city, and on Long Island. Spymaster Tallmadge coordinated the passing of information to and from agents. One network, known as "Culper," was a spy ring that kept British headquarters under constant surveillance and was able to identify visiting Loyalists who had been posing as Patriots. Tallmadge was a central figure in uncovering the treasonous plot of Benedict Arnold in 1780.

Dragoon commander Major Benjamin Tallmadge of Connecticut, one of Washington's most dependable officers, coordinated secret communications with espionage agents in and around New York. Tallmadge was instrumental in the unmasking of André's plans, but he was too late to apprehend Arnold, who eluded capture.

Q: What turned Benedict Arnold, the most notorious traitor of the Revolutionary War, against the Americans?

A: In 1778, Arnold commanded the Philadelphia garrison while he recuperated from wounds suffered at Saratoga. Before long, he was court-martialed and reprimanded for using his official position for personal profit. (His corruption, however, was later proved to have been much more serious.) Resentful, and also angry at how Congress had been slow to honor his military achievements, Arnold opened secret negotiations with General Clinton. They arranged for Arnold to surrender the strategic

Margaret "Peggy" Shippen Arnold is pictured holding Edward, the first of her five children with Benedict Arnold, whom she married in April 1779. Peggy was just eighteen when she married Arnold, who was a thirty-eight-year-old widower.

Margaret "Peggy" Shippen

fortress at West Point, where Arnold took command in 1780. In return, he would receive $20,000 and be commissioned a high-ranking officer.

The conspiracy failed when Arnold's go-between with Clinton, Major John André, was captured in civilian disguise and found to be carrying a plan of West Point's fortifications. Interrogated by Major Tallmadge, André confessed, was tried, and hanged.

Q: How did Major André become involved in Arnold's plot?

A: André was Clinton's trusted aide, but he also had a previous personal connection to Arnold's family. While stationed in Philadelphia during the 1777–78 occupation, André had courted Peggy Shippen, the daughter of a prominent Loyalist. That courtship did not blossom, however, and the British evacuated the city. Peggy soon married Benedict Arnold, Patriot garrison commander.

Q: Why did Washington allow the execution of Major André rather than exchange him for a British prisoner?

A: Washington believed in setting an example that would warn others who might be considering similar dangerous conspiracies. There was much sympathy on both sides for the dashing André, including a personal appeal for

tary leader, Arnold was shunned by most British officers, who considered him a dishonorable turncoat. In addition, he had little success in raising large numbers of Loyalists to his command, which disappointed Clinton.

Arnold's wife, Peggy, and their children were permitted to leave America unmolested, and eventually the family settled permanently in England.

André is stopped by David Williams and Isaac Van Wart at Tarrytown, New York, on September 23, 1780. They find, in his boot, secret papers from Benedict Arnold for the betrayal of West Point. The men who caught André were likely robbers who realized he would fetch a handsome reward if brought to the Patriot lines.

mercy from General Clinton. Washington, however, adhered to his commander in chief's duty, regretfully accepting the sentence of the military tribunal that tried André. The execution was proof that the American revolutionaries were deadly serious, resolved to follow the strictest military protocol, even in the most tragic situations. As with young Nathan Hale, executed by Howe in 1776, there would be no clemency for spies.

Q: What happened to Arnold after his conspiracy was discovered?

A: Arnold escaped down the Hudson on a British warship to safety in New York and soon became a British army brigadier general. His new career was short-lived, involving destructive raids in Virginia and Connecticut. For all his ability as a mili-

"The unfortunate death of Major André (adjutant general to the English army) at head quarters in New York, Octr. 2, 1780, who was found within the American lines in the character of a spy," is the period description of this English engraving of the execution. Both sides mourned André's death, as they had in 1776 at the execution of Nathan Hale.

> ❝ The request I have to make [is that] I am branded with nothing dishonourable, as no motive could be mine but the service of my king. ❞
> —ANDRÉ TO WASHINGTON

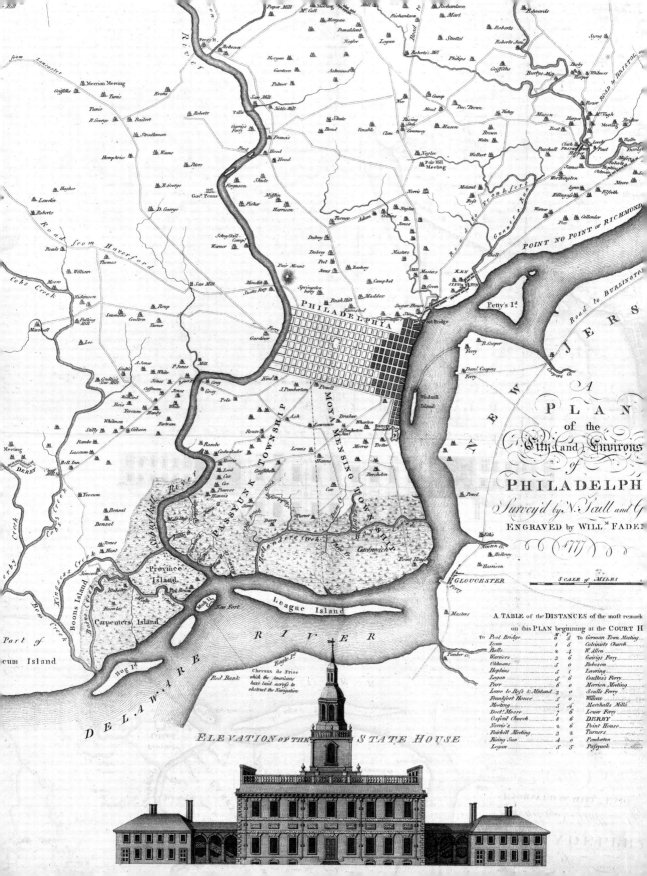

10

IN CONVENTION ASSEMBLED

At the beginning of America's war for indepen-dence, one of the most serious shortcomings facing the revolutionaries was the lack of a central government. Americans could well govern themselves, but until the months leading up to the war, communication between the colonial legislatures had been limited. Colonial relations were contentious as each jealously competed for government favors, control of western lands, and commercial advantage.

The need for treaties with the native peoples and for unified action in the French and Indian War had stim-ulated colonial cooperation, and the despised Stamp Act of 1765 had compelled the legislatures to hold the Stamp Act Congress. Asserting rights and grievances as a congress—a meeting—of colonial delegates had forced the home government to relent. When, in 1774, relations with Britain worsened, the First Continental Congress gathered "in convention assembled" to appeal to the king. When matters remained unresolved, the Second Continental Congress convened in May 1775, but now it was a war congress, and the delegates were risking their fortunes, liberty, and lives if they failed.

Dangerous to Royalty

Q: What were the duties and powers of the Second Continental Congress?

A: There was no legal precedent for creating an American congress with war-making or financial powers, so the delegates had to create their own regulations. They employed their members' considerable legal, financial, and military expertise, with one of the most important steps being the preparation for military action.

In 1777, Alexander Purdie of Williamsburg, Virginia, printed the "Articles of Confederation and perpetual union between the states of New Hampshire, Massachusetts Bay, Rhode Island, and Providence plantations, Connecticut, New York, New Jersey, Pennsylvania, Delaware, Maryland, Virginia, North Carolina, South Carolina, and Georgia."

This meant granting authorization to the Continental Army—adopting the army besieging Boston—as well as naming George Washington commander in chief and appointing other generals. Regulations and rules for the army had to be formulated, as did an address appealing to Canadians to join the revolution. Also, Congress authorized bills of credit to borrow $2 million to finance the war, appointed commissioners to negotiate with the Indians, and established an intercolonial postal service.

When, late in 1775, the king refused Congress's petition to make peace, secret committees were established to negotiate with foreign powers. The crucial need to open diplomatic links with France, Spain, the Netherlands, Prussia, and Tuscany required much planning and debate. Even a Continental flag had to be approved and designed.

As the war progressed, Congress had to approve treaties and alliances, find the means to finance the war, confer with Washington on strategies, supply, and the appointment of commanders, establish commercial and legislative protocols and policies for a new nation, and negotiate a peace.

In the fall of 1777, Congress adopted the Articles of Confederation, which established the central government and would serve as a foundation for the future United States.

> **Whereas many of our subjects . . . in North America, misled by dangerous and ill-designing men [have] proceeded to open and avowed rebellion . . .**
>
> —*KING GEORGE III*
>
> *in his 1775 proclamation declaring America in a state of rebellion and accusing the leaders as traitors*

Q: What were the Articles of Confederation?

A: These thirteen articles were the basis for governing the United States from March 1781 until March 1789, when the first Congress under the Constitution convened.

First presented to Congress on July 12, 1776, after a year of committee work and study, the Articles of Confederation underwent yet another year of debate until formally adopted in November 1777. The key issues covered the number of state representatives and their terms, the system of voting, how expenses were to be paid, and the future of western lands. There was to be a single-house Congress with each state having one vote, and although the states kept their own sovereignty, Congress had authority over foreign affairs. There was no power of taxation, which the states did not want to give to a central authority after enduring so much animosity over Parliament's taxation policies.

When the Articles of Confederation went into effect on March 2, 1781, the Second Continental Congress ceased to exist. The new Congress now became known as "The United States in Congress Assembled."

Q: What personal difficulties did members of Congress face once the war began?

A: Not only did the "rebel leaders" in Congress risk execution by hanging as traitors if the war failed and they were captured, but they also faced setbacks and disasters in their home communities. While they were away at Congress, many had their properties attacked by political opponents, and their families were threatened or banished. Even when Congress's armies were victorious on the battlefield, civil strife might erupt anywhere, and members of Congress were prime targets for attack. Members were often in danger of pursuit and arrest or worse as they moved about a country wracked with revolt and civil war.

By the close of the war, more than half the members had property looted or destroyed—sometimes by British army incursions, and often by Loyalist mobs and gangs. Likewise, those who were merchants and traders were always at risk of losing their wares, buildings, and ships to acts of war.

Connecticut's Roger Sherman, a legal expert for the Continental Congress, was the only delegate to sign all four great documents: the 1774 Articles of Association, the Declaration, the Articles of Confederation, and the Constitution.

Prominent leaders of the Continental Congress, left to right: John Adams, Gouverneur Morris, Alexander Hamilton, and Thomas Jefferson.

Presidents and "Patrioteers"

Q: Who were the wartime presidents of the Second Continental Congress?

A: Peyton Randolph of Virginia, the first president of the First Continental Congress, was elected president of the second Congress in May 1775. Randolph fell ill after two weeks in office and was replaced by John Hancock of Massachusetts.

Hancock presided during the 1776 Declaration of Independence. Although he was bitterly disappointed not to be named commander in chief of the army, Hancock served as president until October 1777. He remained a delegate until 1780, when he became governor of Massachusetts. The next president was Henry Laurens of South Carolina, one of Washington's most trusted allies in Congress.

Laurens had recently served in the defense of Charleston, and as the respected vice president of his state he had been instrumental in preventing the eruption of open civil war there. Resigning the presidency of Congress in 1778, he sailed for Europe to arrange for loans but was captured aboard ship and imprisoned in the Tower of London, charged with high treason. After fifteen months in severe conditions—twice refusing pardons if he would serve the British—Laurens was released on bail and finally exchanged for Cornwallis. He remained in Europe as a peace commissioner.

New York attorney John Jay was the next president, serving until September 1779, when he became minister to Spain. After June 1782, Jay went to Paris as a peace commissioner. Samuel Huntington of Connecticut, a member of Congress from 1775 to 1784, was president until mid-1781, when he resigned for poor health. Delaware's Thomas McKean served until November 1781, and John Hanson of Maryland was president until November 1782.

Next was New Jersey's Elias Boudinot, who of all the wartime presidents was perhaps closest to Washington. Having aided the general in the field with crucial supplies—personally contributing $30,000 to their cost—Boudinot also had worked conscientiously as commissary-general of prisoners. He was well known to Washington, whom he revered. Boudinot was in office until November 1783 and signed the peace treaty with Britain.

This portrait of South Carolina's Henry Laurens was painted by Bostonian John Singleton Copley, who lived in England during the war and remained neutral.

I do _____ _____ that I will faithfully, truly and impartially execute the office of _____ to which I am appointed, and render a true account, when thereunto required, of all public monies by me received or expended, and of all ſtores or other effects to me intruſted, which belong to the U N I T E D S T A T E S, and will, in all reſpects, diſcharge the truſt repoſed in me with juſtice and integrity, to the beſt of my ſkill and underſtanding.

This oath, published in Philadelphia in 1778, was required by Congress for all United States officials: "I [blank] do [blank] that I will faithfully, truly and impartially execute the office of [blank] to which I am appointed . . ."

Q: How did the character of the Second Continental Congress change as the war progressed?

A: As early as 1778, many of the 1775 delegates had retired or taken up arms, and revolutionary passions had been dampened by the tedious and difficult work of prosecuting the war. While most members of Congress were of unimpeachable integrity and devoted to the cause, others were profiting from the conflict.

Nicknamed "patrioteers," these men put personal gain, not the cause, as their first interest. While more idealistic men fought and died, these individuals operated behind the scenes, seldom known to history. Some took advantage of inside information regarding military needs to buy and sell supplies at immense profit. Others rested on their laurels as delegates but did not attend sessions of Congress, making it difficult for the governing body to function. Many Patriots worried that the "spirit of avarice" was undermining all their efforts.

Q: What did Alexander Hamilton, then Washington's aide, say when he learned a member of Congress had made an immense profit from selling military supplies?

A: "[He] ought to be detested as a traitor of the worst and most dangerous kind," wrote the twenty-year-old Lieutenant Colonel Hamilton to an associate in 1778. Hamilton was expressing outrage felt by many regarding a secret profit made by Maryland congressman Samuel Chase, who provided grain for the French navy. Hamilton publicly denounced Chase, who until then had been a staunch proponent of price controls but in this transaction had behaved like a war profiteer and "a degenerate character."

" The exorbitant price of every article, and the depreciation upon our currency, are evils derived essentially from this source. "

—*HAMILTON*

accusing war profiteers as monopolists and extortionists

Washington's Enemies

Philadelphia physician Benjamin Rush, a signer of the Declaration of Independence, criticized Washington's generalship; this portrait is by Charles Willson Peale.

Q: What was the "Conway Cabal"?

A: This was an aborted conspiracy in late 1777 to replace Washington with Horatio Gates as commander in chief. Although the alleged "cabal" never achieved a final, organized form, it involved members and former members of Congress and army officers who blamed Washington for failure in the field. Gates, meanwhile, was being lavished with credit for Saratoga, a campaign actually won by Arnold and other commanders.

At the center of the brew was Thomas Conway, an Irish-born French colonel who offered his services in 1777 and was made a general by Congress. Conway had little opportunity to show his prowess before corresponding with Gates, praising him and belittling Washington. Learning from one of his officers about Conway's letter and its insults, Washington realized a collaboration was afoot to discredit him. The faction in Congress that considered Washington inept and unable to win a major battle included Samuel Adams and John Adams and their fast friend, Richard Henry Lee of Virginia. Also involved were former member of Congress Benjamin Rush, like the Adamses from Massachusetts, and the army's quartermaster

Virginian Richard Henry Lee, a signer of the Declaration, was an ally of the anti-Washington faction in Congress that included John Adams. Lee opposed a strong central government and helped create the Bill of Rights. Portrait by Peale.

general—in charge of supply—Thomas Mifflin of Pennsylvania.

Rush expressed their feelings when he declared, "I am sick of Fabian systems in all quarters!" He was referring to the delaying tactics of Roman general Quintus Fabius, who harassed the more powerful Hannibal and avoided pitched battle. (Fabius was, in fact, successful with this strategy.) Gates pretended to Washington that he was above the fray, but the impetuous Conway pushed himself to the forefront, persuading Congress to promote him over twenty-three generals who were senior to him. Conway became inspector general of the Continental Army, a rank with prerogatives beyond Washington's authority. Also, Congress appointed a new Board of War to oversee the military. Mifflin became a member of the board, and none other than Gates was its president.

Washington and his leading commanders received Inspector General Conway icily. Conway complained to Congress, accusing Washington of failing to support him in the execution of his duties. This inexcusable near-insubordination, coupled with the anger of the generals who had been passed over, weakened Conway's position.

Gates, meanwhile, accused one of Washington's staff (Hamilton) of having "stealingly copied" Conway's letters and revealed the insults to Washington. Apparently Gates did not know that it was one of his own staff who, while drunk, had shown the letter to an officer loyal to Washington. When this was revealed to Congress, Gates was embarrassed. The combination of Conway's unbearable arrogance and Gates's unfounded accusations unmasked the developing "cabal." The army's fierce loyalty to Washington, however, was not to be trifled with by Congress, and the would-be conspirators were silenced.

Q: What was the "Canada Invasion" of 1778?

A: This was a planned campaign that turned out to be final proof that the Congressional Board of War was incompetent either to administer military affairs or plan strategy. While the Conway cabal was unfolding in late 1777, the Board of War began laying the groundwork for an invasion of Canada. Washington was not informed about these plans until January 1778. Lafayette was chosen to lead the invasion, but when he went to Albany, where men and supplies were supposedly assembled, he found preparations woefully inadequate. He called for abandonment of the plans, and Congress agreed.

In the midst of all this, Lafayette had refused to accept Thomas Conway as his second in command. Furious, Conway complained to Congress and threatened to resign if not given a fitting field command. By now the members were tired of the controversy and intrigues and realized that many commanders despised Conway. His resignation was accepted. Before departing for France, Conway was wounded in a pistol duel with a Continental officer who was infuriated by his insults to Washington.

Peale painted this portrait of fellow Pennsylvanian Thomas Mifflin, a former aide to Washington, and later a bitter adversary; Mifflin became president of Congress near the end of the war and received the commander in chief's resignation.

"A Gates, a Lee, or a Conway would in a few weeks render [Washington's army] an irresistible body of men."

—BENJAMIN RUSH
to Patrick Henry in 1778, criticizing Washington as incompetent

Congress in Crisis

Q: **Did many members of Congress serve in the military?**

A: Yes. Few governing bodies have had so many sitting members take up arms for their country. It is remarkable that even though most delegates were older than forty years of age, a total of 134 out of the 342 elected from 1774 to 1787 served in the military. Many left Congress to join the Continental Army or the militia—often when their home districts were under attack.

One member was killed in action,

This period French print illustrates a meeting of delegates to the Continental Congress.

twelve seriously wounded, and twenty-three were taken prisoner. The loss of its early delegates to the military deprived Congress of some of its best minds and most patriotic members. The replacements were not always up to the high-minded responsibilities that had inspired the first delegates.

Q: **What did Congress do when faced with imminent capture by the British?**

A: With Washington in full retreat across New Jersey in late 1776 and Philadelphia threatened, Congress fled to Baltimore. There it was difficult assembling enough members, because fewer than twenty-five went to Baltimore, less than half the number who had decided the momentous issues of 1775–76. Congress returned to Philadelphia in March 1777, but that fall, as Howe's army approached, it again fled the city, this time to Lancaster and then to York, Pennsylvania.

Congress fled again as the war was coming to a close in June 1783. Several hundred angry soldiers marched on Philadelphia and threatened violence if their pay and other compensation were not guaranteed. Congress went to Princeton and then to Annapolis, Maryland, where it greeted the end of the war.

" **Desperate diseases require desperate remedies and I with truth declare, that I have no lust after power.** "

—*WASHINGTON IN 1776*

soliciting increased command authority from Congress

To Congress.

Camp above Trenton Falls Dec. 20. 1776

Sir

I have waited with much impatience to know the determinations of Congress on the propositions made some

Q: What were General Washington's "dictatorial powers"?

A: At first, members of Congress too often interfered in military business. Fearing Washington might assume too much authority, they worked to prevent it, often at a price to his stature as commanding general. He was expected to turn to Congress for approval of all he wished to do. Further complicating matters, state governments gave their own orders to their regiments and chose their own generals. The commander in chief found himself caught between Congress and the states and at times even was unaware of orders legislative bodies had issued.

Washington acquired supreme authority during the crisis of 1776, when Philadelphia was threatened and Congress fled to Baltimore. These so-called "dictatorial powers" gave him the freedom to deal with this crisis without referring every matter to Congress. "Ten days will put an end to the existence of our army," he declared as he requested authority to command without constant consultation. He received that authority, which made his task immensely easier.

Now Washington totally reorganized the army so it would be under his, not the states', control. He appointed officers of his own choosing, up to brigadier general, and raised, officered, and equipped thousands of cavalry, regiments of artillery, and a corps of engineers. These powers also permitted him to apply directly to the states when he needed militia support. In addition, he could confiscate—after paying a fair price—what he needed from civilians who refused to sell, and could arrest and confine those who refused to accept Continental currency or proved dangerously "disaffected to the American cause."

Officially, these powers were given Washington for only six months, but they were never seriously challenged for the rest of the war. Although they did not impart "dictatorial" authority by any means, they gave Washington the ability to create a true army under his undivided command.

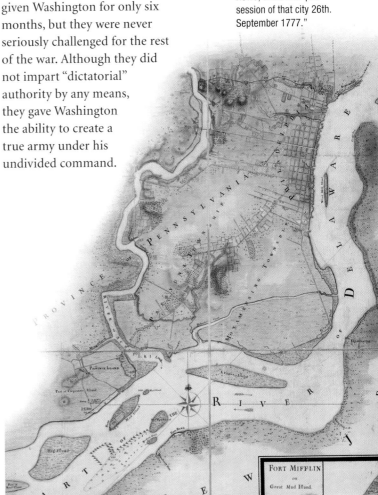

THE WAR ROAD TO YORKTOWN

When hostilities broke out in 1775 the British army had no troops in the South. Patriots moved rapidly to take control of colonial capitals and to warn Loyalists against arming. Early in 1776 pro-British forces in the Carolinas rose up to unite with the seaborne expedition against Charleston, but the expedition failed, leaving the Loyalists without support. After 1,700 Loyalists were defeated in February at Moore's Creek Bridge in North Carolina, southern Loyalists remained inactive until 1778, when the British again took the offensive.

By 1780 the South was the war's major theater, as Clinton took Charleston and Cornwallis led expeditions to crush Patriot resistance. Inconclusive campaigns in the South closed with Cornwallis occupying Yorktown, Virginia, in late summer 1781. There he waited for the British navy to arrive and reinforce him. Instead, it was the French navy and an American and French army that came to Yorktown, and Cornwallis was trapped.

Left: Redcoated British officers led by General Charles O'Hara, Cornwallis's second-in-command, surrender at Yorktown to Washington's second-in-command, General Benjamin Lincoln, on horseback.

Above: This distant view of Charleston, capital of South Carolina, was engraved in London in 1776; a British ship sails in the foreground.

The Southern Theater of War

Q: What did Washington do to counter the British strategy of pacifying and occupying the South?

A: When Horatio Gates was routed at Camden in August 1780, Washington asked General Nathanael Greene, a Rhode Islander, to go south and stir up a flame of resistance from the ashes of defeat. The commander in chief dared not go south himself in case Clinton sallied out from New York with his army. Greene's mission seemed impossible, but it would not be the first time he had answered such an appeal from Washington.

Greene's most remarkable accomplishment thus far had been the reorganizing of the quartermaster's department during the army's starving time at Valley Forge in 1777–78. The previous quartermaster general, Thomas Mifflin, had failed miserably to provide for the army. Mifflin was unable to procure enough food or manage the movement and storage of what supplies and equipment were available.

Greene assumed the post of quartermaster general at a time when there were no uniforms, no shoes, and no shelter. He much preferred to be a general in the field, yet as an administrator he was a dynamo, resourceful and decisive. Not only did he shake up a department that was in disarray, but he enforced the legal obligation of Pennsylvania farmers and merchants to accept Continental money, which they were reluctant to do. Greene also found supplies and equipment that had been misplaced. In one case, hundreds of tents had been stored in distant barns and forgotten. By mid-February, as Von Steuben began to train the troops, Greene had solved the shortages of food, although there was still not enough clothing, even for officers. With the timely arrival of French equipment and uniforms, the American army was ready to resume campaigning in mid-1778.

Q: Who won the most battles in the Southern Theater from December 1778 to October 1781?

A: The British and Loyalists won the most engagements, but they were never able to corner and destroy the American forces in the field. As long as bodies of determined fighting men remained intact—especially those under Greene and Lafayette—the potential Loyalist counterrevolution would remain suppressed. Without the rising of Loyalist sympathizers that the British hoped for, there were too few king's troops to wipe out the revolutionaries.

These years saw major British victories, including the capture

Right: Polish nobleman Count Casimir Pulaski fled Russian occupation of his native Poland in 1772 and five years later joined the American forces. A cavalryman and military engineer, Pulaski was killed leading a mounted charge at Savannah in 1779.

Far right: American expatriate and member of the prominent Cruger family of New York City, Henry Cruger served in Parliament and as mayor of Bristol. He was a fierce opponent of British colonial policy in America. Returning to New York in 1790, he was elected to the state senate.

Count Casimir Pulaski

Henry Cruger

of Savannah in December 1778, the defeat of the American and French siege of Savannah in 1779, and the capture of Charleston in May 1780. This last was the greatest British victory of the war. Then the destruction of Gates's army at Camden in August 1780 seemed the final stroke needed to clear the South of Patriot forces. These triumphs were indeed devastating to the revolutionary cause, especially when combined with demoralizing Patriot defeats in many skirmishes, such as at Waxhaws in May, where Tarleton's men massacred Virginia Continentals. Each time, however, the Patriots stubbornly recovered to fight on.

With backcountry Loyalists mustering in mid-1780, and the ambitious Cornwallis on the offensive in the Carolinas, the course of war seemed to have swung in favor of the British. Then, in October, came the crushing defeat of Major Patrick Ferguson's Loyalists at King's Mountain, a disaster that struck fear into the hearts of many who might have rallied to the king's colors. This Patriot triumph occurred as Nathanael Greene was about to take command of the tattered rebel army in the South.

In January 1781, Tarleton attacked a force under Daniel Morgan at the Cowpens, South Carolina, and was defeated. Cornwallis drove Greene from the field at Guilford Court House in March, but at great cost in irreplaceable troops. In April, Greene was again defeated at Hobkirk's Hill, but his army fought on. In June he was repulsed at the strategic Loyalist stronghold of Ninety-Six in South Carolina, and he closed his southern campaign in September, again defeated, at Eutaw Springs.

Yet Greene had won the campaign. His army was intact, the British and Loyalists had been severely bloodied, and Cornwallis was moving toward Yorktown.

American sergeants William Jasper and John Newton rescue prisoners from British guards in August 1779; the sergeants were on a scout for Francis Marion's partisan raiders when they discovered prisoners and families being led to nearby Savannah for confinement.

> "We fight, get beat, rise, and fight again."
> —*GREENE IN 1780*
> *describing his southern campaigns*

Closing Chapters

Q: Whom did Washington consider his best general?

Washington's favorite commander, General Nathanael Greene of Rhode Island won the crucial southern campaign of 1780–81 without recording a victory. Greene skillfully maneuvered against and fought Cornwallis, preventing British control of the Carolinas and influencing his adversary's final move to Yorktown and defeat.

A: If Washington's behavior when he was deathly sick counts for anything, then he wanted Nathanael Greene to replace him if the time came.

At the Morristown cantonment in the spring of 1777 Washington fell so seriously ill that his officers feared for his life. As he weakened, wracked with fever and unable to speak, the senior generals gathered anxiously at his bedside. One gently asked the question that troubled them all:

Who should assume command if it were necessary?

Summoning his strength, Washington looked from man to man until he came to Greene, and his gaze fixed on him. Greene gasped and took Washington's hand, then made a casual, light comment, to relieve the heaviness of the moment. It was apparent that Washington had nominated Greene as his successor.

As it turned out, to everyone's relief, Washington was much improved the next day. Furthermore, news came that Martha was on her way from Mount Vernon to nurse him back to health.

Q: Why were the settlers of the Blue Ridge Mountains so determined to destroy Ferguson and the Loyalists mustering at King's Mountain, South Carolina?

A: This blood feud was typical of the animosity between Patriots and Loyalists who had been hostile to each other before the war. The "Over Mountain Men" of the Kentucky region were Scotch-Irish, while the Loyalists raised by Ferguson were Scottish for the most part. Although these folk had a common heritage, there was a tradition of prejudice and resentment that caused a rift between them. When they chose opposite sides in the war, that rift worsened. Ferguson, a Scottish officer lacking knowledge of these people, fanned that resentment into fiery anger when he rashly threatened to punish the Over Mountain Men and their families if they supported the Patriot cause. He wrote to militia leader Isaac Shelby that if he

British Major Patrick Ferguson improved the breechloading mechanism being used in some sporting guns, and adapted it to this military rifle. In 1776, he tested the Ferguson Rifle, which proved accurate at two hundred and fifty yards, five times farther than the musket.

Issac Shelby

and his men did not "desist from their opposition to British arms," Ferguson would "march his army over the mountains, hang their leaders, and lay their country waste with fire and sword."

Perhaps Ferguson was flushed with confidence after the British victory at Camden and had overestimated the number of new Loyalist recruits. Unwittingly, he had stirred Shelby's people into a fury that was vented at King's Mountain, where the Loyalists were wiped out.

Q: What did Cornwallis think about recruiting Loyalists from the South?

A: Cornwallis had little confidence in them. Although British strategy in 1780 depended on large number of Loyalists

uniting to take control of North Carolina, Cornwallis wrote Clinton that he thought this unlikely: "[Patrick] Ferguson is to move . . . with some militia whom he says he is sure he can depend on for doing their duty; but I am sorry to say that his own experience, as well as that of every other officer, is totally against him."

Some historians believe the war was lost by the British because they did not put enough trust in the fighting ability of the Loyalists. Perhaps if more British commanders had encouraged the Loyalists and shown them respect, as did Ferguson, the Loyalists would have had more confidence in the British, and the war's outcome would have been different. In fact, Ferguson's doomed Loyalists at King's Mountain fought courageously, as did many others like them in other engagements.

In 1780 frontier commander Isaac Shelby led his "Over Mountain Men" into battle at King's Mountain, South Carolina. Shelby became the first governor of Kentucky in 1792.

Andrew Pickens, a native Pennsylvanian brought up in South Carolina, joined expeditions against the Indian nations before the war. Pickens served as a patriot militia general and was a key leader in several important actions, including the 1781 victory at Cowpens, South Carolina.

" I could not help turning away from the scene before me with horror and, although exulting in victory, could not refrain from shedding tears. "

—PATRIOT JAMES P. COLLINS
observing the dead and wounded Loyalists at King's Mountain

Patriot and Loyalist Raiders

Q: Which partisan leader most frustrated Cornwallis after his victory at Camden in 1780?

A: After Camden, Cornwallis attempted to wipe out all partisan activity harrying his flanks and rear. The most dangerous partisan was South Carolina's Francis Marion, whose raids on British lines of communication with Charleston were costly in terms of men and supplies. The audacity and skill of Marion, known as the "Swamp Fox," infuriated Cornwallis.

After the shock of King's Mountain, Cornwallis sent Banastre Tarleton, commander of Loyalist dragoons, in pursuit of Marion, intending to assert British domination of the region. Tarleton pursued the Swamp Fox through the backcountry and into swamps and forests, but without success. It is said that when Tarleton gave up he had never even caught sight of any of Marion's raiders.

Q: Which battle confirmed that Continental troops from southern regiments were able to stand up to British regiments?

A: The Cowpens in January 1781. After the King's Mountain loss, Cornwallis moved deeper inland, trying to bring Greene to a decisive action. Although Greene had only a few thousand men under his command, he took the risk of detaching a strong force to harass Cornwallis's supply lines. He gave command to Daniel Morgan, a hero of Saratoga whose regiment of riflemen had been lethal against Burgoyne's officers. Determined to destroy enemy forces operating against his communications, Cornwallis sent Tarleton with more than a thousand crack troops in pursuit of Morgan.

In Tarleton's force were the vaunted light infantry of the Seventy-first Highland Regiment, plus another regular British regiment, and cavalry of the famous British Seventeenth Dragoons. Tarleton's own Loyalist Queen's Rangers dragoons were proud of their reputation. Although unable to

A legendary incident from Marion's career is portrayed in this painting of the partisan commander inviting a banished Loyalist officer to share a meal. The officer had returned to South Carolina to plead his case for forgiveness and reinstatement as a neutral citizen.

snare Marion, they had been wreaking havoc with small bodies of Continentals and militia, winning a reputation for hard-hitting attacks. There was every reason to believe that Morgan's days were numbered. He appeared to be retreating, and Tarleton pushed his men hard, giving them little sleep. He engaged Morgan at a place called the Cowpens, where the Americans had stopped to feed their hungry horses and cattle.

Morgan had six hundred veteran Virginia Continentals and a few hundred untested South Carolina militia. His tactic was to put the militia in front, have them fire a couple of volleys and then retreat behind the main line. Tarleton immediately attacked. His unsuspecting troops pursed the fleeing militia and then crashed into Morgan's main line of Continentals. The slaughter of Tarleton's best troops commenced, followed by a counterattack by dragoons under Colonel William Washington to complete the rout. The Cowpens cost the British 100 killed, 229 wounded (all captured), and an additional 600 captured. More than sixty British officers were lost, a severe blow to Cornwallis.

Henry Lee

Q: Which Loyalist commander led a major raid into Virginia in early 1781 to prevent that state from continuing to support Greene's operations?

A: Benedict Arnold. In his first important command since going over to the British, Arnold arrived from New York by sea at Hampton Roads, Virginia, with twelve hundred troops, many of them Loyalists led by Colonel John Simcoe. Arnold, now a British general, captured some vessels and set off up the James River to take lightly defended Richmond. The invaders forced the state government, including Governor Thomas Jefferson, to flee, and they also destroyed valuable stores of tobacco that Patriots intended to sell to raise funds for the war. Arnold and Simcoe were joined by two thousand troops under their senior, General William Phillips, a veteran of the Burgoyne campaign who had been exchanged. With Cornwallis closing in on Greene in the Carolinas and Phillips and Arnold ravaging Virginia, the war in the South again seemed to be going against the Patriots.

Henry Lee, a staunch supporter of fellow Virginian George Washington, won the title "Light-Horse Harry" for his daring leadership of Continental cavalry throughout the war. This portrait, by Charles Willson Peale, is likely from 1782.

As for this damned old fox, the devil himself could not catch him.

—*TARLETON*
after giving up pursuit of guerrilla leader Francis Marion, 1780

British Hesitation

Q: Which battle in the South proved the war would not end just because the British won the most victories in the field?

Below: Nathanael Greene's militia stand in the army's front ranks at Guilford Court House, North Carolina, preparing to give battle against Cornwallis's regulars while Patriot cavalry move into action from the rear. Greene was forced to retreat, but he inflicted heavy losses on Cornwallis's forces.

Right: A soldier's cup, made from a cow horn and inscribed with the initials "WCW," was discovered on the Guilford Court House battlefield site. It is about six inches tall and three inches wide.

A: Guilford Court House, North Carolina, in March 1781. Cornwallis could not shake the partisan harassment of his supplies, and Tarleton's disaster at the Cowpens compounded the general's frustration. Determined to strike a blow that would redeem the British cause in the South, he went after Morgan. Burning his wagons and extra gear to lighten his army's load, Cornwallis tried to keep Morgan from joining Greene. But Morgan was faster, eluding him and uniting with Greene, who withdrew. Cornwallis stayed in pursuit. Now Greene maneuvered onto a field of battle that would favor the Patriots. Militia rallied to Greene, but Morgan left the army, claiming he was ill. Some historians believe he opposed Greene's strategy to bring on a battle with Cornwallis's nineteen hundred veterans. With forty-three hundred men—seventeen hundred

Continentals and the rest mostly Carolina and Virginia militia—Greene prepared for Cornwallis at Guilford Court House on March 15. Greene arrayed his men in much the same way as Morgan had at the Cowpens: militia in front, with orders to fire and then retreat behind the Continentals.

The first line, Carolina militia, who had no bayonets to defend against British steel, showed remarkable courage in the face of the assault. They fired a volley at one hundred and fifty yards then reloaded for a second. At forty yards, the British attack slowed and stopped, the regulars seeming mesmerized as they saw the civilian riflemen taking careful aim at them.

"Come on, my brave Fusiliers!" roared the British colonel, and on they charged, but many were cut down by rifle fire before the militia retreated.

Now Cornwallis's assault was slowed by gunfire from the flanks, and he had to commit his reserves, leaving no force for a decisive breakthrough. His main attack came up against a second line, this one of Virginia militia. The fighting was in a woods, which made massed bayonets impractical. The British forced the Americans back until they hit the main line

Soldier's cup

> **Their whole force had their arms presented and resting on a rail fence . . . They were taking aim with the nicest precision.**
>
> **—A SERGEANT OF THE ROYAL WELSH FUSILIERS**
> *describing the hesitation of the regulars at Guilford Court House*

of Continentals. Among the defenders was the First Maryland, considered the finest regiment in the Continental Army. They fired into the British, then mounted a bayonet attack that forced a retreat. Greene resisted the temptation to order a general assault,

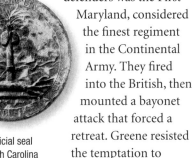

The official seal of South Carolina

knowing it was most important to keep his army in the field and not risk total defeat. Cornwallis regrouped and continued his offensive, and the battle raged, with both sides exhibiting fierce courage and determination. After an hour and a half, the British captured some American guns, the militia dispersed, and the Continentals withdrew in good order.

Greene retreated after dark, and the British were too exhausted and bloodied to pursue. Cornwallis held the field, calling it "a glorious day," but it cost him 140 dead and 380 wounded, including a large proportion of officers. Greene lost 261 killed and wounded. Cornwallis then withdrew, marching to Wilmington, on the coast. Greene, meanwhile, was still in the field.

Q: **Who won, strategically, in the contest between Cornwallis and Greene?**

A: Greene succeeded in his strategy of maintaining his army in the field, while Cornwallis failed in his strategy of finding and destroying the main Patriot forces.

Instead of achieving complete victory, Cornwallis had decimated and exhausted his forces and left much of the South to his opponent. Greene now orchestrated the operations of Patriot forces in the region as they attacked enemy garrisons one by one. Another British force of two thousand men was isolated at Camden, vulnerable to an attack.

Above: Operations in the Carolinas are indicated in this nineteenth-century map showing Greene's campaign against British forces under Cornwallis and Rawdon. Important battles were fought at Guilford Court House and Eutaw Springs.

The War in Virginia

Right: Friedrich Wilhelm von Steuben became one of Washington's key commanders after joining the revolutionary forces in 1778.

Below: George Washington commissioned Charles Willson Peale to paint this portrait of the Marquis de Lafayette, the young French nobleman who volunteered for the American army in 1777.

Q: How did Washington respond to the enemy depredations in his home state of Virginia in 1781?

A: Washington had very few men to spare when Arnold, Simcoe, and Phillips were ravaging the region. Most of Virginia's best Continentals were serving with Washington in the siege of New York or were with Greene in the Carolinas, so British prospects for taking control of Virginia looked favorable. First,

Washington sent Baron von Steuben to Virginia to train newly recruited Virginia Continentals. Next he ordered Lafayette and twelve hundred Continentals into the campaign with orders to avoid full-scale battle.

Baron von Steuben

That spring Cornwallis took his fifteen hundred men northward and assumed command of the force operating in Virginia. Additional reinforcements from New York brought Cornwallis's army to seventy-two hundred men, but he lost the able Phillips, who died of illness, and Arnold returned to New York, hoping to be given his own command. Throughout the steamy summer of 1781, Cornwallis attempted to lure Lafayette, who was only twenty-three years of age, into a decisive battle. Cornwallis once declared, "The boy cannot escape me," but Lafayette narrowly did so, and kept fighting.

In June, Anthony Wayne arrived with a thousand veteran Continentals to reinforce Lafayette, providing enough troops to oppose the destructive raids Cornwallis had been launching. The British in Virginia no longer had the freedom of maneuver, and Cornwallis began to concentrate his forces on the Yorktown Peninsula. There he could be reinforced and resupplied by sea for the next offensive.

Q: What was the military consequence of Cornwallis's move to Virginia in 1781?

A: He virtually abandoned the Carolinas and Georgia, leaving Greene to operate against weakened British forces. In April, as many British troops were trying to catch Francis Marion, Greene brought on a battle at Hobkirk's Hill, South Carolina, but he was forced to retreat by the young British commander, Lord Francis Rawdon.

The two armies met again in early September at Eutaw Springs, South Carolina. Rawdon had fallen ill and been replaced by Colonel Alexander Stewart, whose two thousand British were surprised by Greene's twenty-two hundred men and driven from their camp. When the hungry Americans stopped to loot the enemy tents and gobble the food, the British counterattacked and eventually won the day. Greene had 522 casualties, while Stewart suffered almost 700, including several hundred taken prisoner.

Severely weakened, Stewart withdrew to Charleston. Charleston, Savannah, and Wilmington were now the only remaining British strongholds south of Virginia. Greene had won another campaign.

Q: What policy of Congress was considered a blot upon its reputation?

A: Keeping the "Convention Army" captive. Burgoyne's capitulation terms at Saratoga in 1777 were officially named a "convention" rather than a surrender. His almost five thousand troops, called the Convention Army, were supposed to have been marched to Boston and returned to Britain. The officers and soldiers had promised never to serve in America during the war. Congress, however, objected to these terms, since the troops would surely take the place of others who would be released to come to America.

Congress suspended the evacuation and found legalistic excuses for evading the terms of the convention. The soldiers languished in captivity, were moved around the country on a three-month march, and ended up in Virginia. As Cornwallis approached in 1781, they were shifted again, some as far away as Vermont. Only half the original number remained by war's end—many Germans had been allowed to escape—when they were freed after six years in captivity.

Historians have described this episode as a discredit to Congress. At the same time, it has come to light that General Howe, commanding at New York in 1777, had definite plans to exchange the Convention Army for the thousands of American prisoners he held.

Above: General Francis Rawdon-Hastings was an able subordinate to Cornwallis. Only in his mid-twenties, Lord Rawdon showed excellent leadership.

Below: This postwar English engraving shows the encampment of the "Convention Army," imprisoned at Charlottesville, Virginia, in 1780. The scene shows prisoners engaged in subsistence farming.

The March to Yorktown

Q: Who was winning the Revolutionary War in the late summer of 1781?

A: The Patriots, although there was no clear end in sight to the hostilities. In August, Clinton in New York had been reinforced to fifteen thousand troops, facing Washington's thirty-five hundred Continentals, four thousand French in Rhode Island, and thousands of militia, who would rise if the British attacked. Further, there were rumors of another British invasion from Canada.

For his part, Clinton feared a combined French-American assault on New York, which was indeed brewing. Washington was trying to persuade his ally, Rochambeau, to arrange for a movement of the French fleet and for troop reinforcements, in order to strike that fall.

The difficulties facing Clinton

George Rodney

included contradictory instructions coming from the government in London, which favored Cornwallis over himself. Cornwallis had directly disobeyed Clinton by leaving the Carolinas—and what was worse, had falsely reported that he had defeated the rebellion in that quarter. Encouraged, the government wished to give Cornwallis an independent command, believing he could win the war by taking the offensive instead of following Clinton's defensive strategy. Clinton was so furious that he had decided to resign his command soon.

The Americans, too, faced difficulties, foremost among them the lack of hard cash to pay the troops, who were increasingly disgruntled and war-weary. French loans and outright gifts would resolve that shortcoming, however. And south of Virginia the war had turned in favor of the Americans. Still, at Yorktown, Cornwallis was strong, now with more than nine thousand veterans. If reinforced by Clinton, he would have a formidable field force.

Yet considering the dissension in the high command and the political opposition to the war back home, the hard-pressed British field commanders were not in enviable positions. Washington, on the other hand, was at the height of influence and power, and Rochambeau was committed to doing all he could to sup-

Right: Admiral George Rodney deserves considerable blame for the failure of the British fleet at Yorktown. In August 1781 he took most of his ships to England, leaving admirals Samuel Hood and Thomas Graves without enough strength to prevent the French blockade of Cornwallis.

Below: This fanciful French illustration of the period depicts the surrender of Cornwallis to the armies of Washington and Rochambeau. Yorktown is portrayed as a walled medieval town instead of the coastal village that had never before seen the clash of armies.

port his ally. If the Americans and French could either take New York or capture Cornwallis, the British cause might be dealt a fatal blow.

Q: Why did Cornwallis believe Yorktown was the best place to bring his army?

A: Cornwallis's troops were exhausted from their grueling campaigning and were in need of reequipping and rest. Supplies could come by sea from New York or the West Indies, where the British navy was more powerful than the French.

Q: Why did the British at New York fail to anticipate the siege of Yorktown?

A: Clinton was tricked into believing there would be an all-out assault on New York. Washington used his counterespionage agents and methods to reinforce the British belief that New York was his objective. In mid-August, as he and Rochambeau put their men into motion southward, marching into northern New Jersey, Clinton readied for an attack. Even the allied troops were led to believe this was the plan. Suddenly, on August

Charles Cornwallis

30, Washington and Rochambeau began their forced march by three parallel routes to Yorktown, 450 miles south. Had Clinton learned the truth earlier and attacked from New York, the allied troops would have been vulnerable in their extended columns.

It was not until early September, with the main body of allied troops passing Philadelphia, that Clinton realized the truth. Expecting the British navy would arrive shortly in Yorktown, Clinton began to make preparations to reinforce Cornwallis. The British fleet, however, was unaware of the situation and was not hurrying to General Cornwallis's aid.

Lord Charles Cornwallis was an active and skillful commander who faced long odds in America, which was far too large to be held by even the most hard-hitting expeditionary force. After Yorktown, Cornwallis went on to a successful career as governor-general in India, where his military prowess won important British victories.

The terms of the British surrender would have been written with a portable writing set such as this one, carried on campaign by American commanding officers. Generals kept careful written records and exchanged regular correspondence with subordinates and headquarters.

> "Ostensibly an [attack on] the city of New York is in contemplation—preparations in all quarters for some months past indicate this to be the object of our combined operations."
>
> —AUGUST 15, 1781
> *entry in the journal of Dr. James Thacher of the Continental Army*

Cornwallis Is Trapped

Q: Who unexpectedly joined Washington's headquarters staff on the eve of Yorktown?

A: Washington's adopted son, Jacky Custis. Before going to Yorktown, the American and French general staffs met at Mount Vernon, where Custis, his wife, and their children came to visit. In his early thirties, Custis had never served with Washington, but now he pleaded to be an aide. Washington worried that the young man was not conditioned to the arduous physical demands of campaigning. With Martha taking his side, Custis persuaded his reluctant stepfather to accept him. Custis, a skilled horseman, took to his duties enthusiastically.

Right: Charles Willson Peale painted Alexander Hamilton's portrait from life in the 1790s, when the former headquarters aide and elite infantry colonel was secretary of the treasury. A few years later, in 1804, Hamilton was killed in a duel with vice president Aaron Burr.

Below: Admiral Francois Joseph Paul Comte de Grasse, led the French fleet to a timely victory over the British off the Virginia (or Chesapeake) capes in September 1781. De Grasse prevented seaborne reinforcement of Cornwallis, who was besieged at Yorktown by a French-American army that forced his surrender in October.

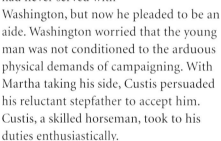

Alexander Hamilton

Q: Which navy, British or French, reached Chesapeake Bay first?

A: A British squadron under Admiral Samuel Hood reached the Chesapeake three days before de Grasse but, finding no enemy vessels in sight, turned northward to New York. Had the squadron taken a position at the mouth of the Chesapeake, it could have kept the French fleet away from Yorktown. Although British intelligence had reported that de Grasse was moving toward the mainland, Hood had no idea whether the enemy was heading to New York or to the Virginia coast.

At New York, Hood joined another squadron under Admiral Thomas Graves, his senior. The British now learned of de Grasse's arrival at the Chesapeake and also that a second French squadron from Newport was heading southward, and carrying siege guns. With Graves in command, the British fleet hurried southward while Clinton continued to ready the relief force.

Q: How important were French troops at Yorktown?

A: The campaign could not have been carried out without them. After reinforcements, Rochambeau had eighty-eight hundred men. Washington's forces swelled to more than eleven thousand as the militia mustered. The allied total at the height of the siege, which began in late September, was twenty thousand troops.

Q: How did the French navy turn the tide at Yorktown?

A: As Graves and Hood approached the Chesapeake, they found the French fleet ready for them. On September 5, the momentous Battle of the Chesapeake (or Virginia) Capes began. De Grasse's twenty-four ships of the line outnumbered Graves's nineteen, but the English commander attacked. The sea battle was ended by darkness after two and a half hours, with the French preventing Graves from entering the bay.

During the next two days the fleets jockeyed for position and for a favorable wind. In this time the French squadron from Newport slipped into the Chesapeake with much-needed artillery and supplies for Washington and Rochambeau, whose forces were closing in on Yorktown. De Grasse now sailed into Chesapeake Bay and took up defensive positions. The outdone British fleet returned to New York to escort the relief expedition for Yorktown. Each side in the naval combat had suffered fewer than three hundred casualties, and although many vessels were damaged, only one, a British sixty-four-gun ship of the line, was lost.

Cornwallis, securely blockaded, was doomed by the slow progress in mounting the relief expedition. As late as October 14, a few days before Cornwallis surrendered, Admiral Graves was hesitant to urge haste, for he was in doubt as to whether a relief expedition could even be attempted.

Q: Which former Washington protégé, who had fallen out with the general, became a hero at Yorktown?

A: Alexander Hamilton. Once a key headquarters secretary and aide, Hamilton had chafed for a field command, but Washington needed him on his staff. At last, in February 1781, the two argued, and Hamilton indignantly resigned. He was soon given his command, however. The men were reconciled at Yorktown, where Washington allowed Hamilton to lead an important night attack to capture a British redoubt. Its fall, along with another redoubt taken by the French, resulted in Cornwallis's surrender.

Above: British admiral Sir Samuel Hood was an outstanding naval commander, but during the Yorktown campaign was frustrated by the poor decisions of his superior officers. Hood was unable to prevent de Grasse from blockading Yorktown, but he later brilliantly won major actions in the Caribbean.

Left: Hamilton showed his ability as a battlefield commander by leading this successful night attack on a British strongpoint at Yorktown in 1781. A simultaneous French attack also succeeded, allowing the allies to fire cannon from these strongpoints into Cornwallis's positions. The British soon surrendered.

> **I think very meanly of the ability of the present commanding officer.**
> —*Hood, October 14, 1781*
> *angrily complaining about Graves's reluctance to embark to save Cornwallis*

The Last Battle

Q: What essential armament made the difference in the siege of Yorktown—a weapon that had not been available to Washington before?

A: The French provided massive siege guns that bombarded the British defenses from long range. The Americans had never before possessed such powerful weapons. On October 9 the Continental colors were run up a staff to fly over the American-manned batteries, and the white flag of the French was raised over theirs. This was the signal to open the bombardment, and Washington had the honor of firing the first heavy gun.

The British replied in kind with their own artillery, but the French and American bombardment was devastating. British vessels anchored off Yorktown were especially vulnerable. The week-long barrage, night and day, destroyed Cornwallis's guns, one by one, and killed the crews. Yorktown was a hell for the more than eight thousand soldiers and hundreds of civilians trapped under the rain of explosive shells and the battering of iron cannonballs.

The French-American siege works were moved steadily closer, as British strongpoints were stormed by surprise night attacks. Eventually, even captured British guns were being turned against the town. On the morning of October 17, a solitary British drummer boy appeared bravely on a parapet and began to beat out

a signal that requested a parley. Cornwallis was prepared to surrender.

Q: What message did Washington send to Congress announcing his victory?

A: After Cornwallis's surrender on October 19, 1781, Washington wrote the briefest of official reports to Congress in Philadelphia. Characteristically, he scarcely mentioned himself: "I have the honor to inform Congress, that the Reduction of the British Army under the Command of Lord Cornwallis, is most happily effected. The unremitting Ardor which actuated every Officer and Soldier in the combined Army in this Occasion, has principally led to this Important Event, at an earlier period than my most sanguine Hope had induced me to expect."

Q: What personal tragedy did the Washingtons endure at the moment of triumph at Yorktown?

A: Jacky Custis fell ill while serving with his father during the campaign. At the moment of Washington's triumph, as Cornwallis's troops were laying down their arms in surrender ceremonies, Custis was lying in a carriage, watching. He was suffering severe "camp fever," a common ailment to new soldiers. A normally self-indulgent young man, Custis had made his mother and stepfather

During his final illness in 1799—suffering from a severely infected throat—Washington was bled as part of common medical practice of the time. This surgeon's bloodletting set was similar to instruments used then. The more than four cups of blood taken in twenty-four hours from Washington likely contributed to his death.

Bloodletting set

The British surrender at Yorktown on October 19, 1781, painted by Patriot artist John Trumbull of Connecticut, shows General Benjamin Lincoln mounted at center with the British officers—Cornwallis was ill and not present. The French officers are at left, and the Americans, led by Washington, are at right. Trumbull was a head-quarters aide to Washington.

proud that he had performed so selflessly throughout the campaign.

As the surrender continued, Custis was taken away to be cared for by Dr. James Craik, Washington's longtime friend and physician. A few days later, after essential military affairs were put in order and Cornwallis had embarked aboard ship under parole, Washington rushed to Custis's bedside. Within hours, the young man died. While the great victory of Yorktown was being celebrated by a joyous America, the Washington and Custis families were in deep mourning.

Q: **What were Washington's main concerns after Yorktown?**

A: Washington worried that Americans would become complacent—especially Congress and the state governments. He also was concerned that once the French departed, the British would seize the first opportunity to strike back. He was also concerned that the French might attempt to take Quebec if the British were weakened enough. He did not favor a return of the French to Canada, where they might renew their claims on the Northwest.

> My greatest Fear is, that Congress viewing this stroke in too important a point of Light, may think our Work too nearly closed, and will fall into a State of Languor and Relaxation; to prevent this Error I shall employ every Means in my Power, and if unhappily we sink into that fatal Mistake, no part of the Blame shall be mine.
>
> —*Washington to Nathanael Greene, November 17, 1781*

CHAPTER 12

FOUNDING THE REPUBLIC

After the triumph at Yorktown it appeared that victory was won. Washington, however, warned the members of Congress and his army officers not to underestimate the capacity of the British to return in force and resume the war. As peace negotiations slowly proceeded in Europe, Washington struggled to keep his army together and to compel Congress to meet its obligations to his men.

Once the peace treaty was signed in late 1783, Congress and the states turned to the task of establishing a federal government and adopting a constitution. Again Washington found himself in the forefront, as the "Father of the Country" and its first president. George Washington was the man most trusted to guide the new United States of America as it took its rightful place in a world dominated by kings and prime ministers—jealous rulers who did not love independent republics and would gladly see them overthrown.

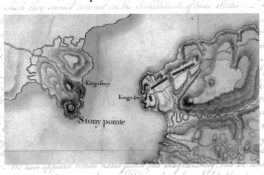

Left: Painted on ivory and just seven inches tall, this watercolor of Washington was adapted from an original by Trumbull. It was commissioned in 1791 by Charleston, South Carolina, to commemorate Washington's visit there.

Above: This 1782 map shows a detail of New York's Hudson River Valley, where Washington's army was encamped during the last months of the war.

The War after Yorktown

Q: How did Washington hold the war-weary army together after Yorktown?

A: Washington refused to rest on his laurels, for he knew the army had to be maintained to prevent a British return in force. After spending the winter of 1781–82 in Philadelphia, meeting with members of Congress and urging them not to be overconfident, he rejoined the army at its encampment in the Hudson River Valley. He would remain vigilant until the peace had been signed and all British troops had left the thirteen states. Washington's presence with the troops was needed until then.

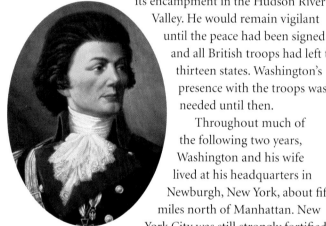

Throughout much of the following two years, Washington and his wife lived at his headquarters in Newburgh, New York, about fifty miles north of Manhattan. New York City was still strongly fortified by the British under a new commander —Clinton had been replaced. With Washington was his most dependable staff officer, Henry Knox, the army's chief artillery officer and the American second-in-command. Although by 1782 hostilities in the region had come to an end, the army's encampment, at nearby New Windsor, was maintained under strict discipline. There was sporadic action in the South, where Nathanael Greene was in overall command, with the mandate to

Above: A native of Polish-governed Lithuania and a trained military engineer and artillerist, Thaddeus Kosciuszko offered his services to Congress in 1776. He later served as a cavalry leader in the South.

Right: Comte de Vergennes, foreign minister of King Louis XVI, was the leading French proponent of supporting the revolutionary cause in America.

keep an army in the field until the last British soldiers had gone.

Washington, Knox, and Greene were greatly respected by the officers and men, and their remaining with the army inspired many others to do the same. If the American forces had melted away, the British and Loyalists might well have seized new footholds from which to resume the war.

Q: Did fighting continue after Yorktown and during peace negotiations?

A: Yes. France and Britain remained at war and battled on the high seas as well as in their far-flung colonies. In America, raiding continued between Loyalists and Patriots around New York, and small but fierce clashes continued in the South. There the British maintained control of only Charleston and Savannah, which were besieged by forces under Greene. In 1782, in an action near Charleston, John Laurens, the former close aide to Washington, was killed. With peace negotiations progressing in Paris, such a loss was especially sorrowful for Washington.

The British evacuated Savannah in July 1782 and Charleston in December. Most of the troops were shipped to New York, where the commander was preparing to evacuate once final instructions arrived from London. Greene remained headquartered in Charleston until August 1783, when the dispatch

Comte de Vergennes

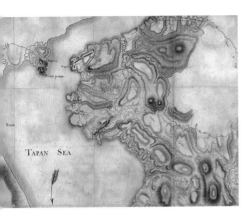

TAPAN SEA

Left: The positions of French and American forces are seen in this 1782 map, which shows Kings Ferry, one of the strategic crossing places on the Hudson River for traffic to and from New England.

announcing the peace treaty arrived and he departed at last for his home in Rhode Island.

Q: What international controversy near the end of the war threatened to turn world opinion against Washington and the Continental Congress?

A: This was known as the Asgill Affair, and it involved a twenty-year-old captured British officer who in mid-1782 had been condemned to death in reprisal for the murder of a Patriot by Loyalists. Loyalist raiders from New York had hanged a New Jersey militiaman to avenge an earlier murder of one of their own. This cold-blooded killing was a sign of the continued hatred between Loyalist and Patriot in America.

Congress ordered Washington to select a prisoner for execution in retaliation. Chosen by lottery was a lowly ensign, Charles Asgill, the only son of an English nobleman. Washington did not want to go

through with the execution, but Congress would not yield despite pleas from the British and also many Americans to spare the young man's life. The general was slow to carry out the sentence, hoping some change in circumstances would allow him to call it off. The case became known around the world, placing Congress in a harsh light. Likewise, Washington was in danger of being characterized as the cold-blooded executioner of a victim who did not deserve to die.

As the execution date approached, Asgill's mother appealed to a family friend, none other than France's Comte de Vergennes, the leading proponent of his country's support of the American revolutionaries. Vergennes sent Lady Asgill's letter to King Louis and Queen Marie Antoinette, who personally asked Congress for clemency. Unable to ignore the French monarch's request, Congress agreed to free the prisoner, and Washington, relieved, promptly did so.

Below: Washington's headquarters in 1780 was at Newburgh, on the Hudson River, while his main army's cantonment was nearby at New Windsor.

The Path to Peace

Q: How did Washington prevent a mutiny by disgruntled, unpaid Continental officers who were threatening to march on Congress?

Right: New York statesman and diplomat John Jay urged Franklin to sign a separate peace with the British rather than await French negotiations that might be less favorable to America. Jay later became chief justice of the United States.

A: In the early spring of 1783 officers at the Newburgh, New York, cantonment gathered to complain about back pay they were due, the lack of funds for food and clothing, and the failure of Congress to arrange for their promised pensions. Many officers were deeply in debt because of their service, and even Washington worried that when they got home they would be thrown in debtor's prisons.

Leading officers communicated with some members of Congress who sympathized with their cause or who saw a road to political power by winning the goodwill of the army. Since the officers had met without Washington's permission, there was an air of mutiny about their efforts, which became known as the Newburgh Conspiracy. Another factor that troubled the officers was Congress's plan to disband the army without back pay and without addressing their complaints. They threatened to refuse to disband and to confront Congress in Philadelphia. One of the officers even proposed that Washington lead them and be anointed king, which shocked and angered the general. Other officers,

John Jay

knowing that Washington would refuse to march at their head against Congress, went to Horatio Gates—still under a cloud for his defeat at Camden—who seemed willing to lead them.

Washington saw this as a potential revolt in the officer corps. He well knew that if he confronted the officers with threats, they would resign, and there would be no army left.

In a meeting with his officers, Washington appealed to them not to take "any measures which, viewed in the calm light of reason, will lessen the dignity and sully the glory you have hitherto maintained."

In the end, the officers accepted his assurance that he would see that Congress kept its promises. Gates

These silver candlesticks, made in Sheffield, England, were used at the signing of the September 1783 treaty in Paris, ending the American War of Independence.

Left: Artist Thomas Sully painted Thomas Jefferson from life in 1821 on a commission from the United States Military Academy at West Point, which was established by Jefferson.

with John Adams in the Netherlands, Thomas Jefferson in America, and John Jay in Spain. Henry Laurens journeyed to France after being released from imprisonment in Britain, and Ben Franklin was in Paris most of this time.

Q: What was the French position during the negotiations?

A: Reaching a settlement was complicated by ongoing French and Spanish negotiations with Britain, because the United States was expected to delay signing a peace treaty until all parties were in agreement. Congress was concerned that France might reacquire her former territory in America. This would be unacceptable to the United States, which did not want the French back in Canada. The American commissioners, therefore, met privately with the British to make a preliminary peace agreement, which was done by November 1782. Learning this, the French objected to the Americans' signing a separate agreement with the British. France wished to come to terms with the British as speedily as possible, but Spanish negotiations had to be completed first. Preliminary terms were agreed to by these combatants in January 1783.

Congress ratified the treaty in April 1783, and it was finally signed by commissioners in Paris that September, officially ending the American War of Independence.

stepped back from leading the officers, and the potential mutiny was averted.

Q: Who were the American delegates to the final peace negotiations in Paris?

A: Peace negotiations had been ongoing since 1780, and a committee had existed since June of 1781 to negotiate for Congress. During much of the negotiations, American commission members were in various places,

Commissioners for the peace negotiations with Britain were, left to right, John Adams, Benjamin Franklin, John Jay, and Henry Laurens. Also pictured are British commissioners David Hartley and Richard Oswald.

A Curtain of Separation

Q: What were the final peace terms between the United States of America and Great Britain?

A: Known as the Peace Treaty of September 3, 1783, the agreement had nine articles, ranging from formal recognition of the United States to the restoration of any land taken in the hostilities—specifically, British-held New York City and surroundings would be evacuated. Boundaries were established between the United States and Canada, fishing rights were confirmed, and private debts owed by the citizens of one country to creditors in the other were to be paid. Also, navigation of the Mississippi would "remain forever free."

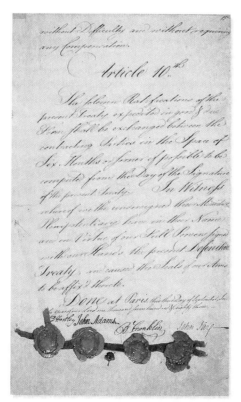

Several important peace treaties were signed in Paris; the agreement that ended the Revolutionary War was termed the "Peace Treaty of 3 September 1783."

Q: When did Londoners first see the Stars and Stripes?

A: On February 6, 1783, even before peace terms were signed, a vessel that was docked at the London customs house attracted considerable attention because she flew a flag with "thirteen rebellious stripes," according to a local publication. Carrying a cargo of whale oil, the Yankee ship *Bedford* was the first American vessel to put in at the London docks since the hostilities began seven years earlier. King George III had recognized the independence of the thirteen states back in December, so the *Bedford* was in no danger of being confiscated. She was tied up within sight of the Tower of London, where American peace commissioner Henry Laurens had been imprisoned until a few months previous.

One magazine reported: "She is American-built, manned wholly by American seamen, wears the rebel colors and belongs to Massachusetts. This is the first vessel which has displayed the thirteen stripes of America in any British port."

The *London Chronicle* took a humorous tack: "There is a vessel in the harbour with a very strange flag. Thirteen is a peculiar number to rebels. A party of prisoners, lately returned from Jersey, say that rations among the rebels are thirteen dried clams a day . . . It takes thirteen Congress paper dollars to equal one shilling sterling . . . Every well-organized rebel household has thirteen children, all of whom expect to be major generals or members of the high and mighty Congress of the United States when they

attain the age of thirteen . . . and Mrs. Washington has a tomcat with thirteen yellow rings around its tail. His flaunting it suggested the Congress the same number of stripes for the rebel flag."

Q: When and why did the British fire a salute in honor of Washington before the war was over?

A: After the official cessation of hostilities, Washington met with Guy Carleton, who had taken command at New York. On May 8, 1783, Carleton invited Washington aboard his ship, anchored in the Hudson River north of New York. As the general boarded the British vessel to dine with Carleton, he was greeted with full military honors, and as he departed he was saluted by the firing of seventeen guns.

This was the first complimentary salute fired by the British for an officer of the United States.

Q: How did Washington deliver his farewell address to the army?

A: Washington's farewell to the army was given by proclamation, which was read in communities around the thirteen states. The army had been disbanded by the summer of 1783, and Washington bid his formal farewell after most of the men had gone home.

The proclamation was issued on November 2 from the general's headquarters at Rocky Hill, New Jersey. Washington recalled the army's difficulties and successes over the course of the war, describing final victory as "little short of a standing Miracle." He described the army as "one patriotic band of Brothers," and hoped the returning soldiers would prove themselves "virtuous and useful as Citizens." Speaking of himself in the third person, Washington said the commander in chief would soon "retire from service— The Curtain of Separation will soon be drawn—and the military scene will be closed to him forever."

Left: This six-foot-tall stained glass portrait of George Washington was created by artist Maria Herndl for the 1904 St. Louis Exposition. It was later acquired by the United States government for display in the Capitol Building.

Below: America celebrates independence while her allies—France, the Netherlands, and Spain—complain at receiving no compensation for their support. King George III is at left, and Ireland, demanding her own freedom, floats in the clouds.

The BELLIGERANT PLENIPO'S

Closing Scenes

Q: Who led the triumphal entry of the Americans into New York City?

Right: As secretary of state for the American colonies, George Sackville—Lord Germain—was most responsible for British policies during the American War of Independence. He died in 1785.

Below: The mouth of the Hudson, or North River, New York City, and eastern New Jersey are shown in this 1778 French map, which also indicates navigation routes.

A: A small procession of a few hundred troops and a few dozen mounted officers and dignitaries was led by New York State's governor, George Clinton, a former Continental general and a good friend of Washington's. Rather than present a display of military triumph, Washington favored stressing the leadership of civilian government. He accompanied Clinton on that late November day in 1783, but it was the governor, not the general, who had the honor of liberating the city.

New York was run-down and dirty, suffering from seven years of siege and shortages and from occupation by thousands of soldiers with their horses, livestock, latrines, and barracks. Churches had been commandeered for stables, and public buildings had been turned into quarters for troops. New Yorkers were worried as the Patriots rode in and the last British rowed out to their waiting ships. Would the victors rampage through the city, attacking former Loyalists and looting homes and businesses? Washington and Clinton, however, had given strict orders to maintain law and order and to protect those Loyalists who had remained instead of sailing away with the British fleet.

New York's transition to American control was peaceful. As was characteristic of Washington, he gave Clinton all the glory for liberating the city that the commander in chief had doggedly besieged for so long.

Lord Germain

Q: What prank did the British soldiers play on the Americans as New York City was being evacuated?

A: Knowing the Americans would ceremonially raise the Stars and Stripes at the fort on the tip of Manhattan Island, some soldiers nailed a British Union Jack to the top of the flagpole. Next they cut down

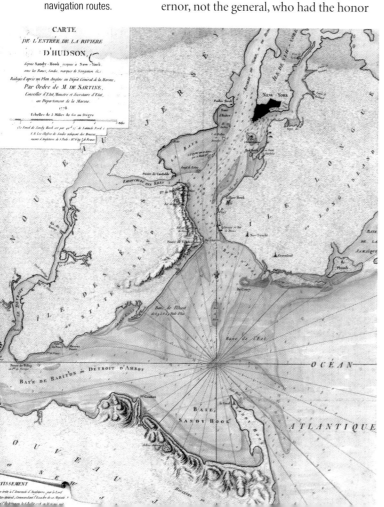

CARTE DE L'ENTRÉE DE LA RIVIÈRE D'HUDSON,

depuis Sandy-Hook jusques a New-York,
avec les Bancs, Sondes, marques de Navigation, &c.

Rédigée d'après un Plan Anglais au Dépôt Général de la Marine.

Par Ordre de M. DE SARTINE,
Conseiller d'État, Ministre et Secrétaire d'État,
au Département de la Marine.
1778.

the halyard—the rope and pulley—needed to raise the American flag, and then they coated the pole with grease. When the first Americans arrived at the flagpole, they hurried to replace the halyard before General Washington and Governor Clinton arrived for the flag-raising. Men tried to shinny up the pole, but the grease made them slide down after a few feet. It seemed the lobsterbacks would have the last laugh.

Then someone fetched a long ladder, and up went a young New York sailor carrying a halyard, hammer, nails, and a batch of wooden slats. As a growing crowd cheered him on, the sailor nailed on the slats for rungs and climbed steadily higher until he could reach the British flag, which he yanked down. Then he replaced the halyard, and the Stars and Stripes immediately rose. Cannon began firing thirteen times in salute.

Nearby was General Washington, who had been standing unnoticed for some time, observing it all with considerable pleasure.

Q: What was Washington's last act as commander in chief?

A: Resignation of his officer's commission. After bidding farewell in New York to his few remaining officers, Washington rode southward to Annapolis, Maryland, where Congress was in session. A few months previously in Philadelphia a Pennsylvania line regiment had mutinied, threatening the delegates if they did not take action to make sure the army was paid. Fearing for their lives, members of

Congress had adjourned to Annapolis, and there Washington arrived in mid-December 1783, with only one aide de camp and Baron von Steuben as escort.

Congress convened, and Washington was received. A brief expression of thanks was given by the president of Congress, Thomas Mifflin of Pennsylvania—the former general who had been a failure as a quartermaster during the Valley Forge ordeal and a longstanding opponent of Washington's. Then Washington gave his own brief address, which was an expression of thanks to Congress. Immediately after shaking hands with the members, Washington mounted his horse and rode home to Martha at Mount Vernon, fully intending to live out his life in peaceful retirement.

Below: A New York sailor secures the Stars and Stripes to a flagpole in Manhattan after British troops evacuated the city on November 25, 1783.

Bottom: John Trumbull painted this portrayal of Washington resigning his commander in chief's commission before Congress at Annapolis, Maryland, in December 1783.

New Country, New Government

Q: **What dramatic step did King George III take when he knew the former colonies were finally lost to the empire?**

A: King George wrote an abdication statement, but it was never delivered to Parliament, which would have been required to make abdication official. The king later reconciled himself with "the separation," as he described America's independence, telling American ambassador John Adams, "I would be the first to meet the friendship of the United States as an independent power."

Phillip John Schuyler

Q: **What was the most important task of the Congress of the United States after the war was over?**

A: Adopting a constitution for a federal government. The Articles of Confederation that had guided the Continental Congress during the Revolutionary War required revisions to function as a federal system.

With this in mind, a convention of representatives from the states, with Washington as president, met in Philadelphia in 1787 and drafted a proposed constitution that was adopted by Congress in September. The drafting committee stated:

"The friends of our country have long seen and desired that the power of making war, peace, and treaties, that of levying money, and regulating commerce, and the correspondent executive and judicial authorities, should be fully and effectually vested in the General Government of the Union; but the impropriety of delegating such extensive trust to one body of men is evident: hence results the necessity of a different organization."

The preamble to the Constitution read: "We, the People of the United States, in Order to form a more perfect Union, establish Justice, ensure domestic Tranquility, provide for the common defence, promote the general Welfare, and secure the Blessings of Liberty to ourselves

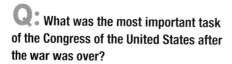

Q: What is the Bill of Rights?

A: During the debates on the adoption of the Constitution, delegates were concerned about too much power being placed in the central government. The memory of British violations of American civil rights before and during the Revolution urged the delegates to demand a "bill of rights" that would protect the liberties of individual citizens from a tyrannical government. As the Constitution was being ratified—formally approved—by the state legislatures, several delegates asked for amending, or changing, the document to include these basic rights. The Bill of Rights was added as the first ten amendments to the Constitution.

In 1789, the First Congress of the United States proposed—and the state legislatures later ratified—the Bill of Rights. These amendments assert that Congress shall make no laws regarding the free exercise of religion or that prevent freedom of speech, of the press, or of the right to peaceably assemble. They also guarantee the right to bear arms, freedom from illegal government searches, the right to trial by jury, and to a speedy trial.

and our Posterity, do ordain and establish this Constitution for the United States of America."

Q: Who was the leading figure in the writing of the Constitution of the United States?

A: James Madison of Virginia. One of the most accomplished congressmen, Madison had been skillful at solving legal difficulties that blocked the creation of a federal government. These included issues such as states giving up their claims to the western lands. Madison was also the primary author of the Bill of Rights. While he favored a strong central government, the primary aim of the Constitution was to create an elected government that was responsive to the will of the people. Madison faced opposition in this aim from many of the "Founding Fathers," who believed the new government needed to be insulated from the changing whims of the people.

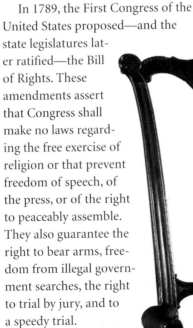

Below: George Washington used this "Rising Sun" mahogany armchair during the Constitutional Convention of 1787. Benjamin Franklin reportedly was at first unsure whether the sun was rising or setting. He later said, "It is a rising . . . sun."

Father of the Country

Right: George Washington's epaulets were made of gold bullion thread tassels with gilt sequins and twisted bullion bows. Epaulets were worn on the shoulders of a uniform coat and indicated general officers.

Below: Gilbert Stuart's second life portrait of George Washington, painted in 1796, is best known as the image on the one-dollar bill. Washington sat for Stuart in Philadelphia for this, the most famous portrait of the first president.

Q: What role did Washington play in the creation of the republic?

A: After resigning his command in 1783, Washington hoped to be able to retire from public life, but he continued to be involved in regional affairs. Mount Vernon was the site of a commission organized by Virginia and Maryland to decide on the regulations for the navigation of the Chesapeake and Potomac rivers. This commission,

Washington's epaulets

with Washington as the presiding officer, led to the "Annapolis Convention," with broader regional representation to decide pressing commercial and legal issues that involved several neighboring states. In turn, this convention stimulated the 1787 Federal Convention in Philadelphia, which met to revise the Articles of Confederation.

Washington reluctantly assumed the position of presiding officer in Philadelphia. He was the one most trusted to be fair and objective as president of the convention. In April 1789, after the new American government was organized, Washington was elected unanimously as the first president of the United States. Sworn in at New York City, Washington served two terms, but when elected to a third term, he declined. As president, he strengthened the power of the central government by firmly putting down the 1794 Whiskey Rebellion, an uprising in Pennsylvania that attempted to prevent government regulation and taxation of whiskey making. Washington sent troops to quell the disturbance, making it clear the new government would oppose by force any attempt to ignore its authority.

Washington strictly maintained America's neutrality in overseas conflicts and refused to be drawn into hostilities—even though the French-American treaty of 1778 called for a military alliance. He fostered diplomatic ties with Great Britain while also sending troops into the Northwest to put down Indian uprisings,

which in part were encouraged by the British, who maintained several fur-trading posts that were supposed to have been evacuated after the war.

Washington strongly opposed party politics—a stand that made political enemies who harshly criticized him; but the people still adored Washington by the time he left office in September 1797.

Q: Who first called Washington the "Father of the Country"?

A: The earliest known written use of this expression was in a German-language almanac titled *Nord-Americanische Kalender,* printed in Lancaster, Pennsylvania, in 1779. The almanac had a picture of Washington on the frontispiece and spelled his name "Waschington." Also on the page is the figure of "Fame" and a trumpet from which came the words "Des Landes Vater," or Father of the Country.

This expression was well known in America, as indicated in March 1781 when Washington was heralded by a crowd in the streets of Providence, Rhode Island. A French officer attached to the general's headquarters later wrote: "The whole of the population had assembled from the suburbs, [and] we were surrounded by a crowd of children carrying torches, reciting the acclamation of the citizens, all ... eager to approach the

person of him whom they called their father, and pressed so closely around us that they hindered us from proceeding. General Washington, who was much affected, stopped a few moments, and pressing my hand said, 'We may be beaten by the English; it is the chance of war; but behold an army which they can never conquer.' "

Q: What famous phrase describing Washington was first stated after his death?

A: "First in war, first in peace, first in the hearts of his countrymen." This sentiment was expressed by former Revolutionary War cavalry leader Henry Lee, a fellow Virginian and the future father of Robert E. Lee, Confederate commander in chief in the Civil War. After Washington died on December 14, 1799, Henry Lee used this enduring phrase in a eulogy for his former commander.

Historical artist Howard Pyle depicted the farewell of Washington to his remaining officers at New York's Fraunces' Tavern in December 1783. Pyle's drawing appeared in *Harper's Weekly* in 1883.

Glossary

AMERICAN REVOLUTION. The social, political, and military events that took place in North America from 1763 to 1787, as Americans cast off British rule and established the United States of America.

BILL OF RIGHTS. The first ten amendments to the United States Constitution, adopted to guarantee civil liberties for Americans.

BRITISH AMERICA. In 1775 this included the former New France—Canada, Nova Scotia, and Newfoundland—thirteen colonies along the Atlantic seaboard, and East and West Florida.

CAMP FOLLOWERS. Civilians, mostly women, who accompanied an army and attended to the needs of the troops. Many were wives or daughters of soldiers.

COLONIES. Communities in undeveloped lands that have been planted by a mother country and are tied to that country economically, culturally, and politically. Colonies differed in terms of government and purpose, with most being permanent "plantations" of settlers, while others were established as commercial ventures controlled by business interests, termed proprietors.

COMMITTEES OF OBSERVATION AND SAFETY. First appointed in 1774 by Massachusetts, these committees were empowered to call out militia and assemble military supplies. The prewar effort in the colonies to build a military force was guided by Committees of Safety established throughout the colonies.

CONSTITUTION. The fundamental principles of governing that are accepted by a social group, government, state, or confederation of independent states.

CONTINENTAL ARMY. The organization of land troops created by the Continental Congress. Soldiers who served in it were considered "regulars," long-term professionals, not short-term volunteer militia, and were known as "Continentals."

CONTINENTAL CONGRESS. The political organization that led the revolutionaries throughout the War of American Independence. The 1774 convention of representatives from the thirteen colonies, who met in Philadelphia, was the First Continental Congress. The Second Continental Congress, which declared independence and prosecuted the war, sat from 1775 to 1781.

CONTINENTAL NAVY. A small naval force of frigates, gunboats, and minor vessels created by Congress during the war.

DECLARATION OF INDEPENDENCE. The official statement, or declaration, of the Second Continental Congress adopted on July 4, 1776, asserting the independence of the thirteen former British colonies.

EDGED WEAPONS. Bladed weaponry with sharp cutting edges: swords, daggers, and bayonets were the common edged weapons of mid–eighteenth century warfare.

FREE BLACKS. Americans of African origin who were nonslaves, although their social entitlements and political rights were sharply limited. By 1790, 60,000 free blacks lived in the newly established United States.

GRENADIER. Originally soldiers assigned to throw grenades, grenadiers later became elite troops who were organized into companies that were often combined into fighting units such as battalions.

HESSIANS. The term for mercenary troops hired by the British from German principalities to fight American revolutionaries. Most came from Hesse, although many were from Brunswick.

INDIAN NATIONS IN THE REVOLUTION. Most native peoples managed to remain neutral, but the American victory effectively voided British peace treaties and territorial agreements with the nations, opening Indian lands to settlement.

INTOLERABLE ACTS, or COERCIVE ACTS. These 1774 acts of Parliament were intended to force Americans to accept British colonial and taxation policies. Widespread colonial hostility to them led to the First Continental Congress and eventual open warfare.

LOYALISTS. Americans who opposed revolution and supported the British government. As many as eighty thousand left for Canada and England after the war.

MILITIA. Civilian volunteers who were prepared to defend their communities when needed. Militia units served short-term when called out for campaigns.

MINUTEMEN. Militia units organized to respond "at a minute's notice" to an emergency. Even before hostilities broke out, the Minutemen mustered to confront British troops searching for militia military stores.

MUSKET. A smoothbore, muzzle-loaded firearm that could be rapidly loaded and fired by trained troops.

PARLIAMENT. The governing body of Great Britain and the empire, with two houses—the elected House of Commons and the hereditary House of Lords. Members of Parliament select ministers to run the government.

PARTISAN. A guerrilla fighter who operates behind enemy lines, raiding supplies and attacking small units by surprise.

PATRIOT. The preferred term for revolutionaries who fought for American independence. "Rebel" was a derogatory term to Patriots, who considered themselves to be fighting for legitimate rights.

PRESIDENT OF CONGRESS. The individual elected to preside over meetings of the Continental Congress.

REGULAR. A professional soldier who enlists in a national or government army for several years and is thoroughly trained.

REVOLUTIONARY WAR, or WAR OF INDEPENDENCE. The military phase, from 1775 to 1783, of the American Revolution.

RIFLE. A shoulder-held firearm that, unlike the smoothbore musket, has spiral grooves inside the rifle barrel—"rifling"—which causes the bullet to spin and fly accurately at long range.

"TAXATION WITHOUT REPRESENTATION IS TYRANNY." A longstanding British slogan meaning that only subjects who were represented in Parliament may be taxed. Taxation without political rights was tyranny.

TORY. The conservative, pro-royalist British political party that was in power during much of the American Revolution. Loyalists were termed "Tories," although this was often inaccurate.

WHIG. The British political party that opposed military action in America, but which was out of power during the Revolutionary War.

Further Reading

Books

Bird, Harrison. *March to Saratoga: General Burgoyne and the American Campaign.* New York: Oxford University Press, 1963.

Boatner, Mark M. III. *Encyclopedia of the American Revolution.* Mechanicsburg, PA: Stackpole Books, 1994.

Chartrand, René. *American War of Independence Commanders.* Oxford: Osprey Publishing, Ltd., 2003.

Commager, Henry Steele, and Richard B. Morris. *The Spirit of 'Seventy-six.* New York and London: Harper & Row Publishers, 1958.

Editors et al. *The Revolution.* New York: American Heritage Publishing Co., 1958.

Faragher, John M. *Encyclopedia of Colonial and Revolutionary America.* New York: Facts on File, 1990.

Fitzpatrick, John C. *The Writings of Washington from the Original Manuscript Sources 1745–1799, 39 vols.* Washington, D.C.: Government Printing Office, 1931–1944. Reprint, New York: Greenwood Press, 1970.

Flexner, James Thomas. *George Washington. 4 Vols.* Boston: Little, Brown, 1965–1972.

Freeman, Douglas Southall. *George Washington, A Biography, 7 vols.* New York: Scribner, 1948–1957.

Jones, Maldwyn A. *George Washington's Generals and Opponents: Their Exploits and Leadership.* New York: De Capo Press, 1994.

Lossing, Benson J. *The Pictorial Field Book of the American Revolution.* New York: Harper & Brothers, 1860.

McKelden, Theodore Roosevelt. *Washington Bowed.* Excerpted in *American Heritage Magazine,* August 1956.

Moore, Frank. *Diary of the American Revolution.* New York: Washington Square Press, 1967.

Morris, Richard B. *The Forging of the Union, 1781–1789.* New York: Harper and Row, 1987.

Murray, Aaron R. *American Revolution Battles and Leaders.* London and New York: DK Publishing, Inc., 2004.

Murray, Stuart. *American Revolution.* London and New York: DK Publishing, Inc. in association with the Smithsonian Institution, 2002.

———. *America's Song: The Story of "Yankee Doodle."* Bennington, VT: Images from the Past, 1999.

Randall, Willard Sterne. *Benedict Arnold: Patriot and Traitor.* New York: Morrow, 1990.

Scheer, George F., and Hugh F. Rankin. *Rebels and Redcoats.* New York: New American Library, 1957.

Thane, Elswyth. *Washington's Lady.* Mattuck, NY: Aeonian Press, 1977.

Thatcher, James. *A Military Journal During the American Revolutionary War. 2nd ed.* Boston: Cottons & Barnard, 1827.

Van Doren, Carl. *Secret History of the American Revolution.* New York: The Viking Press, 1941.

Web sites

Smithsonian Institution web sites on the War of American Independence:
americanhistory.si.edu/militaryhistory
americanhistory.si.edu
www.npg.si.edu

The American Revolution
www.theamericanrevolution.org

Women in the Revolution
www.americanrevolution.org

The American Revolution 1775–1783:
The Complete History of the
American Revolution
www.americanrevolution.com

Library of Congress: American
Memory—Helpful teachers' aids
memory.loc.gov/learn/features/timeline/
amrev/amrev.html

The Writings of George Washington from
the Original Manuscript Sources 1745–
1799; edited by John C. Fitzpatrick
etext.virginia.edu/washington/fitzpatrick/

U.S. Army Center of Military History
www.army.mil/cmh

U.S. Army Center of Military History:
"Rangers in Colonial and Revolutionary
America." Article traces the evolution
of the ranger tradition from the
seventeenth century wars between
colonists and Native American tribes
through the Revolutionary War
www.army.mil/cmh-pg/documents/
revwar/revra.htm.

The On-Line Institute for Advanced
Loyalist Studies
www.royalprovincial.com

At the Smithsonian

The Smithsonian's National Museum of American History, Behring Center, is located on the Mall in Washington, D.C. The Museum's collections and scholarship are dedicated to inspiring a broader understanding of the United States and its many peoples. Exhibitions explore major themes in American life, from the end of the American Revolution to the present day.

The Smithsonian Institution in Washington, D.C., features many fascinating items from the American War of Independence in its "Price of Freedom" collection, which includes hundreds of artifacts related to America's military history. A number of the artifacts on display are pictured in this volume.

The "Price of Freedom," at the National Museum of American History, Behring Center, examines how wars have shaped the nation's history and transformed American society. It highlights the service and sacrifice of generations of American men and women. The American War of Independence exhibit includes a painting of General Washington by Charles Willson Peale, Washington's sword and scabbard, and his postwar uniform.

This exhibit surveys the history of America's military from the colonial era to the present, exploring how wars have been defining episodes in American history. Using hundreds of original artifacts and graphic images, it tells how Americans have fought to establish the nation's independence, determine its borders, shape its values of freedom and

opportunity, and define its leading role in world affairs. These stories go beyond a survey of battles to examine the social as well as military aspects of wars. The exhibition also looks at the relationships of wars to American political leadership, social values, technological innovation, and personal sacrifice.

In the War of American Independence exhibit are soldier accoutrements, artillery pieces, art, animal heroes, military caps and hats, civilian clothes, edged weapons, ephemera, equipment, espionage instruments, explosives, firearms, flags, insignia, medals, medical equipment, uniforms, documents, models, music, naval vessels, prisoner of war items, relics, religious objects, toys, and vehicles.

The Smithsonian Institution is the world's largest museum complex and research organization. Composed of seventeen museums and the National Zoo in the Washington, D.C., metropolitan area, and two museums in New York City, the Smithsonian's exhibitions offer visitors a glimpse into

These porcelain dishes are decorated with an angel representing "Fame" holding the order of the Society of the Cincinnati, an association of Continental officers who fought in the Revolutionary War.

This miter cap was worn by a member of the Newport, Rhode Island, Light Infantry company, established in October 1774 as a one-hundred-strong unit. At the top of the miter is the motto, "Hope," and below is the British royal cipher or monogram "GR" for *Georgeus Rex* or King George.

A view of the Quadrangle museum complex behind the Smithsonian Castle on the Mall in Washington. The Quadrangle contains the International Center, the Arthur M. Sackler Gallery (Asian Art Museum); and the National Museum of African Art, all in a multilevel underground complex. The complex is topped by the Enid Haupt Garden.

its vast collection, numbering more than 142 million objects. The National Portrait Gallery's collection includes paintings of famous figures from the Revolutionary period, including the best-known Gilbert Stuart portrait of Washington.

Visitors can begin at the Smithsonian Information Center in the Institution's first building, popularly known as the Castle, which is open daily 8:30 a.m.–5:30 p.m. This distinctive red sandstone building sits on the National Mall. The Center serves as the focal point for information about the Institution's museums and the National Zoo. Visitors may choose from several information options, and helpful volunteers are on hand to answer questions and provide direction. A video orientation is shown throughout the day, and interactive video programs about

the Smithsonian Institution (in various languages) convey information at a touch.

Smithsonian tours are offered on a scheduled basis Tuesday through Saturday. On Sundays and Mondays, tours are given as announced by docent only. No tours are available on federal holidays. Visitors can check at the information desk for tour times. Admission is free for the Smithsonian Institution, with normal operating hours 10 a.m. to 5:30 p.m. daily. E-mail info@si.edu or phone (202) 633-1000.

George Washington and his staff used this headquarters tent during the Revolutionary War. It is made of heavy, unbleached linen and measures eighteen by twenty-eight feet. At the end of the war, the tent was shipped to Washington's home in Mount Vernon, and after his death in 1799 a relation donated it to the United States government.

Index

Acknowledgments & Picture Credits

The author's sincere gratitude goes out to the many individuals who have contributed to, and shared, his lifelong interest in the War of American Independence.

The author and publisher also offer thanks to those closely involved in the creation of this volume: curator Dik Daso of the National Air and Space Museum, Smithsonian Institution; Ellen Nanney, Senior Brand Manager and Katie Mann, with Smithsonian Business Ventures; Collins Reference executive editor Donna Sanzone, editor Lisa Hacken, and editorial assistant Stephanie Meyers; Glenn Novak, copyeditor and military history enthusiast; Hydra Publishing president Sean Moore, publishing director Karen Prince, editorial director Aaron Murray, art director Edwin Kuo, designers Rachel Maloney, Mariel Morris, Gus Yoo, Greg Lum, La Tricia Watford, Erika Lubowicki, editors Marcel Brousseau, Lisa Purcell, Suzanne Lander, Gail Greiner, Ward Calhoun, Emily Beekman, picture researcher Ben Dewalt, production manager Sarah Reilly, production director Wayne Ellis, and indexer Jessie Shiers; David Burgevin, Smithsonian Images; artist Don Troiani, Historical Art Prints, www.historicalartprints.com; Joan Mathys, of MJM Picture and Film Research; Renee Klish, curator, U.S. Army Art Collection; Andrea Ashby, Independence National Historical Park; Amy Burton, U.S. Senate Collection; Maurice Boren, Composition Systems, Inc.; Amber Young, Museum Management Program, National Park Service.

PICTURE CREDITS

The following abbreviations are used: NMAH/SI—National Museum of American History, Behring Center, Smithsonian Institution; NPG/SI—National Portrait Gallery, Smithsonian Institution; LoC—Library of Congress; NA—National Archives; VAFO—Courtesy National Park Service, Museum Management Program and *Valley Forge National Historical Park*; GUCO—Courtesy National Park Service, Museum Management Program and *Guilford Courthouse National Historical Park*; MORR—Courtesy National Park Service, Museum Management Program and *Morristown National Historical Park*; INHP—*Independence National Historical Park*; FISKE—*The American Revolution*, by John Fiske, The Riverside Press; USAAC—Courtesy of the National Museum of the U.S. Army, Army Art Collection; DT/HAP—Paintings by Don Troiani, www.historicalartprints.com; DOVER—*The American Revolution: A Picture Sourcebook*, by Dover Publications, Inc.

(t=top; b=bottom; l=left; r=right; c=center)

The American War for Independence
IIII DT/HAP IIIc Smithsonian American Art Museum IIIr USAAC IV Smithsonian American Art Museum IV-Vbackground LoC Vt Armed Forces History, Division of History of Technology, NMAH/SI [2004-40563] Vr GUCO Vb Armed Forces History, Division of History of Technology, NMAH/SI [2004-50686] VI LoC 1 GUCO 2 Courtesy of Morristown National Historical Park 3 Architect of the Capitol

Chapter 1: The Colonial Era
4 LoC 5background NA 5r LoC 6c Armed Forces History, Division of History of Technology, NMAH/SI [2004-40524] 6b Armed Forces History, Division of History of Technology, NMAH/SI [2004-26292.05] 7 LoC 8 LoC 9t LoC 9b Armed Forces History, Division of History of Technology, NMAH/SI [2004-40564] 10t Armed Forces History, Division of History of Technology, NMAH/SI [97-781] 10b Wisconsin Historical Society—Whi-1900 11t LoC 11b VAFO 12t Armed Forces History, Division of History of Technology, NMAH/SI [2004-20293] 12b LoC 13tl Armed Forces History, Division of History of Technology, NMAH/SI [2004-49222.09] 13tr NPG/SI 13b Armed Forces History, Division of History of Technology, NMAH/SI [2004-51193] 14bl LoC 14tr The Colonial Williamsburg Foundation 15t LoC 15c Washington-Custis-Lee Collection, Washington and Lee University, Lexington, VA

Chapter 2: Causes of the Revolution
16 LoC 18b Photo courtesy of The Marblehead Museum & Historical Society, Marblehead, MA 19t LoC 19r INHP 20l LoC

20bl GUCO 20br GUCO 21t LoC 21r LoC 22br Division of Politics and Reform, NMAH/SI [2000-9747] 22tl LoC 23 LoC 24t FISKE 24l Division of Home and Community Life, NMAH/SI [79-8546] 24b LoC 25tl LoC 25r LoC 26tl Photo Courtesy Dumbarton House/ The National Society of the Colonial Dames of America 26tr LoC 26b LoC 27t U.S. Senate Collection 27b Armed Forces History, Division of History of Technology, NMAH/SI [2004-55406]

Chapter 3: War Breaks Out
28 LoC 29tr USAAC 30tr INHP 30b LoC 31 LoC 32 LoC 33t INHP 33b LoC 34 Architect of the Capitol 35tl LoC 35tr LoC 36t INHP 36b NA 37t Armed Forces History, Division of History of Technology, NMAH/SI [2004-22494.08] 37b NA 38 LoC 39t LoC 39b NA 40 DT/HAP 41 Armed Forces History, Division of History of Technology, NMAH/SI [2004-51187] 42 Delaware Art Museum 43t LoC 43b LoC 44t USAAC 44b LoC 45c INHP 45b NA 46 USAAC 47tr LoC 47bl LoC

Chapter 4: The First Struggles
48 LoC 49 LoC 50 USAAC 51tr LoC 51b LoC 52c NA 52bl Armed Forces History, Division of History of Technology, NMAH/SI [90-7408] 53 Armed Forces History, Division of History of Technology, NMAH/SI [93-5844] 54 U.S. Senate Collection 55 DOVER 56 LoC 57t LoC 57b NA 58l VAFO 58br NA 59 LoC 60 USAAC 61 NA 62 LoC 63t INHP 63b MORR 64l INHP 64tr LoC 65t LoC 65b NPG/SI

Chapter 5: Declaring Independence
66 LoC 67 Photograph by Dan Smith—Wikipedia Commons 68 LoC 69t INHP 69b NA 70tl NPG/SI 70br Division of Social History, NMAH/SI [2000-3209] 71 LoC 72 INHP 73t LoC 73b LoC 74t LoC 74b LoC 75 Collection of the New-York Historical Society

Chapter 6: The Forces of King and Congress
76 Howard Pyle (1853-1911); *The Nation Makers, 1903*; Oil on canvas; Collection of Brandywine Museum; Purchased through a grant from the Mabel Pew Myrin trust, 1984 78 DT/HAP 79t LoC 79b Armed Forces History, Division of History of Technology, NMAH/SI [2004-29585.16] 80tl Armed Forces History, Division of History of Technology, NMAH/SI [2004-22549.03] 80br NA 81tl LoC 81br Armed Forces History, Division of History of Technology, NMAH/SI [2004-22552.07] 82tl LoC 82br DT/HAP 83 DT/HAP 84 LoC 85t DT/HAP 85b NA 86 INHP 87l USAAC 87r INHP 88t USAAC 88b NA 89 National Park Service

Ready Reference
Background U.S. Senate Collection 90tl Architect of the Capitol 90tr FISKE 90cr FISKE 90bl Courtesy of the National Park Service, Kings Mountain National Park 91tl INHP 91tc LoC 91tr INHP 91bl FISKE 91br FISKE 92tl Architect of the Capitol 92tr FISKE 92tr FISKE 92br FISKE 93tl Courtesy of Dean G. Jahns 93tc NA 93tr DOVER 93bl LoC 93br © 2006 Jupiterimages Corporation 94tl INHP 94tc INHP 94tr INHP 94bl FISKE 94bc FISKE 94br FISKE 95tl INHP 95tr INHP 95bl FISKE 95br NA 96bl DT/HAP 96tr MORR 97cl Anne S. K. Brown Military Collection, Brown University Library 97bl MORR 97br DOVER 98tl GUCO 98tr VAFO 98cl GUCO 98cr VAFO 98bt MORR 98bm Armed Forces History, Division of History of Technology, NMAH/SI [2004-29587.15] 98b Armed Forces History, Division of History of Technology, NMAH/SI [2004-26276.03] 99t DOVER 99clt Armed Forces History, Division of History of Technology, NMAH/SI [2004-40564] 99cl Armed Forces History, Division of History of Technology, NMAH/SI [2004-40569] 99clb Armed Forces History, Division of History of Technology, NMAH/SI [2004-51197] 99crt MORR 99cr GUCO 99crb VAFO 99br Armed Forces History, Division of History of Technology, NMAH/SI [MAH-49621] 100 DOVER 101 DOVER 102l DT/HAP 102br DOVER 103 Architect of the Capitol 104l FISKE 104r FISKE 104b FISKE 105tl LoC 105br LoC 106t FISKE 106bl FISKE 106br LoC 107 LoC

Chapter 7: Heroism, Legend and Lore
108 INHP 110tr Architect of the Capitol 110l Armed Forces History, Division of History of Technology, NMAH/SI [2004-

20295] 111 NA 112t Skillman Library/ Lafayette College 112b NA 113 Armed Forces History, Division of History of Technology, NMAH/SI [2004-51833] 114t LoC 114b Armed Forces History, Division of History of Technology, NMAH/SI [2004-50686] 115l VAFO 115r INHP 116 LoC 117 DT/HAP 118bl NA 118r INHP 119 GUCO 120l INHP 120r NA 121 Tennessee State Museum 122 INHP 123t USAAC 123b INHP 124 LoC 125 LoC 126 U.S. Senate Collection 127r Armed Forces History, Division of History of Technology, NMAH/SI [2000-10747.08] 127bl Armed Forces History, Division of History of Technology, NMAH/SI [99-4030]

Chapter 8: France and the War at Sea
128 LoC 130 FISKE 131 LoC 132t Armed Forces History, Division of History of Technology, NMAH/SI [2004-39200.11] 132b DT/HAP 133t Armed Forces History, Division of History of Technology, NMAH/SI [2004-40568] 133br INHP 134t INHP 134br USAAC 135 LoC 136tl LoC 136br NA 137 Armed Forces History, Division of History of Technology, NMAH/SI [2004-51194] 138 INHP 139l Anne S. K. Brown Military Collection, Brown University Library 139r DOVER 140 DOVER 141tr INHP 141b Armed Forces History, Division of History of Technology, NMAH/SI [2004-40532]

Chapter 9: The Home Front and Behind the Lines
142 U.S. Senate Collection 144 LoC 145tl GUCO 145cr LoC 146 DT/HAP 147 LoC 148 LoC 149 DOVER 150 LoC 151tr DT/HAP 151b GUCO 152 NA 153tl NPG/SI 153br National Numismatic Collection, NMAH/SI 154tl National Numismatic Collection, NMAH/SI [2005-27299] 154bl National Numismatic Collection, NMAH/SI [2005-27298] 154tr National Numismatic Collection, NMAH/SI [2005-27379] 154br National Numismatic Collection, NMAH/SI [2005-27380] 155 DOVER 156 LoC 157c DT/HAP 157r LoC 158 LoC 159 Armed Forces History, Division of History of Technology, NMAH/SI [2004-20294] 160 LoC 161t Armed Forces History, Division of History of Technology, NMAH/SI [2004-19460.08] 161br NPG/SI 162tl DOVER 162b NA 163t LoC 163br LoC

Chapter 10: In Convention Assembled
164 LoC 166 NA 167bl LoC 167tr NPG/SI 168 NPG/SI 169 LoC 170bl INHP 170tr INHP 171 INHP 172 LoC 173t LoC 173br LoC

Chapter 11: The War Road to Yorktown
174 Architect of the Capitol 175 LoC 176bl INHP 176br INHP 177 U.S. Senate Collection 178 INHP 179tl Armed Forces History, Division of History of Technology, NMAH/SI [2004-26282.02] 179c FISKE 179br FISKE 180 U.S. Senate Collection 181 INHP 182bl USAAC 182br GUCO 183tl FISKE 183r FISKE 184bl Washington-Custis-Lee Collection, Washington and Lee University, Lexington, VA 184tr INHP 185tr FISKE 185br LoC 186bl LoC 186tr FISKE 187t FISKE 187br VAFO 188t INHP 188bl FISKE 189bl USAAC 189tr FISKE 190 Medical Science, Division of Science, Medicine, and Society, NMAH/SI [2004-49228] 191 Architect of the Capitol

Chapter 12: Founding the Republic
192 Smithsonian American Art Museum 193 LoC 194l INHP 194br FISKE 195tl LoC 195br LoC 196bl Political History, Division of Social History, NMAH/SI [2004-51178] 196tr INHP 197t U.S. Senate Collection 197b U.S. Senate Collection 198 NA 199t U.S. Senate Collection 199b LoC 200bl LoC 200tr FISKE 201tr LoC 201br Architect of the Capitol 202bl DOVER 202tr INHP 203tl NA 203br INHP 204bl U.S. Senate Collection 204t Armed Forces History, Division of History of Technology, NMAH/SI [2004-50203] 205 DOVER

At the Smithsonian
210 Smithsonian Photographic Services [82-8967] 211t Political History, Division of Social History, NMAH/SI [2004-47116] 211b Armed Forces History, Division of History of Technology, NMAH/SI [2004-22549.09] 212 Smithsonian Photographic Services [90-6258] 213 Armed Forces History, Division of History of Technology, NMAH/SI [74-4423]